The Sociology of Intellectual Life

Theory, Culture & Society

Theory, Culture & Society caters for the resurgence of interest in culture within contemporary social science and the humanities. Building on the heritage of classical social theory, the book series examines ways in which this tradition has been reshaped by a new generation of theorists. It also publishes theoretically informed analyses of everyday life, popular culture, and new intellectual movements.

EDITOR: Mike Featherstone, *Nottingham Trent University*

THE TCS CENTRE
The *Theory, Culture & Society* book series, the journals *Theory, Culture & Society* and *Body & Society*, and related conference, seminar and postgraduate programmes operate from the TCS Centre at Nottingham Trent University. For further details of the TCS Centre's activities please contact:

The TCS Centre
School of Arts and Humanities
Nottingham Trent University
Clifton Lane, Nottingham, NG11 8NS, UK
e-mail: tcs@ntu.ac.uk
web: http://sagepub.net/tcs/

Recent volumes include:

Informalization: Manners and Emotions Since 1890
Cas Wouters

The Culture of Speed: The Coming of Immediacy
Jom Tomlinson

The Dressed Society: Clothing, the Body and Some Meanings of the World
Peter Corrigan

Advertising in Modern and Postmodern Times
Pamela Odih

The Saturated Society: Regulating Lifestyles in Consumer Capitalism
Pekka Sulkunen

Globalization and Football: A Critical Sociology
Richard Giulianotti & Roland Roberton

The Sociology of Intellectual Life

The Career of the Mind in and around the Academy

Steve Fuller

Los Angeles | London | New Delhi
Singapore | Washington DC

First published 2009
Reprinted 2010

Published in association with *Theory, Culture & Society,*
Nottingham Trent University

SAGE Publications Ltd
1 Oliver's Yard
55 City Road
London EC1Y 1SP

SAGE Publications Inc.
2455 Teller Road
Thousand Oaks, California 91320

SAGE Publications India Pvt Ltd
B 1/I 1 Mohan Cooperative Industrial Area
Mathura Road, Post Bag 7
New Delhi 110 044

SAGE Publications Asia-Pacific Pte Ltd
33 Pekin Street #02–01
Far East Square
Singapore 048763

Library of Congress Control Number: 2008943694

British Library Cataloguing in Publication data

A catalogue record for this book is available from
the British Library

ISBN 978-1-4129-2838-0
ISBN 978-1-4129-2839-7(pbk)

Typeset by C&M Digitals (P) Ltd, Chennai, India
Printed in the UK by the MPG Books Group
Printed on paper from sustainable resources

Mixed Sources
Product group from well-managed
forests and other controlled sources
www.fsc.org Cert no. SA-COC-1565
© 1996 Forest Stewardship Council
FSC

Contents

Introduction

This may be the most self-exemplifying of my books to date: the strands of thought and writing drawn together in these pages stem from my participation in the very roles, capacities and arenas that they examine. Their overall effect has led to me to conclude that an edifying life may be led by becoming the sort of person one writes about with favour. It amounts to a kind of method acting in which the author functions as both author and performer of the script. Thus, not only do I need to thank professional academics – Stefan Gattei, Ivor Goodson, Alan Haworth, Ian Jarvie, Ouyang Kang, Douglas Kellner, Gregor McClennan, Hugo Mendes, Tom Osborne, Raphael Sassower and Nico Stehr – for prompting my thinking in many useful directions, but also such decidedly extra-academic personalities and media represented by Julian Baggini (*The Philosopher's Magazine*), George Reisch (Open Court Press's Popular Culture and Philosophy series), Project Syndicate (a worldwide press organization associated with George Soros's Open Society Institute) and *The Times Higher Education* (London).

The Sociology of Intellectual Life is divided into four chapters guided by my own version of social epistemology. 'Social epistemology' is an inter-disciplinary field concerned with the empirical and normative bases for producing and distributing knowledge. My own version has focused largely on the organized forms of knowledge associated with academic disciplines. The social epistemological thesis pursued in this book can be stated in a way that makes sense of the arrangement of the four chapters. Historically speaking, a specific institution has best promoted a form of intellectual freedom that has managed to serve as a vehicle for the progressive transformation of society. That institution is the university, especially in its nineteenth-century reincarnation as the seat of 'academic freedom', as theorized by 'philosophy', understood as both the foundation and the ultimate unifier of all specialized forms of knowledge. This idea was largely the invention of Wilhelm von Humboldt, who saw himself as applying the lessons of Immanuel Kant's critical philosophy, which formalized many aspects of the previous century's Enlightenment movement. Humboldt envisaged that as increasing numbers of people received a university education, they would become intellectually empowered, so as to take decisions of public import for themselves in democratic forums. Thus, this book has three main chapters, each devoted to a part of Humboldt's original vision: one to the university, one to philosophy, one to the intellectual.

However, Humboldt's vision did not go quite to plan in many respects. Over the past 200 years academic life has become a victim of its own success. It has trained people so well and its research has become so socially relevant that it has constantly had to resist economic and political curbs on its spirit of free inquiry. This resistance has often assumed the sort of studied anti-disciplinary stance that characterizes improvisational forms of expression – that unholy alliance of plagiarism and bullshit by which clever academics routinely overreach for the truth. Hopefully once readers have considered the stormy 'career of the mind in and out of the academy' in the main body of the text, Chapter 4 will provide comic relief, if not an outright catharsis.

1

The Place of Intellectual Life
The University

The University as an Institutional Solution to the Problem of Knowledge

At least since Descartes, the problem of knowledge has been posed *inside out*, that is as a problem for each individual to solve by approximating an external standard to which the individual may or may not have conscious access. There is no sense that epistemic access may be a scarce good, with one individual's access to knowledge perhaps impeding, competing with, or making demands on the epistemic access of some other individual. Rather, knowledge is regarded as what welfare economists call a *public good*, namely, one whose value does not diminish as access increases (Samuelson 1969). In contrast, my own version of social epistemology poses the problem of knowledge *outside in*, that is, in terms of the individual having to choose between two or more alternative courses of action, in full awareness that resources are limited and that other individuals will be simultaneously making similar decisions, the consequences of which will realize certain possibilities at the expense of others. I have called this the problem of *epistemic justice* (Fuller 2007a: 24–9). It implies an image of the knower as a 'bounded rationalist' engaged in 'knowledge management'. This line of thought has run throughout my work in social epistemology, even in my doctoral dissertation (Fuller 1985) and certainly from Fuller (1988) onward. It presupposes that knowledge is a *positional good* (Hirsch 1977). This point has significant implications both for the interpretation of the time-honoured equation 'knowledge is power' and the design of knowledge-bearing institutions, especially universities.

In the slogan 'knowledge is power' (or '*savoir est pouvoir*' or '*Wissens ist Kraft*'), power involves *both* the expansion and contraction of possibilities for action. Knowledge is supposed to expand the knower's possibilities for action by contracting the possible actions of others. These 'others' may range from fellow knowers to non-knowing natural and artificial entities. This broad understanding of the slogan encompasses the interests of all who have embraced it, including Plato, Bacon, Comte and Foucault. But differences arise over the normative spin given to the slogan: should the stress be placed on the *opening* or the *closing* of possibilities for action? If the former, then the range of knowers is likely to be restricted; if the latter, then the range is likely to be extended. After all, my knowledge provides an advantage over you only if you do not already possess it; hence, knowledge is a 'positional good'. This concept also helps to explain the rather schizoid attitudes toward the production and distribution of knowledge that are epitomized in the constitution of universities. In short, we do research to expand our own capacity to act, but we teach in order to free our students from the actions that have been and could be taken by others.

By virtue of their dual role as producers and distributors of knowledge, universities are engaged in an endless cycle of creating and destroying *social capital*, that is, the comparative advantage that a group or network enjoys by virtue of its collective capacity to act on a form of knowledge (Stehr 1994). Thus, as researchers, academics create social capital because intellectual innovation necessarily begins life as an elite product available only to those on 'the cutting edge'. However, as teachers, academics destroy social capital by making the innovation publicly available, thereby diminishing whatever advantage was originally afforded to those on the cutting edge. Recalling Joseph Schumpeter's (1950) definition of the entrepreneur as the 'creative destroyer' of capitalist markets, the university may be similarly regarded as a 'meta-entrepreneurial' institution that functions as the crucible for larger societal change.

However, if the university is taken out of this systemic context, its effects can appear perverse. A clear example is the tendency for credentials to depreciate as more people seek them. The fact that a Bachelor's, or even a Master's, degree does not offer the same labour-market advantage as in the past is sometimes blamed on low-quality academic instruction or the irrelevance of academic to vocational training. More likely, though, the loss of advantage is simply a straightforward result of more job-seekers now possessing the relevant degrees, and hence cannot be so easily discriminated just on that basis. In this case, knowledge has lost its former power. A natural academic response is to call for more research, so as either to discriminate more effectively among current degree-holders or to establish yet still higher degrees in which the new knowledge is taught in the Sisyphean struggle for credentials (Collins 1979). Moreover, this strategy is deployed even within academia, as the PhD is now virtually required to hold any regular teaching post, even though doctoral candidates are still selected in terms of their research potential and trained with a research career in view.

Although research has always been an elite activity, the closeness – ideally the identity – of researchers and teachers in universities tended to overturn whatever initial advantage was enjoyed by the creators and funders of new knowledge. The ideal governing this cycle of creative destruction received its clearest philosophical justification with Wilhelm von Humboldt's reinvention of the university in early nineteenth-century Germany. It aspires to a form of knowledge that is 'universal' in both its potential applications and its potential appliers. Over the past half century, this ideal was recast as serving the welfare state's dual economic function of subsidizing capitalist production (research) and redistributing its surplus (teaching). Not surprisingly, while universities magnified in size and significance during this period, the welfare state's recent devolution has thrown them into financial and wider institutional uncertainty (Krause 1996). The recent drive to have universities mimic business firms as generators of intellectual property amounts to no less than a campaign of institutional dismemberment, in which the university's research function is severed from the teaching function. Thus, we have seen the emergence of quasi-private 'science parks' whose profitable ventures threaten to arrest the normal flow of knowledge and to provide a legal framework for the creation of a knowledge-based class structure that is nowadays sometimes called *information feudalism*. The full implications of this phenomenon are treated in the next section. In the section after that, I explain it as an instance of *capitalism of the third order*, which is paradoxically an attempt to reproduce within capitalism the kind of social structure that capitalism is designed to eliminate.

The Alienability of Knowledge in Our So-called Knowledge Society

Consider the strangeness of 'knowledge society' as a label for what is supposedly distinctive about our times. To anyone innocent of social theory, it should be perfectly obvious that knowledge has always played an important role in the organization and advancement of society. What is new, however, is what the expression 'knowledge society' is meant to *conceal*. An easy way to see this point is to examine the other words that inhabit the same semantic universe as 'knowledge' in knowledge-society discourse: *expertise, credentials, intellectual property* are the sorts of things that denizens of the knowledge society either possess or can acquire. These three words have been listed in order of increasing *alienability*. Let us start with the least alienable: expertise.

The knowledge embodied in my expertise inheres to me in ways that make it not clearly distinguishable from other aspects of my personality. Indeed, the relatively inalienable state of my expertise renders it less tractable to the classical philosophical treatments of knowledge than to what I have called *phlogistemology*, named for that protean eighteenth-century chemical substance *phlogiston*, whose properties were defined exclusively in terms of whatever was left after all the other known factors have been removed or accounted for in a combustion experiment. The defining moment in the Chemical Revolution was when Lavoisier realized that what chemists called 'phlogiston' was sometimes oxygen and sometimes nitrogen, depending on the context of combustion. By analogy, 'expertise' probably refers, not to some unique quality of mind, but to a variety of behavioural dispositions that share little more than our current state of mystification about them.

More specifically, expertise is phlogistemic in the following senses, adapted from Fuller (1996):

(1) Expertise is not reducible to a formal procedure or set of behavioural indicators, yet those who possess expertise can make appropriate socio-epistemic judgements in real life settings.

(2) The same act may be counted as manifesting or not manifesting expertise, depending on the social status of the agent (e.g., a novice's error may count as an innovation if committed by an expert practitioner).

(3) There is little direct evidence for the presence of expertise. Rather, it is 'pre-supposed' in the lack of disruption in one's day-to-day activities.

(4) Conversely, expertise operates as a default explanation for one's basic competence when one's thoughts or actions are otherwise under dispute (e.g., the fact that you disagree with me on this point does not lead you to conclude that I am generally off the mark).

(5) The denial of expertise to someone is taken to be at least as much a moral judgement as a social or epistemic one, thereby inviting the charge that the denier is not merely critical, but uncharitable to the point of misunderstanding the person under scrutiny.

Expertise can be placed on a continuum of alienability that leads naturally to credentials and intellectual property via the common knowledge society locution that expertise can be 'acquired'. This peculiar feature is captured in point (2) above. It means that if I demonstrate that I have undergone a certain regime, then my actions are given much greater significance than they would be given otherwise. In order to appreciate the phlogistemic character of this process, consider that the actions themselves, as pieces of behaviour, may not have changed much before and after the application of the regime. Rather, what has changed is the context, and hence the range of responses, that are likely to follow the performance of those actions. This point was elevated to a metaphysical conundrum at the dawn of the knowledge society in the form of the 'Turing Test', which hypothesized that it may be impossible to tell the difference between human and machine utterance, short of being told which was which. Knowing that a given sentence was uttered by a *bona fide* human rather than an 'artificially' intelligent machine licenses one to confer virtually limitless semantic depth on the former utterance, while reducing the latter utterance to a superficial, programmed response (Fuller 2002a: chap. 3).

However, we need not breach the human–nonhuman divide to make the point. Students typically (and perhaps justifiably!) fail to understand why they cannot get away with saying the more radical things contained in the texts they are assigned to read. The pat answer is to say that the assigned authors can back up their radical utterances, whereas students would be unable to justify their own versions of the same utterances. Of course, we teachers rarely, if ever, put this hypothesis to a direct test. Rather, we treat the hypothesis as a presumption: experts must fail by some canonically sanctioned test before we question their expertise, yet these tests tend to be administered indirectly and their results are always contestable (e.g. fading citations count as measures of invalidity or even irrelevance). In contrast, students must pass tests that are clearly defined, frequently administered, and still largely uncontested, before they are declared expert. We typically let the fact that the expert authors assigned in a course graduated from good universities, hold good jobs, and publish in good places, and are regarded highly by other such experts pass as grounds for supposing that they possess a depth in knowledge that is lacking in the student. Moreover, a consequence of possessing such credentials is that the expert is given the licence to make statements about things that have little to do with the content of one's qualifying examinations or even one's last book.

Once knowledge has begun to be alienated from the knower, such that one needs to acquire something not already possessed, the *content* of what one needs to acquire is no longer salient in explaining how credentials confer expertise on people. This point is clear to those who seek university degrees mainly to get credit for knowledge they have already come to possess by virtue of their job or other life experience. That alone makes 'knowledge society' an extremely misleading expression, since knowledge is usually defined in terms of its content, i.e. some more-or-less valid and reliable representation of reality, without which one could not function. But it would seem that the *containers* of knowledge are really what matter in the knowledge society, e.g. whether what is said comes from the mouth of a Harvard PhD or a high-school dropout. The validity and reliability of one's knowledge may not substantially rise between the start and finish of an academic degree programme, but the likelihood that one's knowledge will be recognized as possessing those qualities does. (However, the speech of a Harvard dropout may carry authority, too, if there is sufficient capital backing and product delivery: witness Bill Gates.)

Thus, the expression 'knowledge society' may be informative, after all – namely, of the means by which social structure is reproduced. Alma Mater has replaced birthright as the biggest determiner of one's place in society, which means that academics have replaced the family and the clergy as the premier custodians of social status. This transition reflects not only the fact that a formal education is required for doing virtually anything of social significance, but perhaps more importantly that it has crowded out most alternative paths of social advancement (Ringer 1979). While knowledge society rhetoric extols the virtues of 'lifelong learning' and apparently extends a hand to those returning to school after having made their way in the 'real world', in reality these adult learners are compelled to return in order to translate their life experience into the hard currency of credentials.

It may be useful at this point to take an aerial view of the alienation of knowledge. In trendier terms, what are the 'spatial flows' that define the knowledge society (Urry 2000)? The natural home of expertise is the workplace, where the requisite tacit knowledge is incubated and transmitted. However, the next stage, that of credentials, forces people out of their disparate workplaces to a central location, the university classroom, where their expertise is converted into something of a generally recognizable social value by means of formal discipline. The final stage of epistemic alienation, intellectual property, involves a further move out of the classroom into the ultimate site of commodification, 'research', which immediately calls to mind laboratories but is hardly confined to those bastions of natural science authority. The social sciences have their own version, as epitomized in the work of the Austro-American sociologist Paul Lazarsfeld. Lazarsfeld's public opinion surveys enabled the extraction of tacit social knowledge to occur at the sites where they are naturally produced (typically, the household), the results of which are then used (or sold) to inform the manufacture of products and policies aimed at generating consumer demand or voter interest, depending on whether the client is in the private or public sector. In the former case, it is called 'advertising', in the latter 'campaigning'. In one clear sense, the social-scientific extraction of raw knowledge material is more efficient than its natural scientific counterpart, namely, that the only instruction required prior to the extraction of social knowledge is telling subjects the constraints within which they must reply to the survey questions.

What distinguishes the knowledge society from the conversion of labour to technology that has characterized the bulk of human history is the presence of academic 'middlemen' who ease the conversion from human to artifact by subjecting the former to explicit procedures. When the academics are civil servants, they provide a moment of mercantilism in what would otherwise be a straightforward account of capitalist appropriation. However, the analogy with mercantilism is not perfect. Universities have never enjoyed – and certainly do not now – a monopoly on the disposition of knowledge products. Moreover, the semi-privatized character of higher education (long-standing in the USA and increasing in Europe) and the proliferation of corporate-sponsored science parks adjoining university campuses serve ultimately to render academia the tail of innovation that is mistakenly thought to be wagging the capitalist dog. In fact, intellectual mercantilism's last stand is the teaching function of the university, which remains (at least for the time being) under the control of the state, even as the university's research function is increasingly devolved to the private sector.

The result partly resembles what Marx originally called 'Oriental Despotism', whose 'Asiatic' mode of production consists of an imperial power taxing its subject-nations, while leaving their local modes of production and social relations largely intact. This corresponds to the role of academics who, empowered by the state, can command the time and money of workers in need of credentials for career advancement, usually without transforming the workplace or sometimes even the workers' substantive knowledge. Under Oriental Despotism, the collected taxes were originally fed back into large-scale public works projects that solidified the empire's power. Here too there is an analogy in the history of the knowledge society, namely, the efforts taken by what Alvin Gouldner (1970) tellingly called the 'welfare-warfare state' at the height of the Cold War era to consolidate the citizenry with comprehensive healthcare coverage and educational access, at the same time as it increased surveillance and military capabilities through the construction of vast electronic information and communication networks. These nation-building projects called forth the first burst of the technically trained personnel of the post-World War II generation, especially in the wake of Sputnik in 1957.

However, with the decline of superpower hostilities in the 1990s revealing large state budgetary burdens, both large corporations and special interest groups have increasingly appropriated these projects for their own uses. The resulting political devolution and normative fragmentation are associated with the ideological emergence of 'postmodernism' and 'neo-liberal' forms of governance. These developments are normally cast as the continued penetration of capitalism into spheres of society previously protected by the welfare state. Without denying the considerable truth of this claim, once we see the original construction of the knowledge society's infrastructure as a latter-day version of Oriental Despotism, the privatization of the great information and communication networks starts to look more like the breakdown of the Roman Empire into the feudal fiefdoms and free cities that characterized the Middle Ages in Europe.

Not surprisingly, then, on the margins of the knowledge society's boosters has flourished a clutch of foreboding theorists of the oncoming 'information feudalism' (Drahos 1995). What might count as evidence for this atavistic turn of events? The following three points will have to suffice for an answer here:

1   Human labour becomes increasingly transitory as a source of value, but only in part because more efficient mechanical means are developed to replace it. The other part of the story is that these new machines – e.g. expert systems – are increasingly protected by intellectual property law, which enables the holder of the relevant property rights (i.e. patent, copyright or trademark) to extract rents from those who would try to lower their own overall production costs. In the name of encouraging innovation, the legal system effectively converts the capitalist profit-seeking motive to a feudal rent-seeking one. This conversion had not occurred at the onset of the Industrial Revolution because, before the US Constitution explicitly prescribed the state's interest in systematically licensing innovation, the granting of intellectual property rights had been subject to the ruler's discretion, typically as a personal favour. There had been no expectation that eventually all of intellectual space would be divided into discrete domains as physical space had been under feudalism. For their part, the American Founding Fathers were mainly concerned with ensuring individual free expression (which required protection not only from censure but also from imitation) and collective wealth production (assuming that the nation that had registered a patent stood to gain most from the invention's economic benefits). Given capital's increasingly transnational mobility over the last two centuries, intellectual property legislation would seem to meet the former aim at the expense of the latter.

2   The more that credentials are required for employment, the less the knowledge content associated with obtaining those credentials matters to prospective employment. This is largely because credentials are no longer sufficient but merely necessary to securing a position. Thus, from being a principle of empowerment, credentials are now marks of exclusion. Under the circumstances, they have succeeded race and class as the premier mechanism for discriminating and stratifying a population. And like race and class, credentials turn out not to be an especially good job performance indicator but merely a lightning rod for resentment. As this feudal residue of credentials is revealed, private sector non-academic training centres emerge to undermine the virtual monopoly enjoyed by universities. But more importantly, and ironically, the surfeit of academically qualified people gives a competitive edge to those who possess traditionally *non-academic*, specifically entrepreneurial, forms of knowledge. This is no more evident than in the natural sciences. The 'expert' scientist enters and exits lines of research just ahead of the pack, invests in skills and equipment that are usable in the widest variety of projects, and constructs her knowledge products so as to extract a certain 'tribute' (be it an attribution in a citation list or a financial tribute in patent royalties) from their users. 'Knowledge engineers' design computers that simulate a field's expertise to eliminate still more academic competitors. The raw material for these simulations is of course the experts themselves, who gladly sell their knowledge in the face of eventual obsolescence, once it has yielded most of its anticipated return. Here we see, perhaps most clearly, the wedge that the knowledge society drives between the two main functions of the university – teaching and research – for instead of feeding back into teaching, research either circumvents the educational process through privatization or renders it obsolete through automation (Fuller 2002a: chap. 3).

3   The surfeit of available information often described as an 'explosion' turns out to have the same effect as scarcity had in pre-capitalist times, namely, to slow the overall pace of intellectual progress. Before Johannes Gutenberg perfected and commercialized moveable type printing in the mid-fifteenth century, books could not be produced in large quantities; hence authors could not reasonably suppose that their readers had access to a library. This meant that the bulk of most texts was given over to acquainting readers with all the knowledge they would need to have in order to understand the author's distinctive contribution. Unfortunately, the propaedeutic task was usually so laborious that more energy was spent in summarizing and criticizing the past than in pushing forward the frontiers of knowledge (Eisenstein 1979). Little wonder, then, that the Copernican Revolution began only after Gutenberg, even though various heliocentric astronomies had already challenged the geocentric orthodoxy for over a thousand years. However, now we suffer from the opposite problem, as the speed at which texts are put on the market makes it impossible for anyone to catch up with all of them first hand. Consequently, instead

of running ahead of the pack, academics run interference within the pack, each trying to show his or her own indispensability to understanding what the others are doing. In this respect, the recently growing awareness of complexity in reality is nothing more than a projection of academics who need to define themselves in terms of their colleagues in order to occupy any recognizable intellectual position whatsoever (Fuller 2000a: chap. 5). Such a regime, perhaps most closely associated with Pierre Bourdieu's sociology of knowledge, ensures that innovation will occur only within the narrow confines of professionally sanctioned discourse, thereby minimizing the prospects for ideas being the source of major societal change (Fuller 1997: chap. 7).

Readers who doubt this gloomy prognosis should consider the recent computerization of the medieval practice of anonymous writing, or 'hypertext'. As was true generally of texts in the Middle Ages, the authority of the hypertext rests on the circulation patterns revealed by the superimposition of layers of commentary. Because the ultimate source of such a text is often unknown and its exegetical accretions are often at odds with each other, it is nearly impossible to subject the text to any focused criticism (i.e. to oppose a thesis that it asserts). Instead, one is forced to 'write against' or 'resist' the hypertext, which in turn unleashes another hypertext into its own separate electronic orbit.

The feudal precedent for the above developments is obscured by the dual sense of history that informs the continual condensing and surveying of texts that together artificially maintain the knowledge society's sense of its own originality. This duality consists of a *telescoping* and a *stereoscoping* phase.

On the one hand, the history of the relatively distant past is *telescoped* so that knowledge-based social movements from the past that have been at least as complex and wide-ranging as the knowledge society are collapsed into a uniformly distributed ideal type – say, 'Protestantism', 'Enlightenment', 'Socialism' (Wuthnow 1989) – that is chosen more for its distinctiveness than its representativeness. Although a reasonable methodological principle when it was first introduced to enable sociology to formulate general hypotheses on the basis of historical data, it has since become a strategy for legitimating historical amnesia in an archivally saturated world. Therefore, any awareness of anticipations of contemporary developments is bound to be lost.

On the other hand, for the history of the relatively recent past, events are *stereoscoped*: that is, a wedge is driven between two closely connected developments, making them appear to be on opposite sides of a fabricated divide. Perhaps the clearest case in point is the alleged distinction between 'Mode 1' and 'Mode 2' knowledge production that is now so popular among European science's policy gurus (Gibbons et al. 1994). Applied mainly to the laboratory-based natural sciences's, Mode 1 stands for discipline-based research and Mode 2 for a hybridized sense of research that blends together the interests of academia, the state, and industry. Seen stereoscopically, the origins of Mode 1 are pushed back to the founding of the Royal Society in the seventeenth century (if not to the ancient Greek philosophers), while the roots of Mode 2 are brought up to the period starting with the Manhattan Project that built the first atomic bomb (if not the post-Cold War devolution of the welfare-warfare state). However, historically speaking, it is only in the last quarter of the nineteenth century that *both* Modes come into being, almost simultaneously, in Germany. Laboratories had been traditionally excluded from universities (and confined to polytechnics) for reasons that amounted to an intellectualized class snobbery (i.e. lab work required a manual dexterity that was alien to the hands-free world of liberally educated elites). Yet, once the laboratory sciences were ensconced on campuses, they quickly made alliances with state and industry clients, most notably in the Kaiser Wilhelm Gesellschaften.

Indeed, what had made the laboratory sciences so alien to the classical constitution of the university *also* enabled them, once inside the university, to adapt well to externally oriented research projects. Here it is worth recalling a salient feature of Kuhn's (1970) account of science, which is based almost entirely on the laboratory sciences (with astronomy as the important exception): the 'normal science' conducted by a paradigm's practitioners is autonomous not only from practical applications but also from the research trajectories of other academic disciplines. In that respect, a paradigm is a *doubly alienated* form of knowledge – a self-contained module of inquiry that does not require the institutional setting of the university for its existence or even its legitimation. Little wonder – though also little noticed – that Kuhn says next to nothing about academia as a site for the conduct of normal science. Only doctoral training programmes are worthy of some discussion. In contrast, the university's traditional nerve centre has been its undergraduate curriculum committee, as the site where the relevance of each discipline's major discoveries to a liberal education is regularly negotiated, resulting in 'the creative destruction of social capital' discussed in the first section of this chapter. The humanities, which until about 1900 had dominated the universities, were never as narrowly insular as Mode 1 implies but neither as readily adaptive to external pressures as Mode 2 implies (Fuller and Collier 2004: chap. 2).

The Knowledge Society as Capitalism of the Third Order

To understand the integral role of universities to the latest phase of capitalism, consider two general ways of thinking about the nature of capitalism. The more familiar one is a first-order account about how producers are engaged in a perpetual – and largely self-defeating (according to Marxists) – competition to make the most out of the least, and thereby generate the greatest return on investment, a.k.a. 'profits'. Whatever its other merits, this account takes for granted that the relative standing of competing producers is self-evident, so that no additional work is required to identify the 'market leaders'. But in fact, such work *is* needed. This second-order account of how producers publicly demonstrate their productivity is the context in which 'capitalism' was coined by Max Weber's great German rival Werner Sombart in 1902 (Grundmann and Stehr 2001). What contemporaries, notably Thorstein Veblen, derided as the 'conspicuous consumption' of successful capitalists, Sombart treated as the principal means by which capitalists displayed their social standing in a world where social structure was no longer reproduced as a system of fixed heritable differences. Thus, capitalists had to spend more in order to appear more successful.

However, it would be misleading to think of these expenditures as allowing capitalists to luxuriate in their success. On the contrary, it spurred them to be more productive in the ordinary, first-order sense, since their competitors were quickly acquiring comparable, if not better, consumer goods. Indeed, before long, the competition was so intense that it became necessary to spend on acquiring the connoisseurship needed to purchase goods that will be seen – by those who know how to see – as ahead of the competition's purchases. By the time we reach this 'third-order' capitalism, we are at the frontier of the knowledge society. That the 'knowledge society' might be a more polite way of referring to third-order capitalism should not be *prima facie* surprising. After all, the founding father of scientometrics, Derek de Solla Price, trawled through the welter of national economic statistics, only to find that the indicator that showed the strongest positive correlation with research productivity was not a measure of industrial productivity, but of electricity consumption per capita (Price 1978; see also Fuller 2002a: chap. 1).

A certain vision of economic history is implied in the above account of capitalism. In pre-capitalist times, consumption was done at the expense of production, which explained (for example) the fleeting success of Spain and Portugal as imperial powers. They failed to reinvest the wealth they gained from overseas; they simply squandered it. In contrast, capitalist consumption is second-order production supported on the back of increased first-order production. From a sociological standpoint, the most striking feature of this 'before-and-after' story is its suggestion that capitalism is innovative in altering the sense of responsibility one has for maintaining a common social order. In pre-capitalist times, this responsibility was, so to speak, equally distributed across its members, regardless of status. Lords and serfs equally bore the burden of producing the distinction that enabled lords to dominate serfs. Expressions like 'mutual recognition', 'respect', and 'honour' capture this symmetrical sense of responsibility. However, in capitalist times, it would seem that, like insurance in today's devolved welfare states, individuals bear this burden in proportion to their desire to be protected from status erosion. Thus, those who would be recognized as superior need to devote increasing effort to a demonstration of their superiority.

This last point becomes especially poignant in advanced capitalist societies, where at least in principle the vast majority of people can lead materially adequate lives while spending less time and effort on first-order productive pursuits. However, this situation simply leads people to intensify their efforts at second-order pursuits. As a result, for example, individuals spend more on education and firms on advertising, even though the advantage they gain in terms of first-order production is marginal or temporary. Yet, this expenditure is necessary for one to be seen as 'running with the pack'. Thus, we return to the concept of positional good introduced at the start of this chapter. The logic of producing such goods predicts that, over time, one's relative status will decline, unless it is actively maintained, which usually involves trying to exceed it, thereby raising the absolute standard that everyone needs to meet. Thus, an expanded production of positional goods, combined with increased efficiency in the production of material goods, results in the systemically irrational outcomes that we have come to expect (and perhaps even rationalize) as our 'knowledge society'. Specifically, the resources spent on acquiring credentials and marketing goods come to *exceed* what is spent on the actual work that these activities are meant to enhance, facilitate and communicate.

Of course, such a classic case of means–ends reversal is *not* systemically irrational, if it marks a more-or-less conscious shift in values. Thus, it may not take much to be persuaded that we really do produce in order to have something to sell, and we take up particular jobs in order to have a platform for showing off our credentials. The *struggle for recognition* therefore overtakes the *struggle for survival* – the ultimate triumph of the German over the English tradition in political thought (Fukuyama 1992: chaps 13–19). But this point acquires more of a sting in the case of so-called 'public goods', especially knowledge. In the case of such goods, producers are (supposedly) not only unable to recover fully the costs of production, but they would also incur further costs, were they to restrict consumption of their good. However, I would urge that so-called public goods be analysed as simply the class of positional goods that most effectively hide their production costs, specifically by everyone paying into a fund whose actual beneficiaries are undisclosed, perhaps because they are indeterminate (Fuller 2002a: chap. 1).

This abstract point may be illustrated by answering a concrete question: why was Einstein *not* entitled to a patent for his theories of relativity? The answer is that Einstein's theories were innovative against a body of physical science whose development had been funded by the German state through taxation and other public finance schemes, major beneficiaries of which were institutions of higher education. These institutions were, in turn, open to anyone of sufficient merit, who would then be in a position to contribute to this body of knowledge. Einstein happened to take advantage of this opportunity that was in principle open to all taxpayers. But even if Einstein had not existed, it would have been only a matter of time before someone else would have come along to push back the frontiers of knowledge in a comparable manner. But as long as it remains unclear from what part of the population the next Einstein is to be drawn, the public finance of higher education is justified. In that case, Einstein does not deserve the economic advantage made possible by a patent because he simply exploited an opportunity that had been subsidized by his fellow citizens. I propose this as the 'deep rationale' for the production of public goods like university education and research that have been the hallmarks of welfare-state regimes.

Will the University Survive the Era of Knowledge Management?

Academics are too easily flattered by talk of 'knowledge management'. They often think it points to the central role of universities in society. Yet, the phrase signals quite the opposite – that society is a veritable hotbed of knowledge production, over which universities do not enjoy any special privilege or advantage. Academics have been caught off-guard because they have traditionally treated knowledge as something pursued for its own sake, regardless of cost or consequences. This made sense when universities were elite institutions and independent inquirers were leisured. However, there is increasing global pressure to open universities to the wider public, typically for reasons unrelated to the pure pursuit of knowledge. Today's universities are expected to function as dispensers of credentials and engines of economic growth. Consequently, academics are no longer in full control of their performance standards.

In this context, knowledge managers have their work cut out. Former *Fortune* editor Tom Stewart (1997) has called universities 'dumb organizations' that have too much 'human capital' but not enough 'structural capital'. Behind these buzzwords is the view that a fast-food chain like McDonald's is a 'smart organization' because it makes the most of its relatively ill-trained staff through the alchemy of good management. In contrast, business as usual in academia proceeds almost exactly in reverse, as department heads and deans struggle to keep track of the activities of its overeducated staff. If a McDonald's is much more than the sum of its parts, a university appears to be much less.

Academics remain largely in denial about the impact of knowledge management, even though the sheer increase in the number of university heads drawn from business and industry concedes that McDonald's and MIT may be, at least in principle, judged by the same performance standards. A glaring recent example is Richard Sykes, whose appointment as Rector of Imperial College London was based largely on his successful merger of two transnational drugs companies, Glaxo and Smith-Kline. Not surprisingly, he tried – unsuccessfully as of this writing – to merge Imperial College and University College London to produce the UK's premier research-led university (at least as measured by research income). In any case, Sykes seeded the idea in the UK's academic management culture, resulting in the merger of the University of Manchester and its neighbour UMIST, the largest campus-based UK university (in terms of student numbers), a move advertised at the time as comparable to the hypothetical merger of Harvard and MIT, which are located on opposite ends of Massachusetts Avenue in Cambridge (USA).

And should we automatically think that the next academic generation would resist such changes? Put bluntly: why should we expect the increasing number of academics on short-term contracts to defend the integrity of an institution that cannot promise them job security? Even PhDs quickly acquire the survival skills and attitudes of McDonald's much less-trained and disposable staff, as they become willing and able to move for better pay and work conditions (Jacob and Hellstrom 2000). Indeed, when adaptability to an ever-changing labour market becomes the premier value, the normative force of autonomous work conditions starts to fade. After all, autonomy implies the capacity to say no to external pressures, which in the world of flexible capitalism looks unreasonably rigid. Thus, a signature practice of academic tenure has been the entitlement to teach whatever one happens to be researching – even if it attracts only three students, two of whom are regularly offended by what the teacher says.

However, many academics – and not just professional knowledge managers – have endorsed recent steps taken to disaggregate the unity of teaching and research that has defined the university since its modern reinvention in early nineteenth-century Germany. These steps occur daily with the establishment of each new on-line degree programme and science park – the one reducing the university to a diploma mill, the other to a patent factory. Though they pull in opposing directions, these two 'post-academic' organizations share an overriding interest in benefiting those who can pay at the point of delivery. In this context, universities appear quite vulnerable, as they have always been hard-pressed to justify their existence in such immediate cost–benefit terms. But it would be a mistake to place all the blame for this 'service provider' view of universities on knowledge managers, or even the recent wave of neo-liberal ideology.

Academics who nostalgically recall the flush funding for universities in the heyday of the welfare state often forget that service provision was precisely what lay behind the appeal of academia to policymakers. The public was willing to pay higher taxes because either they (or, more likely, their children) might qualify for a course of study that would enable them to improve their job prospects or academics might come up with a cure or a technique that would improve the quality of life in society. The same mentality operates today, only in an increasingly privatized funding environment.

In short, a Faustian bargain was struck during the era of the welfare–warfare state that was typically cloaked in a social-democratic rhetoric. Universities grew to an unprecedented size and significance, but in return they had become the premier site of socio-economic reproduction. In the long term, this bargain has caused the universities to lose their political – and consequently their intellectual – independence, a point that is increasingly clear with the removal of state legal and financial protection. After having been in the service of all taxpayers and judged by the benefits provided to them, universities are now being thrown into a global market where US universities already enjoy a long history of providing high-quality knowledge-based goods and services on demand.

At least, this is how the shifting political economy of academia appears from the European side of the Atlantic. It is now common for university heads to complain that lingering attachments to the welfare state prevent governments from charging the full student fees needed to compete with US universities on the world stage. They seem to assume that Americans are willing to pay a lot for higher education at the best institutions because these have a long track record of proving themselves in the market-place. However, this does not explain how, say, the Ivy League manages to officially charge the world's highest fees, yet requires only a third of the students to pay them. Time-honoured universalist, democratic and meritocratic ideals may explain *why* the Ivy League has this policy, but the mystery for Europeans is in determining *how* they have pulled it off.

As it turns out, European understanding of the American scene – especially at the elite end – is seriously flawed. What makes the flaw so serious is that it involves forgetting what has historically made universities such a distinctive European contribution to world culture. I shall return to this shortly. But at an even more basic level, this flaw should remind us of the long-term corrosive effect that marginal utility thinking has had on how we conceptualize value. Both welfare-state economics and the current wave of neo-liberalism agree that the economy is built from transactions in which the traders are simultaneously trading with each other and trading off against their own competing interests. Thus, the rational economic agent is willing to accept a certain price, but only for a certain amount of any good or service. Beyond that point, 'diminishing returns' set in and rational agents shift their spending elsewhere. This means that goods and services are judged by the prospect of their impact on the consumer in the relative short term. Such a frame of reference is fundamentally antithetical to the character of the university.

To their credit, welfare economists have long realized that their conception of the economy tends to devalue benefits that accrue only in the long term and especially to others not intimately connected to the agent (Price 1993). As we saw in the previous section, the welfare-state conception of universities as both instances and producers of 'public goods' was meant to address this problem by arguing, in effect, that it is cheaper to indemnify everyone in a society than to target particular citizens for providing the costs and enjoying the benefits. But to unsympathetic neo-liberal ears, this sounds like a concession that higher education is a market with an indeterminate price structure. Could this be because producers and consumers are impeded from effectively communicating with each other? Such a suspicion motivates the knowledge manager's general call for the removal of state barriers to the free competition of universities, which will quickly force them to restructure and perhaps even devolve, in the face of market forces.

However, buried beneath this by now familiar line of thought is its anchoring intuition: the paradigm case of all economic activity is the exchange of goods that might occur in a weekly village market between parties trying to provide for their respective households. From that standpoint, the main practical problem is how to clear the market so that no one is left with unsold goods or unmet needs once the sun goes down. This formulation of the problem makes at least three assumptions that are alien to the economic situation in which the university has (always) found itself:

1 Each trader is both a 'producer' and 'consumer'. In contrast, the two roles are clearly distinguished in any transaction between a university and a prospective client, including a student.
2 No trader wants a surplus of goods, let alone to accumulate as many goods as possible. Unused goods will either rot or become a target for thieves. In contrast, the sheer accumulation of knowledge – be it in books, brains or databanks – is central to a university's mission.
3 There is a cyclical structure to each trader's needs that ideally corresponds to the village market's periodicity. There are no inherently insatiable desires, only recurrent desires that are met as they arise. In contrast, the idea of termination is so foreign to academic inquiry that attempts to arrest or even channel its conduct have tended to be treated as repressive.

However, universities can be managed as other than multi-purpose service providers joined to their clients by discrete transactions that end once the academic goods have been delivered. What originally entitled a university to corporate status under Roman law (*universitas* in Latin) was its pursuit of aims that transcended the personal interests of any of its current members. This enabled universities to raise their own earmarked funds, which were bestowed on individuals who were 'incorporated' into the institution on a non-hereditary basis. Such individuals typically negotiated their identity through examination or election, which required that they be willing to become something other than they already were. Along with universities, the original corporations included churches, religious orders, guilds and cities. In this respect, being a student was very much like being a citizen. Commercial ventures came to be regularly treated as corporations only in the nineteenth century. Before then, a business was either a temporary and targeted venture (akin to a military expedition) or an amplified version of family inheritance, the default mechanism for transmitting social status under Roman law.

The corporate origin of universities is of more than historical interest. The oldest and most successful US universities were founded by British religious dissidents for whom the corporate form of the church was very vivid. From the seventeenth century onward, American graduates were cultivated as 'alumni' who regard their time in university as a life-defining process that they would wish to share with every worthy candidate. The resulting alumni endowments, based on the Protestant 'tithing' of income, have provided a fund for allowing successive generations to enjoy the same opportunity for enrichment. In return, the alumni receive glossy magazines, winning sports teams (which the alumni worship every weekend), free courses and nominal – and occasionally not so nominal – involvement in university policy. Two-thirds of Ivy League students have their education subsidized in this fashion. Moreover, the leading public American universities display similar, and sometimes even stronger, tendencies in the same direction. Thus, UCLA, the University of Michigan and the University of Virginia are 'public universities' that are 70 per cent privately funded, relatively little of which comes from the full payment of student fees.

In contrast, the two main strategies for 'privatizing' the universities in former welfare state regimes – market-driven tuition fees and income-based graduate taxes – operate with a long-term strategy for institutional survival that is nothing more than a series of short-term strategies. At most, these compulsory payment schemes would enable universities to replace the capital they invest in their students, but they would also provide little incentive for graduates to contribute more than had been invested in them. If anything, such fees and taxes could become a source of resentment, non-compliance and even overall fiscal failure, since in a world where knowledge is pursued as a positional good, it becomes harder to justify a high-quality university education on a short-term value-for-money basis.

Therefore, to overcome the knowledge manager's jibe that they are dumb organizations, universities must endeavour to be wholes that are much greater than the sum of their parts. At the very least, this means that a university's value must be measured beyond the short-term benefits it provides for immediate clients, including students. The ideal of uniting teaching and research promised just such a breadth of organizational vision, one worth updating today. After all, universities are unique in producing new knowledge (through research) that is then consolidated and distributed (through teaching). In the former phase, academia generates new forms of social advantage and privilege, while in the latter phase, it eliminates them. This creative destruction of social capital entitles universities to be called the original entrepreneurial organizations. However, universities have been neither produced nor maintained in a social vacuum. With the slow but steady decline of the welfare state, it is time to recover the university as one of the original corporations, whose style of 'privatization' is superior to the 'trade fair' model that has dominated modern economic thought and today threatens the institution's integrity.

Postmodernism as an Anti-university Movement

A telling but little remarked fact about the provenance of Jean-François Lyotard's (1983) coinage of 'postmodernism' is that it occurred in a 1979 'report on the state of knowledge' to the higher education council of Quebec. Lyotard dedicated his report to the 'institute', or department, where he held a chair in one of the new universities of Paris, wishing that it may flourish while the university itself withered away. This sentiment neatly epitomizes the postmodern normative posture – one that celebrates the endless proliferation of inquiries and condemns the submission of this 'information explosion' to the institutional containment of the university, which, after all, presupposes a clearly bounded 'universe of discourse' that is traversed in a 'curriculum'. Put in an historical perspective, Lyotard challenged the last bastion of medievalism in an the modern university, namely, the idea that everything worth saying could be confined within its walls. This image made sense in the thirteenth century, when the physical universe was held to be bounded, with the earth, and humanity more specifically, at its centre. The university was then quite literally a microcosm.

Lyotard's dedication of *The Postmodern Condition* reversed the definition of postmodernism that Daniel Bell (1973) had introduced only a decade earlier as the cultural analogue of 'postindustrialism'. In Bell's usage, postmodernism meant the rise of an academically informed class of public administrators who contained and sublimated the potentially disruptive effects of the information explosion in the name of a benevolent, albeit technocratic, welfare state. Here the comprehensive critical vision of the university – above and beyond specialist knowledge in particular disciplines – was the key point. In this respect, Bell's establishmentarian vision of postmodernism presupposed a future for intellectuals not unlike that of Alvin Gouldner's 'new class', the welfare state's answer to the revolutionary party vanguard in a post-Marxist world (Gouldner 1979). But neither Bell nor Gouldner anticipated the devolution of the welfare state and its associated challenges to the university as a well-formed social entity. Lyotard's crystal ball turned out to be clearer, as his disparagement of the structural power of the university was of a piece with neoliberal calls for unimpeded innovation and Margaret Thatcher's declaration of society's non-existence. This is the postmodern future we got. To be sure, the differences in the postmodern prophecies put forward by Bell, Gouldner and Lyotard can be largely explained by their respective vantage points in higher education.

In 1963 Bell was commissioned by the trustees of Columbia University to diagnose increasing student calls for 'relevance' in an undergraduate curriculum that had been unique in requiring that all students spend the first two years studying the classics of Western philosophy, literature, art and music, followed by two years of intensive study in a traditional academic discipline. The call for 'relevance' was operationalized as proposals for interdisciplinary studies programmes that took as their subject matter a region of the world or an aspect of humanity (i.e. class, race, gender) whose significance had not been adequately represented in the constitution of academic departments. Much to the relief of the trustees, Bell held firm to the classical ideal – bolstered by Thomas Kuhn's trendy 'paradigm' conception of scientific research – that traditional academic departments offered protected space for the autonomous pursuit of fundamental inquiry, on the basis of which secondary inquiries driven by social concerns could then be built at the postgraduate level (Bell 1966). As it turned out, Bell's Solomonic judgment failed to anticipate that by 1968 Columbia would be at the forefront of worldwide student revolts against 'the establishment'.

For his part, Gouldner was struck by the growth of higher education as a credentials mill since the end of World War II. Although most of those passing through academia were not motivated by the ethos of pure inquiry, the occasion of their training provided an opportunity for instructors to enlarge and replenish the public sphere by instilling a critical attitude in whatever fields the students happened to pursue. But Gouldner's sudden death in 1980 prevented him from seeing that once 'proper universities' started to present themselves unabashedly as dispensers of credentials, they would encroach on terrain much more familiar to more locally oriented institutions as polytechnics and colleges. Moreover, the gradual abandonment of the welfare state's meritocratic mentality over the next two decades would compel universities to compete in a buyer's market where, given the ratio of instititutions to matriculants, any pedagogical imposition unrelated to the acquisition of credentials – such as 'critical reflexivity' – could be assured an unwelcomed response.

In striking contrast to Bell and Gouldner, Lyotard took a more cynical view of higher education as a member of a university that had been commissioned by De Gaulle to placate the '68ers', academic radicals who demanded more open admissions to elite institutions. In practice, this had only served to coopt the radicals and compromise the independent standing of academia in French society. From Lyotard's standpoint, the creation of new universities was the state's last desperate attempt at maintaining social order in a world that was quickly exceeding its control. In this context, the appeal to academic standards was often a disguised reactionary ideology for arresting the cross-fertilization of ideas and the novel developments they could breed. This explains Lyotard's profound antipathy for Juergen Habermas's 'ideal speech situation', a projection of the university's founding myth that is unrealizable except through the imposition of closure on an indefinite plurality of cross-cutting discourses. In Lyotard's hands, the university was reduced from a transcendental concept to a cluster of buildings where representatives of these discourses would have chance encounters and set up temporary alliances, subject to the strictures of the buildings' custodians (a.k.a. academic administrators).

What has enabled Lyotard's cynicism to triumph over the opposed yet still idealistic visions of the university espoused by Bell and Gouldner? The key to the answer may be found in the material bases for the expansion of higher education in the modern period. Lyotard, Bell and Gouldner can be seen as reflecting on the same set of developments associated with highly productive capitalist economies married to welfare-state systems. These constitute the blindspot of Marxist political economy, which had provided the classic explanation for the rise of a critical intelligentsia capable of revolutionary leadership. Marx had failed to anticipate that the state would resume a regulatory role in advanced capitalist societies comparable to its role under mercantilist regimes in the seventeenth and eighteenth centuries. Not only would the state provide investments and incentives to capital development, but it would also use its powers of taxation to strengthen welfare-oriented institutions designed to buffer the populace from the effects of business-cycle fluctuations. It would mean a steadier growth curve for the economy, but at the cost of an escalating operating budget for the state.

According to Joseph Schumpeter (1950), who first clearly formulated this scenario, the captains of industry would have little choice but to accept increasing tax rates on their profits as the price for avoiding the mass displacement of workers that would sow the seeds of revolution. In the end, innovation's 'creative destruction' of the marketplace would itself be seen as a threat to economic security. While neither capitalist nor socialist would realize their heroic visions, everyone would be able to survive comfortably in the same world. In short, the future would be Swedish.

For Bell and Gouldner, the Schumpeterian scenario provided plenty of scope for the work of intellectuals, even if it precluded the Second Coming of Lenin. Among the expanding welfarist institutions were the universities and other state-licenced institutes of higher learning, which provided training and employment for intellectuals. Before the mid-nineteenth century, these intellectuals would have been – much like the original Enlightenment *philosophes* – itinerant workers with no particular attachment to the current political economic order. But over the last 150 years, and markedly since the end of World War II, these people have become civil servants who, in the first instance, address each other in jealously guarded ('peer-reviewed') zones of discourse and only then, after that initial filtering process, the larger society. Consequently, their potential for incendiary speech has been domesticated into reasoned cultural critiques and piecemeal policy advice.

Marx would not have been pleased, but Bell and Gouldner saw hope. Because the smooth functioning of advanced capitalism depends on the maintenance of its welfare system, the intellectuals who staff the system collectively hold enormous power in shaping the course of society. In Bell's vision, this would lead to a greater rationalization of the economy, 'the end of ideology', in his memorable phrase, as class conflict would be resolved into specialized administrative tasks. For his part, Gouldner envisaged a somewhat less complete sublimation of ideological conflict. Intellectuals would continue to take it upon themselves to make, in the name of humanity, overarching claims that would invariably contradict each other. However, the increasing specialization of both their knowledge and interests would make the partiality of their claims more apparent than ever, thereby enabling the emergence of a more critical public culture.

However, from Lyotard's Parisian perch, Bell and Gouldner were indulging in wishful thinking, not least because they took for granted that the state could indefinitely translate ever-fragmenting knowledge practices into principles of social structure by employing increasing numbers of intellectuals. What happened instead circumvented both Schumpeter's vision of capitalism's excesses contained by a fully socialized state and its nightmare counterpart, what James R. O'Connor (1973) originally called the 'fiscal crisis of the state', whereby an over-extended social-services budget would lead to a renewed cycle of class conflict, perhaps even on the epic scale originally envisaged by Marx. Those in search of a suitable role for intellectuals in the postmodern world failed to anticipate that the state would simply devolve its central welfare provision, including health and education, thereby enabling capitalism to simply continue apace.

Lyotard's postmodern cynicism has been vindicated by an unholy alliance between academia's classical ethic of autonomous inquiry and the increased disciplinization of the scaled-up modern university. Originally all academics believed they were engaged in *the same* autonomous inquiry, which was driven by some overarching ideal, such as The Truth. The commonality of this ideal gave considerable scope for probing criticism that frequently challenged reigning orthodoxies and crossed disciplinary boundaries. The university provided the institutional space that made these free-ranging inquiries possible. We see remnants of this attitude in public debates towards such 'undisciplined' issues as the existence of God, the meaning of life and even the evolution of human traits. However, that attitude is quite alien to today's professional academic sense of inquiry, in which autonomy is relativized to particular disciplines. Thus, instead of seeking The Truth wherever it may lead, one applies a 'paradigm' or follows through a 'research programme' until its intellectual resources – or, more pointedly, financial resources – have been exhausted. In effect, then, the division of labour in today's academia has modularized, perhaps even decontextualized, the commitment to autonomous inquiry. A vivid reminder of this development is the ease with which the research units of some natural-science departments can be transferred from the institutional setting of the university to another – say, a science park or a corporate facility – without seeming to lose anything in the translation.

The postmodern condition, then, marks the literal *disintegration* of the university, as each discipline becomes increasingly capable of getting on with the business of inquiry without worrying about the fates of other disciplines. Traditionally, the university had the means to check such tendencies toward self-absorption. The most mundane, but no less potent, was a common pool of financial resources from which the various departments would draw their operating budgets, which would then have to be justified, if not to each other, to the university's finance committee, whose default position would favour cross-subsidizing the departments (i.e. the poor benefit from the rich). However, with the emergence and active encouragement of extramural income, this default position is losing its moral suasion, and the finance committee is more generally losing its significance as a forum for discussions of the costs and benefits of pursuing alternative lines of inquiry. The other traditional academic check on disciplinary self-absorption is, of course, the university's principal clientele: *students*. Curriculum planning remains a sobering exercise for evaluating the relative importance of bodies of knowledge and modes of thought for the life of the ordinary individual. Indeed, as we shall see in the next section, this turns out to be the source of leverage that critical intellectuals can exert over the knowledge system.

At this point, a few words are in order about the role of interdisciplinarity in promoting the postmodern condition, since my earlier discussion of Bell and Gouldner suggested that, at least in the 1960s and 1970s, interdisciplinarity promised to revive the university's critical edge. To be sure, appeals to 'interdisciplinarity' remain in vogue across the academy today. However, they have now been given a postmodern spin that was previously lacking (Fuller and Collier 2004: Introduction). This becomes especially clear upon recalling that Humboldt founded the modern university with the liberally educated citizen in mind. From that standpoint, knowledge production was presumed to be 'always already' interdisciplinary. Disciplines as we currently know them – corresponding to departments, journals and dedicated graduate degree programmes – only gradually emerged as institutionalized settlements between clashing research programmes governed by overarching world-views. Thus, people who we now so clearly call physicists, chemists, biologists, physicians and even engineers were quite hard to distinguish for most of the nineteenth century. The same applied even more strongly in the so-called non-natural sciences. Moreover, sophisticated surveys of academic knowledge up to the first third of the twentieth century presupposed this murky and fractious process of disciplinization (e.g. Cassirer 1950; Merz 1965).

However, as disciplinary boundaries hardened in the twentieth century, intellectual gaps between the disciplines began to emerge as blindspots, which interdisciplinary work could then be explicitly dedicated to redress. The Cold War motivated much of this thinking, as national security issues focussed academic minds on both sides of the communist–capitalist divide to organize themselves as a unified whole. In this context, operations research, systems theory and artificial intelligence began to portray the existence of disciplines as obstacles to efficient knowledge flows. By the late 1960s this perspective had come to acquire a radical counterpart in the West as feminists, multiculturalists and others came to see disciplines as actively suppressing politically unruly subjects that prevented the academy from effectively communicating with – and, more to the point, enlightening – the larger society.

The many symbolic and material conflicts that transpired between the establishment and the counterculture during this period occurred against the backdrop of an expanding university sector. However, this began to end with the fall of the Berlin Wall in 1989. Afterward interdisciplinarity started to acquire its current postmodern cast. Travelling under the guise of 'Mode 2' knowledge production, to use the Newspeak preferred in European science-policy circles (Gibbons et al. 1994), interdisciplinarity was became a vehicle for introducing non-academic performance standards designed to break down such normal trappings of academic life as technical language and self-regulating work habits, all of which were presented as glorified 'rent-seeking'. 'Interdisciplinarity' henceforth came to refer to all the 'real world' problems that discipline-based academia routinely ignored or devalued. Thus, research agendas and even degree programmes were urged to include potential 'users and beneficiaries' outside of academia in their very constitution.

The precincts of academia that have flourished in this environment are ones in which 'interdisciplinarity' is expressed mainly through the multiply applicable method, as opposed to the comprehensively explanatory theory. As a point of contrast, consider that the more academically centred of interdisciplinarity had been based on disciplines confronting their theoretical and methodological differences to reach some kind of synthetic resolution, as each recognizes something in the other, which then serves to limit the hegemonic claims of one's own discipline. We might regard such interdisciplinary 'interpenetration' as the *semantic ascent* approach (Fuller and Collier 2004: chap. 2). But in our Brave New World, the biggest obstacle to interdisciplinarity is precisely the theoretical baggage that the different disciplines carry by virtue of their specific histories, as that then makes it difficult to proceed in collaborative inquiry. This is, so to speak, the *semantic descent* approach, which encourages one to head for a lowest empirical common denominator, as in evidence-based policy, in which the different theories – and even methods – used to gather and interpret data are seen as ladders that must be removed once climbed. Striking in this regard is the semantic dissipation of the word 'theory' itself, as in such popular interdisciplinary research tools as 'rational choice theory', 'game theory', 'complexity theory', 'chaos theory', 'actor–network theory' – none of which really explains the patterns they highlight in the data.

Of course, some may say that I pose a false dichotomy with regard to the point of interdisciplinary knowledge production. It need not be either a matter of constructing a higher form of academic knowledge or taking the ends of knowledge out of the hands of academics altogether. It may simply involve learning to appreciate that other disciplines exist with ways of knowing that are valid in their own terms. But that nostrum is a bit like trying to learn modern languages without ever facing the intercultural conflicts generated by their speakers.

To conclude this section, let me put the impending disintegration of the university into what might be called a 'world-historic' perspective. I have elsewhere written of *the post-epistemic condition*, whereby science is pursued as something other than a form of inquiry: e.g. as a strategy for securing employment or a factor in creating wealth (Fuller 2000a: chap. 3). In the post-modern condition, the university is being pulled apart by these alternative pursuits, which effectively disaggregate the teaching from the research function. At its best, the university was a catalyst of social change when its two functions engaged in mutual regulation: teaching curbed the esoteric tendencies of research, while research disrupted the routinizing tendencies of teaching. The result was that each new generation of students would be imparted knowledge that was, in some respects, substantially different from that imparted to earlier generations, thereby providing an initial impetus for larger societal change. However, this delicate balance between the two functions is in danger of being lost. On the one hand, teaching is being reduced to the dispensation of credentials; on the other, research is being privatized as intellectual property: the one driven by the employment market, the other by the futures market.

These developments may be new to the recent past but they are not entirely original to either our period or our culture. In fact, despite its name, the post-epistemic condition has been the normal state-of-affairs in non-Western cultures that have had institutions of higher education for at least as long as the West, most notably China and India. As part of the most extensive comparative sociology of schools of thought ever undertaken, Randall Collins has discovered a most remarkable fact about knowledge production in China and India (Collins 1998: 501–522). These Asian regions had harboured most of the theories and technologies that were relevant to the Scientific Revolution several centuries before their seventeenth-century realization in Europe. However, they lacked the institutions that could bring them together in a constructive confrontation, such that a set of theories might be subject to an experimental test. Instead, the technologies tended to be designed and refined entirely in the context of either large-scale public works projects or specially commissioned artisanship. Moreover, with the exception of some fleeting fertile episodes, even the theoretical schools remained largely immune to the scholastic disputations that marked the first flourishing of the universities in medieval Europe. Rather, the Eastern doctrines would be elaborated in the context of studying for civil-service examinations, just as technical innovations would not be theorized beyond what was necessary to accomplish an appointed task.

In short, teaching and research in the East were developed too closely in relation to separate 'performance standards' to enable a social-epistemic transformation as radical as the West's Scientific Revolution. But is the situation so different today? Might we not be in the process of *undoing* the Western university's distinctive achievement by, say, disjoining the evaluation of research from that of teaching in our academic audits – reducing the former to the number of students graduated and the latter to the number of papers generated, without any concern for what might be the relationship between the two? To be sure, this undoing is bound to occur, at least at first, with few outward signs. After all, the material wealth of the East is generally seen as having outstripped that of the West until the late eighteenth or early nineteenth century, some two or more centuries after the Scientific Revolution is normally said to have begun (Frank 1997).

However, a clear sign of the university's retreat from its public mission is what Lyotard identified as the decline of 'meta-' or 'grand narratives' in academic discourse. These are academically generated stories of how things came to be as they are and how they are likely to turn out in the future. Meta-narratives are typically informed by theoretical frameworks that move beyond, and even challenge, ordinary modes of understanding. The pervasive influence of grand narratives associated with, say, capitalism, socialism or scientific progress more generally, has probably been the best advertisement for the value of critical intellectual work in the nineteenth and twentieth centuries. At the same time, however, these narratives have displayed enormous arrogance, often in disproportion to their basis in fact. Two world wars and countless instances of organized violence over the last 150 years may have been avoided, had such narratives not proven so captivating.

To be sure, some grand narratives continue to make their way out of the university's precincts and into society at large. The biological sciences currently enjoy a great vogue as the source of various genetic and evolutionary just-so stories, most of them minted only after Lyotard's original diagnosis of the postmodern condition (e.g. Wilson 1998; Pinker 2002). Nevertheless, these narratives, though counter-intuitive in plot structure and explanatory strategy, tend to provide legitimation for the dominant beliefs and customs in society. Moreover, the compelling character of these broadly 'sociobiological' tales lies in their removal of human agency from history, such that no one appears especially responsible for their fate. In that sense, they do not function in the same 'critical' fashion as the older meta-narratives. Indeed, it would not be very difficult to connect the ascendancy of sociobiology with the 'orientalizing' of intellectual life suggested above, especially if one understands genetics in karmic terms (Fuller 2006a: Part III). But that would return us to a diagnostic mode, whereas I now wish to suggest a more positive way forward.

Regaining the University's Critical Edge by Historicizing the Curriculum

Historical consciousness is a precondition for critique, a lesson that education researchers have come to learn (Goodson 1999). But to what extent has the curriculum of various academic disciplines cultivated historical consciousness? Let us start with the discipline whose pedagogical mission has probably most self-consciously influenced its research trajectory: *philosophy*. Philosophy is unique in that its deepest problems are routinely presented in introductory courses, with successive courses merely adding more nuanced formulations and sophisticated analyses of these problems without any pretence of resolving them. To a large extent, recent philosophers are presented as occupying roles – e.g. 'realist' or 'relativist' – that have been reproduced for centuries, if not for ever. Students enrolled on philosophy courses are not expected to learn the solutions to philosophical problems, let alone solve such problems themselves; rather, they are to think 'philosophically' about them. For any given problem, the actual history of philosophy is fitted into a cycle of a few competing solutions in a perennial tension. This means that, if we control for differences in language, were Aristotle transported to a contemporary introductory philosophy course, he should have little difficulty understanding the instructor. At least, that is the ideal towards which the philosophy curriculum strives.

Exceptions to this goal are most apparent in those branches of philosophy influenced by the special disciplines, where time's arrow is more directly registered on the curriculum. The role of mathematics in the development of modern logic is the obvious case in point, one where we would not expect

Aristotle to outperform a clever undergraduate without further training. However, the historical character of the maths curriculum is itself rather unique. Roughly speaking, the curriculum recapitulates the history of the discipline, as each branch of mathematics is taught as a generalization or limitation of an historically precedent branch. Arithmetic reflects on counting and geometry on measuring, while algebra reflects on arithmetic and analytic geometry on algebra and geometry, and the rest of the maths specialities reflect on these. Most debates in the history of modern mathematics have turned on the ontological status of the entities and the validity of the propositions generated through these successive reflections, especially if they fail to correspond to the structure of physical space and time, as revealed by either common sense or physics (Collins, 1998: chap. 15). Here mathematics converges with metamathematics, returning the field to its philosophical roots, albeit in a much more technical guise. But students are typically not introduced to these debates, except as a means of shoring up the autonomy of mathematical inquiry in the face of 'naive' objectors.

Despite periodic attempts to present pedagogy in the natural sciences as a recapitulation of disciplinary history, twentieth-century teaching in these fields has been dominated by a 'rational reconstructionist' approach to the past. This means that the curriculum is organized from the perspective of contemporary researchers interested in the most efficient means by which the past can be shown to have issued in the current research frontier. Thus, theoretically the simplest matters are taught first, followed by those which build upon them, all gradually leading towards the research frontier. Only token gestures are made to include bits of the discipline's actual history, typically as concrete examples for abstract points.

Not surprisingly, those trained in a natural-science subject who eventually devote most of their energies to researching the history of their field end up being identified primarily as historians rather than scientists, which is to say, keepers of a dead past that has no bearing on the training of today's science students. A frequently overlooked implication of this point is that the selective appropriation of history for present-day purposes exists symbiotically with the attempt to re-enact the past in order to understand it on its own terms. In effect, the exclusion of history from the natural-science curriculum enables the history of science to exist as an autonomous field of inquiry without the interference of practising scientists.

Attitudes toward history are considerably different, when we turn to the humanities and the social sciences that do not conform to the natural-science model of pedagogy. In the first place, students are introduced to the subject matter in a pre-disciplined form that roughly corresponds to common sense. Thus, students learn about artworks before art theory, literature before literary theory, and so forth. Whereas the first economics course introduces students to the most basic concepts and the simplest models of the economy, the sociology curriculum usually begins by presenting the complexity of social life, which then calls forth the need for an explicitly sociological analysis.

The pedagogical procedure exhibited in the sociology curriculum makes the discipline's perspective appear artificially connected to its putative subject matter, thereby opening the door to students questioning the value that is added by adopting this perspective. In effect, the 'soft sciences' perpetually re-create in the classroom their original struggle for legitimation by drawing attention to this 'unnatural' character of disciplining the subject matter. If the maths or natural-science curriculum were constructed in this fashion, then students would leave such courses knowing a lot about, say, the phenomena of moving objects, but would still left wondering whether physics had much to contribute to a deep understanding of them. However, such students do not exist because physics teachers generally take care to present the richness of physical reality in ways that presuppose the need for the conceptual apparatus of their discipline.

To be sure, in the 100-year period leading up to World War I, there were numerous attempts to establish the natural science curriculum on a basis that closely resembled current practice in the humanities and social sciences. The poet Johann Wolfgang von Goethe and the positivist Ernst Mach can conjure up the broad church of sympathizers with this approach, which (in the days before Husserl) flew under the flag of 'phenomenology', as in 'phenomenological optics', to name a field to which both Goethe and Mach contributed. Moreover, far from being an unfulfilled fantasy, this humanistic approach enabled the natural sciences to make their way from the polytechnics to the universities in the nineteenth century. Indeed, the profound influence of Hegel's rival and proponent of *Naturphilosophie*, F.W.J. Schelling, on successive generations of German experimental scientists is only slowly being rediscovered – and then only by historians of science (e.g. Heidelberger 2004), whose work is carefully cordoned off from the science curriculum. One important exception to this general tendency is the ongoing attempt by Creationists, including Intelligent Design theorists, to restructure the teaching of biology, especially in the United States and Australia, but also increasingly in the United Kingdom.

A key part of the Creationist proposal is that the phenomena associated with the development of life on earth – evidence from palaeontology, morphology, etc. – should be presented separately from the conceptual apparatus of the Neo-Darwinian evolutionary synthesis. The result would make biology textbooks look more like those in sociology, as explanatory frameworks are introduced only once rich accounts of the phenomena have been presented. Students would be positioned as evaluators of competing frameworks, each of which would appear to have certain strengths and weaknesses when judged against the full range of evidence (Meyer et al. 2007). In the Creationist proposal, these alternative frameworks would be taken from biology's otherwise hidden past: Biblical Literalism, Cosmic Perfectionism, Intelligent Design Theory, Lamarckianism, and so forth (Fuller 2007c, 2008).

Those who are both pro and con the Creationist proposal agree that its rhetorical import would be to subvert the pedagogic hegemony enjoyed by

Darwinian evolution through natural selection. Theories previously treated as defunct would receive a new lease on life, as students are forced to weigh Darwinism's actual merits against those that might have followed, had one of the defunct theories enjoyed a comparable level of development. The presence of these historic alternatives would also throw into relief persistent conceptual and empirical difficulties with Darwinism that have been obscured by its paradigmatic status in biology. Radical as this prospect would be for biology, it would be quite familiar to sociology instructors, for whom no theory from the past ever seems to be completely discarded. Indeed, were sociobiology to come to dominate the scientific study of social life in the twenty-first century, one could easily imagine sociologists themselves adapting to their advantage the rhetorical strategy behind the Creationist critique of the biology curriculum.

An important difference in attitudes towards history is brought out in the Creationism controversy. It centres on the perceived reversibility of a discipline's history, especially back to a level of understanding that coheres with 'pre-disciplined' forms of experience. Clearly, evolutionary biologists regard Creationist pedagogical innovations in this respect as a great leap backward. They follow Thomas Kuhn (1970) in holding that the achievement of consensus around a highly elaborated theory like the Neo-Darwinian synthesis is the clearest sign of progress in science. In contrast, the Creationists would establish a curriculum that would seek to undermine this sort of consensualism (Fuller 2008: chap. 1).

But as I have already suggested, one need not be a religious zealot or an intellectual reactionary to argue for such views. For example, Mach was reluctant to make atomic theory central to the teaching of the physical sciences because, while useful in the conceptual and experimental inquiries of professional physicists, the theory's counter-intuitive nature impeded the comprehension and appropriation of physical knowledge by engineers, artisans and other non-experts. For Mach, the estrangement of atomic theory from ordinary experience reflected the idiosyncrasy of the history of physics, which like other fields has developed heuristics that work very well in specialist settings but less well outside of them (Fuller 2000b: chap. 2). Accordingly, the task of education is to release these specialist insights into larger social settings, and *not* to reinforce their original theoretical packaging by treating students as if they were potential recruits to specialist ranks.

The pedagogical tension elaborated in the previous sentence is most clearly played out in those social science disciplines with the longest histories of trying to approximate the methods of the physical sciences, namely, psychology and economics. In these fields, students are routinely exposed to a schizoid curriculum. The foundational courses divide the disciplinary domain into theoretically relevant categories, be they 'sensation', 'perception', and 'cognition' (in the case of psychology) or 'the market', 'the household', and 'the firm' (in the case of economics). However, later courses in 'history and systems' – still often required of all majors – subvert this rational reconstructionist presentation by recalling the discipline's origins in matters closer to the heart of students' interests. Typically, these turn out to be 'conceptually ill-formed' (a.k.a. 'applied') areas that rate low in the current academic value system. Thus, the theoretically driven successes of, say, neoclassical economics or cognitive psychology are offset by their conspicuous silence on issues relating to the economic and psychological aspects of everyday life, which turn out to be the strengths of such 'defunct' movements as institutionalism (in economics) and behaviourism (in psychology). Moreover, this curricular dissonance is easily exacerbated, as academic departments' teaching loads are increasingly borne by those whose interests and training are too far away from the 'cutting edge' to secure large research grants.

No doubt an educational theorist possessing a Panglossian turn of mind will praise this state-of-affairs, since it enables psychology and economics to take advantage of the segmented market for teaching and research: highly research-active staff can remain aloof from students, as long as their less active counterparts engage them in the classroom, even if this means that students will be most animated by inquiries that suffer low status within the discipline. While this strategy may help academic departments survive our current audit culture, it ultimately proves Lyotard's point that the university has become little more than a physical container for disparate activities, each of which may be performed better elsewhere, if allowed to go their own way. Cutting-edge researchers may be given a freer hand in a science park or a think-tank, while popular teachers may likewise be able to pursue their calling without distraction as part of a vocational training programme or the Open University.

To be sure, the reward structure for these different institutionalizations of research and teaching would need to be rendered equitable. But assuming that can be done, what role would remain for the university? None, according to the logic of postmodernism. But I propose a radical solution, one that would reposition the university as the institution responsible for regulating society's knowledge flow. In short, it would redress the problems of 'uneven development' that arise from knowledge production outpacing its distribution.

Affirmative Action as a Strategy for Redressing the Balance Between Research and Teaching

Fuller and Collier (2004) distinguish *plebiscience* and *prolescience* as general knowledge policy orientations. In a nutshell, plebiscience is academia's 'natural attitude' of treating education as little more than an adjunct to research, whereas prolescience is the reverse attitude that involves evaluating research in terms of its teachability. In terms of the role assigned to history in the curriculum, the former approximates the situation in the natural sciences and 'harder' social sciences, the latter in the humanities and 'softer' social sciences.

Plebiscience draws on the meaning of 'plebiscite' in political science as the reduction of suffrage in mass democracies to a formality for ratifying current government initiatives or providing a choice between options, none of which strays far from established policies. This is academia's 'natural attitude' to education, which treats it as the functional equivalent of a plebiscite that has little substantive impact on research. It presumes that the research frontier can never advance too quickly and that education must either raise students to that level or, failing that, instill a sense of deference to the latest developments. Plebiscience is regularly reinforced by histories of science that omit any mention of the mechanisms for distributing new knowledge, implicitly assuming that any friction in the dissemination process must be due to incompetent teachers or backward students. Plebiscientific attitudes run very deep in our thinking about knowledge. Rare is the academic administrator or research funding council that has the temerity to declare the elite inquiries of the research frontier an indulgence rather than the standard. (Usually, a budgetary crisis first needs to intervene.) Thus, the experimental natural sciences come to be valued above all other disciplines for their ability to 'lead from the front' pedagogically, that is, to have their curriculum driven by the research frontier, a point elaborated in the previous section.

From the standpoint of the history of higher education, the problem with using the natural sciences – especially the laboratory-based disciplines – as a general model is that they were amongst the last to be incorporated within the mission of the university, and arguably were never fully assimilated. The location of research laboratories on university grounds in most countries dates no earlier than the third quarter of the nineteenth century. Moreover, this was largely a defensive response to the proven financial benefits of research emanating from laboratory settings that were typically funded by industry and situated in polytechnic institutes. Left to their own devices, universities were still governed by aristocratic prejudices, reaching back to the Greeks, which associated knowledge gained through manual labour with drudgery and even slavery.

But a Faustian bargain had to be struck in order to house these industrially inspired forms of knowledge. The capitalist ethic stipulates a universe of boundless productivity to complement the lack of natural limits to human appetites. One could never innovate too much because there were always new markets to conquer or, more precisely, old markets to reconfigure to one's competitive advantage. Eventually this became the university's own ethic. Its legacy is the mindless preoccupation with the number of writings produced and the number of citations to such writings amassed – all done without consideration of the qualitative significance of these quantitative indicators (Fuller 1997: chap. 4). The epitome of this perverse logic is that universities have increasingly encouraged their staff to secure as many patents as possible, despite the lack of evidence that much commercial value is generated in the process (Hinde 1999).

In contrast, the prolescience perspective starts with the realization that plebiscience is an historical aberration that began when universities felt the need to mimic the value system of capitalism, thereby reducing the public value of knowledge to the (relatively) private conditions of its production. To regain the public character of knowledge, then is, economically speaking, to recover distribution as a mode of production. In more classically academic terms, the classroom experience must be reintegrated into research under the covering term of 'inquiry'. In the previous section, I discussed this strategy as a matter of historicizing the curriculum. As its name implies, 'prolescience' takes its cue from the mass of society, the 'proletariat' in that sense: the state of knowledge in society is measured by what the ordinary citizen, not the expert inquirer, knows. The prolescientific cure for plebiscience involves a shift in the image of knowledge production. Whereas the plebiscientist envisages a clear research frontier at any given moment, which functions like a major river into which tributaries ultimately flow, the prolescientist turns this image on its head, interpreting the presence of a clear research frontier as a monopoly in need of dissolution, much like a major river that flows into a delta. The means for effecting either of these fluvial transformations is, of course, education (Fuller 2000a: chap. 6; Fuller 2000b: Conclusion).

The prolescientific task of inquiry is to render new knowledge claims compatible with as many different background assumptions as possible. Undertaking this task requires dissolving the currently sharp distinction between teaching and research – especially insofar as these activities are evaluated by separate means. In sociological terms, it involves a two-step process: *demystification* and *detraditionalization* (Beck et al. 1994). One would begin by revealing the specific historical reasons that a particular research programme first arrived at a generally valued form of knowledge. That is demystification. Then, one would show that this knowledge can be assimilated and used by a variety of research programmes, often to ends quite different from that of the originator. That is detraditionalization.

In the long run, success for the prolescience perspective would amount to converting the pedagogy of all the academic disciplines into the model followed by the humanities and the softer social sciences. It would make the dissemination of new knowledge in the larger population a prerequisite to any claims to epistemic progress, much as Mach and the Creationists would have it. Education would no longer be the mere handservant of research but rather take an active role in checking the worst tendencies of research to become overspecialized and overcommitted to certain domains of inquiry at the expense of others.

My proposal would take affirmative action legislation to its logical conclusion, extending academia's universalist aspirations from the range of people included in the pursuit of knowledge to the ideas they can legitimately entertain while so engaged. At the moment, affirmative action functions to redistribute the advantages enjoyed by, say, white middle-class males to the rest of the population in matters relating to student admission and academic employment (Cahn 1995). Typically the success of these redistributionist policies is measured in terms of an increase in the proportion of desirable positions held by members of traditionally disadvantaged groups. However, disadvantage continues to be suffered not only by groups of individuals but also, and perhaps more trenchantly, by schools of thought.

Current affirmative action regimes may do much to facilitate the movement of non-whites, the working class and women to highly valued academic positions, but they do relatively little – at least directly – to reorient the values that academics place on various schools of thought. Not surprisingly, the members of subaltern groups who most readily benefit from affirmative action are those whose educational and research interests most neatly conform to the dominant paradigms.

Of course, certain strands of identity politics argue that the mere addition of traditionally unrepresented groups will eventually transform the dominant lines of inquiry, since those groups harbour forms of consciousness that cannot be fully assimilated into mainstream culture. However, the empirical evidence for this hopeful hypothesis is far from obvious. On the contrary, one need only look at the number of people from traditionally disadvantaged groups who balk whenever their success is linked to their ethnic, gender or class identity. These people typically think it is better to have won by 'the rules' than to have changed them. Cultural critics may scoff at this attitude as 'mere' assimilationism that disregards the interests of fellow class members. Yet, it may be that the cultural critics are projecting the value they themselves place on iconoclasm, which may be neither so easy nor desirable for the people they criticize.

A more direct approach to affirmative action at the level of schools of thought would provide incentives for prolescientific pursuits, such that *everyone* is rendered responsible for making new knowledge available to the widest range of people possible. In that way, the university need not relinquish its Enlightenment aspiration to universalism, while at the same time acknowledging the socio-historically situated character of all forms of knowledge. The twist is that this character would now be treated as a problem to be addressed, not a brute fact. One obvious consequence of this policy would be a blurring of the distinction between teaching and research. It is common nowadays to class as 'merely pedagogical' the task of rendering difficult ideas in a form that students can understand. However, in a prolescientific academic regime, this activity would be equally classed as research, as the academic must determine how much of an idea's original mode of expression – especially its theoretical language – must be retained to impart relevant insights for the intended audience.

I envisage this task as comparable to the 'reverse engineering' of technology, whereby an industrial innovation is analysed into its component parts in order to figure out how it works, with an eye to designing an inexpensive and improved version of that product for a target market. When reverse engineering is amplified into a general economic policy, historians of technology speak of the 'Japan Effect', which should serve as a reminder that over the centuries, the balance of world trade has been often redressed by nations capitalizing on the (unplanned) benefits that come from *not* being the first to arrive at an idea, finding or invention (Fuller 1997: chap. 5 ff.).

Academic research remains captive to the cult of priority, even though the material conditions that made it a reasonable attitude toward new knowledge have radically changed. When the pursuit of inquiry was a leisured activity, done only by those not bothered by having to make ends meet, it was treated as a game, in which being the first to achieve a certain result would merit a prize – but not much more, certainly not intellectual property rights in the modern sense of patents and copyrights. Players in this game were presumed to be of roughly equal ability, so that the difference between winners and losers would ultimately turn on matters of chance, not deep issues of personal competence or a commitment to a particular research tradition.

A proper history of how priority came to be destiny in academia would take seriously the transition in the idea of research from leisure to *labour*, specifically one out of which people had to earn their entire living. At that point, the search for new knowledge began to appear more like activities in the primary 'extractive' sector of the economy – mining, fishing, farming – except, of course, for the uncertain nature of the relationship between original effort and ultimate significance. (In that sense, *prospecting* is a better analogue.) Indeed, the attitude toward any knowledge found became *proprietary*. Moreover, it would not be out of line to describe the course of academic inquiry over the last two centuries as a series of attempts to 'colonize' the lifeworld, success at which can be judged by the felt need for the curriculum to play catch up with the research agenda. But is this trend reversible?

I began the section before last by observing that 'postmodernism' in its most widely used sense was born out of a disillusionment with the university's role in state-driven attempts at social control. Specifically, Lyotard saw the teaching function impeding the natural proliferation of research trajectories. And while he may have correctly identified the reactionary social role of the university in his day, the use of the curriculum to curb, reorient and channel research is not in itself reactionary. In fact, it has been a potent vehicle for democratizing social life by inhibiting the emergence of new knowledge-based forms of elitism. I illustrated this point by considering the role of history across the academic curriculum, singling out the humanities and 'softer' social sciences for their pedagogical attentiveness to the contingent character of research developments. If there is a role for critical intellectuals in academic life today, it is in terms of spreading this 'prolescience' mentality in whatever discipline they happen to practise and resisting all attempts to sever the evaluation of research from that of teaching. This amounts to an extension of 'affirmative action' principles from disadvantaged groups to schools of thought.

I have argued that the university is the greatest sociological innovation of the modern era (interview with the *Guardian*, 30 April 2007). It is the institution that has done the most to allow knowledge to be pursued with impunity, while maximizing its impact on society: the 'unity of research and teaching' that characterizes the mission of the modern university. This mission was the brainchild of the Prussian education minister Wilhelm von Humboldt who first applied it to the University of Berlin in 1810.

In today's terms, Humboldt reinvented the university as an institution dedicated to 'the creative destruction of social capital'. On the one hand, research emerges from networks of particular scientists, investors and other stakeholders who are tempted to restrict the flow of benefits to themselves. On the other hand, the university's commitment to education compels that such knowledge be taught to people far removed from this social capital base, who may in turn take what they learn in directions that erase whatever advantage the original network enjoyed. All of this is to the good: it contributes to the overall enlightenment of society, while spurring on the formation of new networks of innovation. Unfortunately, this virtuous cycle is short-circuited as academics are increasingly encouraged to think of teaching and research as necessarily trading against each other.

Academics Rediscover Their Soul: The Rebirth of 'Academic Freedom'

In late 2006, British academics formally discovered the concept of academic freedom with the formation of 'Academics for Academic Freedom' (AFAF) under the leadership of Dennis Hayes, the first president of the UK's consolidated University and College Union, the largest post-compulsory education union in the world. This organization arose in response to several independent developments that had appeared to reinforce a sense of restriction on what academics could teach and research: (1) fears of offending students, who in light of newly imposed tuition fees have come to think of themselves as 'customers' for academic knowledge (where the customer is always right); (2) fears of alienating actual or potential external clients for university research by criticizing, say, government or corporate policies. As a result, several hundred academics signed the following statement:

Statement of Academic Freedom

We, the undersigned, believe the following two principles to be the foundation of academic freedom:

(1) that academics, both inside and outside the classroom, have unrestricted liberty to question and test received wisdom and to put forward controversial and unpopular opinions, whether or not these are deemed offensive, and

(2) that academic institutions have no right to curb the exercise of this freedom by members of their staff, or to use it as grounds for disciplinary action or dismissal.

The media immediately epitomized the movement as aiming to protect 'the right to offend', which places the emphasis on self-expression rather than, say, seeking the truth wherever it may lead. This spin is unsurprising since in the

English-speaking world, freedom of expression is presumed to be a fundamental civil right. Thus, the burden of proof is placed upon those – typically agencies of the state – who would curtail it on behalf of the greater good. Consider Justice Oliver Wendell Holmes's famous example of arbitrarily shouting 'Fire!' in a crowded theatre, taken from his judicial decision in *Schenck v. the United States* (1919). The problem it raises is simply that of licence in liberal societies, solutions to which depend on how much a society can tolerate and who is authorized to judge. While Holmes's example certainly involves speech, there is nothing especially *intellectual* about it. (However, the exact nature of *Schenck* complicates matters, in ways we cannot address here, as it concerned a socialist whose 'shout' consisted in widely distributed leaflets arguing that America's need to enter World War I was a trumped-up false alarm.) Indeed, 'freedom of speech' is probably best understood as naming a set of distinct freedoms that are expressed via a common medium: academic freedom, freedom of worship, freedom of the press, freedom of assembly. The scope of each needs to be justified separately.

In the context of its origins in nineteenth-century Germany, academic freedom is better seen as the prototype for some larger and later notion of intellectual freedom than as a special case of some timeless archetype. In this respect, academic freedom follows the common pattern of universalist projects of extending to the many what had been possessed by the few. Of course, as Hegel was especially fond of observing, various things may be lost and gained in the process of translation. But without an awareness of this process, it is all too easy to slip into metaphysical appeals to 'intellectual freedom' underwritten by chimerical intuitions married to half-baked notions of human nature.

The original German political presumption was clearly authoritarian – namely, that no one has a right to free speech unless it is delegated, which in turn requires legislating a clear sense of the relevant rights *and* obligations. The principled pursuit of truth was defended as a narrow guild right for academics, who were obliged to protect it by ensuring they expressed themselves within the canons of reason and evidence that it is normally their job to uphold. Thus, the AFAF Statement is not claiming that academics can say whatever they want simply because they are academics. As with all guild rights, the issue turns on a proper use of the tools of the trade, and here the phrase 'question and test' is crucial to the scope of the freedom being defended.

Academics should be allowed to argue, either in the classroom or on television, that the Holocaust never took place, that Blacks are intellectually inferior to Whites, or that thermodynamics render evolution impossible – but only under one all-important condition: that they are then obliged to provide arguments that can be subject to critical scrutiny at the same level as publicity. They cannot get away with saying that it is just their opinion or an article of faith, full stop. In fact, very few controversial academics are so reticent with their reasons. But those who refuse to offer reasons debase the currency of academic life – even, I might add, when they assert quite inoffensive positions.

No doubt academics are no different from ordinary people in viscerally holding beliefs that they cannot defend with the tools of their trade. In that case, the terms of academic freedom require that they keep their mouths shut. However, the normative significance of silence is seriously compromised by a climate of political correctness, partly influenced by increased university auditing. Academics nowadays might be reluctant to mobilize the intellectual resources needed (e.g. by applying for grants) to give their more outlandish views a fair public hearing simply because of the censure that voicing such opinions would bring down on them.

As for the more fearless academics who publicly defend offensive positions, at the very least they force opponents to state the precise grounds on which they take offence, which is never a bad thing in a society that fancies itself rational. That the repeated airing of offensive positions might give solace to undesirable political factions is a fair risk for an enlightened society to take. If the words of a controversial academic are touted as supporting such a faction, the academic is obliged to state where he or she stands on the matter. It is not sufficient simply to say one's words are being opportunistically used. This point goes straight to the guild element of protecting the tools of intellectual trade.

In short, to exercise intellectual freedom is to enable our ideas to die in our stead, to recall Karl Popper's neat phrase. This is 'the right to be wrong', the ability to assert now without compromising one's ability to assert in the future, even if one's assertions are shown to be false (Fuller 2000a). Intellectual freedom in this sense presupposes an institutionalized dualism, such that, literally, you do *not* need to put your money where your mouth is: 'speculation' in the intellectual sense is kept apart from 'speculation' in the financial sense. A true believer in intellectual freedom would thus wish for an environment in which one could commit what statisticians call Type I errors with impunity – that is to say, err on the side of boldness ('false positives').

The modern model for this environment is academic tenure, which was originally introduced to simulate the property ownership requirement for citizenship in ancient Athens. This historical link was forged by the founder of the modern university, Wilhelm von Humboldt, to whom Mill's *On Liberty* is dedicated. On the one hand, an Athenian citizen who was voted down in the public forum could return to his estate without concern for his material security; on the other, his economic significance for the city obliged him to offer opinions in the forum at the next opportunity. Citizens who refrained from self-expression were routinely ridiculed as cowards.

Correspondingly, if academic tenure were policed more rigorously for its entailed obligations, then the conditions surrounding its current erosion would not be tolerated. To the increasing number of academics who know only of the current neo-liberal knowledge production regime, tenure looks like an excuse never to stray from one's intellectual comfort zone. But even if many – if not most – tenured academics conform to that stereotype, it is entirely against the spirit of tenure and indeed arguably merits censure.

At the same time, a much more charitable view should be taken towards those tenured academics deemed 'publicity seekers' who self-consciously – yet often sincerely – advance outrageous views in the public forum. These people routinely expose themselves to criticism, in response to which the life of the mind is performed for society at large. Whether they ultimately win or lose these struggles is less important than the occasion they provide for thinking aloud, a process to which others may subsequently contribute, the result of which raises the overall level of social intelligence. The sort of people I have in mind – say, Alan Dershowitz, Bjørn Lomborg, Richard Dawkins – most genuinely embody the spirit of intellectual responsibility. And I would add to this list even more reviled figures, including many Nazi revisionists, eugenicists, racists and Creationists. To believe that society needs to be protected from the views of these people is to concede that it has not earned the right to intellectual freedom.

Consider so-called Holocaust Denial – the hypothesis that the Nazi maltreatment of Jews in World War II did not amount to genocide. The hypothesis is very likely false, yet it deserves to have its strongest version subject to critical scrutiny. Like so many hypotheses of this kind, its falseness is most evident when taken as literally as its advocates would have us do. However, the effort we expend to falsify these hypotheses forces us to turn a diagnostic eye on the *de facto* limits we place on 'free inquiry' in the name of 'political correctness'. After all, the 'six million Jews' figure was originally advanced as a back-of-an-envelope estimate during the 1946 Nuremberg Trial. Normally a figure constructed under such politicized circumstances would be hotly debated, if not treated with outright scepticism. At the very least, researchers with cooler heads in later years would be expected to raise or lower the figure as they weighed up the evidence.

Holocaust deniers make much of the fact that these norms seem to be suspended, or at least attenuated. It is important to understand why they may be right on this point, even if their overall case is wrong and perhaps even malicious. It goes to why 'intellectual freedom' makes no sense other than as a generalization of academic freedom. A society that genuinely enjoyed the freedom we protect in academia would publicly disaggregate various Nazi activities and judge each of them on their own terms, questioning whether they need to be bundled up with the heinous activities historically associated with them (Fuller 2006a: chap. 14). Thus, we should be able to conclude – without fear or loathing – that Nazi sympathizers, regardless of their ulterior motives, deserve credit for, say, sensitizing us to how our desperation for clear moral benchmarks compromises our critical capacities.

Would our moral outrage be diminished, were we to learn that the Nazis exterminated only 6000 rather than 6,000,000 Jews? Perhaps – especially if one did not trust the maturity of our collective moral judgement. Traditionally children and primitives had to be regaled with exaggerated accounts of unspeakable evil out of a fear that they would not otherwise do good. The Enlightenment was all about escaping from this state of 'nonage', as Kant put it in his signature essay on the movement. He wanted people to be legally recognized as adults empowered to discuss and decide matters for themselves through public deliberation. However, Kant's most politically effective follower, Wilhelm von Humboldt, realized that this Enlightenment ideal required an institutional vehicle through which all of society could be slowly but surely encompassed. With that in mind he invented the modern university.

However, so far I have been dwelling on 'academic freedom' as if it referred solely to freedoms enjoyed by professional academics. However, that is only half of the concept – and not necessarily the half that has been historically dominant (Metzger 1955: 123). Humboldt's conception of the modern university incorporated the original medieval idea that both students and faculty are citizens of the university with complementary rights and obligations that must be maintained together. The justification for what the Germans called the freedom to learn (*Lernfreiheit*) as distinct from the freedom to teach (*Lehrfreiheit*) drew on the university's historic rootedness in the guild idea of transmitting an intrinsically worthy form of knowledge (*universitas*), coupled with a more modern *Bildung*-based concern to provide a space that allowed the individual to mature and flourish. All learners are then effectively apprentice teachers who should be respected as such – what social psychologists nowadays call 'legitimate peripheral participants' (Lave and Wenger 1991; cf. Fuller 2000b: 130).

Max Weber's speech to postgraduate students 'Science as a Vocation' (1958) offers a justly famous insight into this matter. For Weber, academic integrity required that the classroom be policed so that the teacher's rights do not supervene upon the learner's, which would mark the illegitimate slide of science into politics. Weber observed that one important way students exercise their freedom to learn is by choosing which lectures to attend, which means that some teachers get many more students than others. This especially applies to academic systems (e.g. Oxbridge) that clearly distinguish the roles of lecturer and examiner, so that students in principle can pass a course without ever attending the corresponding lectures. While Weber found such nascent academic consumerism distasteful, he nevertheless accepted it as an implication of student's freedom to learn. However, what he did not accept was the idea of teachers catering to this tendency. He would thus oppose the use of student enrolments as a criterion for awarding tenure and promotion. In other words, he wanted to give space to the freedom to learn without contaminating the space for the freedom to teach – and vice versa, for which Weber's speech is better known (i.e. that teachers should reveal their biases in weighing the evidence and present opposing opinions fair-mindedly).

Were Weber alive today, he might argue that if there is sufficient student interest and university resources, students are entitled to courses in non-standard and even countercultural topics like Hospitality Management, Sports and Leisure Studies, Astrology and Creationism. After all, courses on heterodox topics historically entered the university curriculum through self-organizing reading groups of students, with or without faculty sponsorship, for which students then sought formal academic credit. If the interest continued across several cohorts of students, there would be grounds to petition the university to establish a regular academic line on the topic. However, this prospect should in no way influence judgements regarding the tenure and promotion of current academic staff, which should be based on the candidates' claimed fields of academic competence. Of course, any university wishing to maintain the delicate balance between *Lehrfreiheit* and *Lernfreiheit* would need a business plan, if not a more formal legal mechanism, for ensuring that student demand did not swamp teacher supply or vice versa.

Enter self-styled US academic freedom campaigner David Horowitz, 1960s student radical turned neo-conservative champion of 'student rights', most notoriously through the promotion of an 'Academic Bill of Rights'. While Horowitz is widely reviled by professional American academics for his list of the '100 most dangerous professors' (Horowitz 2006), he is treated more respectfully in Germany (Schreiterer 2008). With titles like 'Indoctrination U.' (Horowitz 2007), Horowitz's aims to change the minds not of the academics themselves but of students, their tuition-paying parents and alumni. Often working with student unions and alumni associations, Horowitz encourages more detailed, content-driven student evaluations of courses than are normally used for tenure and promotion purposes. In response to claims by academics that they already protect students' freedom to learn by appearing liberal in the classroom, Horowitz argues that such claims should be taken as seriously as corporate public relations claims that big business spontaneously produces goods with consumers' best interests in mind. Thus, as consumers had done in the 1960s, students now need to stand up for their own rights in order not to be force-fed inferior knowledge products from unscrupulous academics – with Horowitz kindly offering his services as the would-be Ralph Nader of academia.

US academia finds itself in the awkward position of having to take seriously someone like Horowitz because the most venerable US professional academic organization, the American Association of University Professors (AAUP), founded in 1915 by the philosophers John Dewey and Arthur Lovejoy, has been almost entirely devoted to protecting the freedom to teach and research, but not the freedom to learn. The AAUP adapted elements of the more complex German notion of academic freedom to prevent the arbitrary dismissal of controversial and otherwise unconventional academics, typically at the behest of senior university administrators, boards of trustees, state legislatures and, yes, students and their parents, who were often the source of alumni donations. Unsurprisingly, AAUP has acquired the self-protective character of a labour union that has endeavoured to tie the idea of academic freedom quite exclusively to disciplinary expertise, understood in strict guild terms as the entitlement of a mature practitioner to secure employment beyond a legally fixed probation period. Especially in times when universities must raise tuition fees to make ends meet, this strict interpretation of academic freedom as a lifelong tenure can easily be cast in a negative light as 'featherbedding' or 'rent-seeking'.

Sociologically speaking, in the US context, neither a students' rights activist like Horowitz nor the avowedly liberal AAUP is in an especially good position to address the animus informing *Lernfreiheit*. For its part, the AAUP problematically treats universities not as organizations with ends of their own, such as the provision of liberal education, but merely as sites for the reproduction of various disciplinary expertises, on behalf of which universities are made to maintain adequate work conditions for appropriately certified disciplinary practitioners. To anyone other than a professional academic, this is an incredibly self-serving way to think about a university. Nevertheless, Horowitz errs as well in thinking that the freedom to learn is something easily resolved in a single classroom by altering teaching practice. On the contrary, as Horowitz's critics rightly point out, that would be to interfere with *Lehrfreiheit*. However, academics do have a responsibility to ensure that procedures are in place for students to organize their own courses and petition for new subjects to be taught. That takes up the challenge of *Lernfeiheit* much more robustly than adopting a superficially liberal, but ultimately patronizing, attitude towards students' cultivation of their own intellectual interests.

2

The Stuff of Intellectual Life
Philosophy

Epistemology as 'Always Already' Social Epistemology

'Epistemology' has been used by philosophers since the mid-nineteenth century for the study of the theoretical foundations of knowledge. It is usually paired with 'ontology', the theory of being, as the two main branches of metaphysics. The Scottish philosopher James Ferrier coined the English word 'epistemology' in 1854 to refer to what we now call 'cognitive science', i.e. the scientific study of the mind (Passmore 1966: 52–53; Fuller 2007b: 31–36). However, in the twentieth century, two other senses of 'epistemology' acquired prominence in English, one originating in *Germany* and the other in *Austria*.

The German sense harks back to Kant's idea that reality cannot be known in itself but only in terms of our various 'cognitive interests'. In the hands of the German idealists, epistemology in this sense became the philosophy of the university, with the unity of knowledge as its goal and the liberal arts curriculum as its realization. However, for the Neo-Kantian philosophers who by 1900 had become the bulwark of German academia, epistemology rationalized the existence of increasingly divergent disciplinary world-views that was matched by the growth of postgraduate degrees (Schnädelbach 1984). Weber's lifelong attempt to reconcile 'interpretivist' and 'positivist' methodological imperatives in the newly recognized social sciences reflects this epistemological perspective, with Habermas (1971) perhaps its last major expression. In this tradition, epistemology is synonymous with the philosophical foundations of the sciences.

The Austrian sense of epistemology, traceable to the late nineteenth-century philosophical psychologist Franz Brentano (one of Freud's teachers), began as a theologically inspired backlash against Kant (Smith 1994). Brentano returned to Aristotle for a sense of consciousness as indicative of our being in the world. Whereas Kant saw our restless quest for knowledge as implying a radical separation from the world, Brentano was more impressed by our fundamental rootedness in the world. This sensibility inspired the later phenomenological tradition, especially the later work of Edmund Husserl (1954) and the entire corpus of his student, Martin Heidegger, who came to see epistemology itself as symptomatic of an existential alienation that was played out in the proliferation of mutually incommensurable academic disciplines.

These two different senses of epistemology are easily obscured in English, which uses the same words – 'know' and 'knowledge' – for, so to speak, the processes and the products of knowing. In French and German philosophical discourse, the difference is more clearly marked: on the one hand, *connaissance* and *Erkenntnis* and, on the other, *savoir* and *Wissenschaft*. We might translate the former pair of terms as 'cognition' and the latter as 'discipline'. For example, the Baconian motto 'knowledge is power' appears in Comte as '*savoir est pouvoir*'.

A consequence of the expressive awkwardness of English in epistemological matters is that anglophone philosophers have tended to regard socially sanctioned knowledge as simply an aggregation of what is known by individuals. Thus, they obscure the facticity of knowledge as a product of collective action and a normative standard that may contradict what individuals believe. In contrast, just this facticity is taken for granted by French and German theorists of knowledge such as Foucault and Habermas. This difference in starting points remains a major source of misunderstanding between contemporary analytic and continental philosophers, which in recent years has led to a call for 'social epistemology' (Fuller 1998), as a field that would not only overcome this incommensurability but also incorporate the empirical findings of the history and sociology of science in aid of a more richly informed knowledge policy. This is the field of science and technology studies, or 'STS' (Fuller and Collier 2004; Fuller 2006b).

Within sociology proper, epistemology has had a chequered career, though the character of the controversy surrounding it has shifted over the years. For Comte sociology was basically applied epistemology, a view he had inherited from the Enlightenment assumption that societies are defined by their legitimating ideas. However, under the influence of Marx, legitimatory forms of knowledge came to be seen as ideologies ripe for demystification by the sociology of knowledge. Nevertheless, Mannheim (1936) stopped short of demystifying the epistemology of science, not least because, following Comte, sociology itself claimed to rest on it.

But by the 1970s, this concern for the reflexive implications of sociological critiques of science created a schism within sociology that continues to this day. On the one hand, sociologists of science openly demystify the epistemology of science, with Bloor (1976) explicitly aspiring to finish the job of a general sociology of knowledge that Mannheim had started. On the other hand, more mainstream sociologists reject epistemology in favour of ontology as the preferred philosophical foundation for social knowledge. Thus, Giddens (1976) wants to credit social agents as 'always already' social theorists whose access to the social world is as valid as that of the social scientists studying them. This view, explicitly indebted to Alfred Schutz, is also consonant with Rorty's (1979), a philosophy-based critique of epistemology that has been influential among postmodernists better disposed to the idea that we inhabit different worlds equally than have differential access to the same world.

At this point, it might be useful to define my position vis-à-vis two paradigmatic attempts to provide a general social epistemology from the heartland of their respective disciplines, one from sociology and one from philosophy: Randall Collins's *The Sociology of Philosophies* (1998) and Alvin Goldman's *Knowledge in a Social World* (1999). Collins and Goldman are both social *epistemologists*, as opposed to social *ontologists*. In other words, neither assumes that the actual state of knowledge production reveals the full limits of its potential. Rather, they take the actual as providing a variable – yet corrigible – record of the conditions under which knowledge may flourish and diminish. They presume that knowers have yet to fathom how it is that they know, and hence their collective efforts to date do not constitute all there is to know. A special inquiry into the matter is therefore needed; hence social epistemology. Collins proceeds in terms of a comparative historical sociology of philosophical cultures in European and Asian spheres of influence over the last 2500 years, whereas Goldman argues in largely aprioristic terms about the sorts of authority structures and communication networks that will tend to encourage and inhibit the production of reliable knowledge.

Neither Collins nor Goldman gives much credence to informal or unofficial knowledge. This is particularly striking in Collins's case, given the comprehensively empirical character of his project. While purporting to offer a 'global theory of intellectual change', to quote the subtitle of Collins (1998) work, it is nevertheless grounded in a content analysis of standard histories of philosophy, which tend to presume that philosophy is something done by philosophers for other philosophers. Consequently, the traditionally formal branches of the discipline – logic, metaphysics and epistemology – lead Collins's narrative to such an extent that Niccolo Machiavelli, whose concerns were grounded in the practice of law, politics and ethics, receives hardly a mention. I will delve into the significance of this point in the next section. For his part, Goldman takes for granted that knowledge in a complex world entails relatively discrete expertises. The main questions for him are how to identify the experts relevant to a given case and the degree to which one should trust their judgement. Interestingly, Goldman tends to conflate the ideas of 'marginal' and 'novel' forms of knowledge, which would seem to deny the possibility that some quite legitimate ways of knowing have remained outside the mainstream for long periods of time.

In highlighting the sense in which Collins and Goldman are both social epistemologists, we begin to see some very significant points of divergence. True to his analytic-philosophical roots, Goldman assumes a pre-sociological sense of 'the social' as the aggregation of individuals. Accordingly, social life occurs only in observable interactions between individuals. Upbringing, training, let alone spatio-temporally distributed patterns of structural domination, do not figure in Goldman's theory. Thus, all of the interesting properties of epistemic communities turn out to be either the intended or unintended consequences of such interaction. While such an account of the relationship between the individual and the social is familiar from the Scottish Enlightenment, through most micro-sociologies, to today's rational choice theory, it presupposes an indeterminacy of the social that is not evidenced in the individual. Individuals are presumed to have clearly identified psychological and biological properties prior to their engagement with others, whereas a society has no clear identity other than that constituted by specific individuals.

In contrast, my original formulation of social epistemology drew attention to two logical fallacies, that of *composition* and *division*, which together deny the possibility of either exhaustively explaining the whole (e.g. a society) in terms of its parts (e.g. the society's members) or vice versa (Fuller 1988: xii–xiii). It follows that a social epistemology based on a well-bounded conception of the individual knower will be substantially different from one that proceeds from a well-bounded conception of society. For his part, Collins proposes a broadly 'constructivist' alternative to this polarity, namely, that the conditions for individual and collective knowledge mutually define each other. This more reflexive approach to social epistemology is captured by Collins's distinction between 'organizational' and 'intellectual' leaders in the history of philosophy. For example, in his capacity as organizational leader, Johann Gottlieb von Fichte defined the field's research frontier in the early nineteenth century, so as to render his teacher Kant the intellectual focus for all subsequent debate. In effect, Fichte gave philosophy a new sense of purpose as the bulwark of the German university system by redefining its relationship to its past.

Another point of divergence between Goldman and Collins concerns what each takes to be the point, or 'function', of the knowledge system. Goldman is loud and clear: the overarching goal is the production of reliable truths about matters of social concern by the most efficient means possible. At one level of analysis, one which Goldman himself promotes, this is the *only* point of the knowledge system *qua* knowledge system. Of course, science, law, journalism, education and other knowledge-oriented institutions have multiple social functions. But from Goldman's standpoint, these can interfere with its specifically epistemic goals. This viewpoint presupposes that, in matters of knowledge, the ends always justify the means. Goldman allows that the best knowledge producing system may be one that concentrates its resources on a few elite inquirers who communicate and otherwise implement their findings in ways that provide the most benefit for society, by manipulating most of the population most of the time, perhaps because (as, say, Plato thought) people find the truth hard to take, both cognitively and emotionally. This explains Goldman's positive (1992) remarks about 'epistemic paternalism', which justifies censorship and deception, if a dissemination of the truth is likely to result in social unrest.

For Goldman, the ultimate normative question is whether the knowledge produced by a given community can command the assent of all sincere knowers, a goal that should be familiar to sociologists from Habermas, which Goldman interprets in terms of the ability of knowledge claims to pass a wide range of validity checks that are conducted outside the original community. Goldman does not presume that knowledge producers are pristine intellects; rather, the validity checks somehow manage to filter out corrupting influences. Goldman's orientation to knowledge production is reminiscent of explanations of wealth production in advanced capitalism, where one finds little concern for those who actually participate in the process and how they are organized. Rather, maximum productivity per se (in this case, of true propositions or correct solutions) is supposed to be good for everyone, as the knowledge produced somehow manages to filter down to those most in need of it. Indeed, Goldman (1986) defines 'epistemic power' as sheer reliable problem-solving effectiveness.

In contrast, Collins treats communities as embodying or enacting the knowledge they produce. Here he expands upon Erving Goffman's concept of 'interaction ritual chains' to capture the mutually reinforcing character of an activity like philosophy, whose participants are at once concerned with truth, esteem, influence and friendship. In this respect, Collins regards the styles of argument that characterize philosophy in its more organized phases – from quick-witted thrust-and-parry in the public square to a more methodical scholastic disputation in the lecture hall – as largely emotive events designed to produce group solidarity (i.e. a 'community of inquiry'), even as they generate tension and conflict among group members. Here Collins draws on his distinctive view of interaction ritual chains as the micro-structure of Emile Durkheim's paradigm case of social life, religion, which similarly displays a range of consolidating practices, from 'low church' informality to 'high church' formality (Collins 2004).

In any case, *contra* Goldman, the idea of independent validity checks to knowledge is alien to Collins's thinking. His key questions are whether the self-recognized knowledge producers dictate their own inquiries and how the products of those inquiries are transmitted to and transformed by later generations of knowledge producers. Although Collins periodically alludes to the larger social and physical environment that shapes and is shaped by the intellectual world, he tends to treat intellectual life as both self-organizing and self-oriented. He focusses less on the sheer productivity of knowledge than on changes to the character of knowledge. Specifically, the more philosophy has been in control of its own agenda, the more abstract and reflexive it has been. But this may reflect either the very high or the very low social standing of the field. The interesting interpretive question concerns how one knows which is which.

For example, Collins sees the general increase in philosophical abstraction in the West after the seventeenth-century Scientific Revolution as evidence for philosophy's retreat from cognitive authority, as substantive empirical ground comes to be ceded to the special sciences. Interestingly, Collins does not cast the shift in terms of the special sciences engaging in inquiries that literally come 'closer' to the phenomena that both philosophy and science try to comprehend. Rather, Collins stresses the ability of scientists to agree on the decision procedures for resolving disputes – typically by conducting specially designed experiments – that will then enable them to move on to the next item on the research agenda. This is 'rapid-discovery science' (Collins 1998: chap. 10). Those who refuse to accept the outcomes of such official procedures become outlaws or exiles, sometimes founding their own disciplines. The interesting epistemological lesson here is that what philosophers of science still call 'empiricism' turns out to be a naturalisation of a position better called 'antirealism' or 'constructivism': that is, experience provides evidence for general knowledge claims only given the sort of social artifice exemplified by a laboratory, which commands the esteem of the body of registered knowers.

Goldman and Collins also instructively differ over what Kuhn (1977a) originally called 'the essential tension' between tradition and innovation: Goldman valorizes the former, Collins the latter. Much like Kuhn himself, Goldman holds that social epistemology needs to explain, not how knowledge systems generate new ideas and discoveries, but how they come to provide a reliable access to socially significant aspects of reality: i.e. the conditions for 'normal science'. While Goldman shows no signs of having conducted what sociologists would regard as empirical research, his terms of reference are nevertheless consonant with the recent stress in social studies of science on the 'resilience' and 'durability' of mundane laboratory practices (Fuller 2006b: chap. 3).

Nevertheless, I prefer Collins's alternative framing of the issue. Even if philosophy is not a 'rapid-discovery' practice, it nevertheless enables zones of creativity by allowing practitioners to address several audiences at work in the course of systematically solving a set of problems. Of course, as Collins rightly stresses, this creativity is often lost in the teaching of philosophy, which reduces each major figure's contribution to a position in a never-ending chess match. In this context, Collins provocatively suggests that the general sociological explanation for the 'depth' of philosophical problems (i.e. their resistance to clear solutions) may be that the discipline's collective attention span is so limited that subtle formulations are easily lost and hence in continual need of reinvention.

If the sociology of religion aims to demystify the 'sacred', and the sociology of science the 'objective', then the sociology of philosophy aims to demystify the 'deep'. How is it that vast numbers of philosophers and their multifarious arguments over the last 2500 years are reducible to a few 'perennial' questions that never seem to get answered, but are only repeatedly explored from a handful of perspectives? Philosophers themselves claim that the intractability of these questions is a mark of their depth. Yet this cannot be the whole, or even most, of the story, since it can be easily shown that posing questions in similar terms does not necessarily mean that a solution is being sought for the same problem, especially when inquirers are separated by space, time, and language (Fuller 1988: 117–62). Seen in Collins's more down-to-earth terms, philosophical depth is a sociological shorthand for the collected means by which philosophers maintain their collective presence in society. It is quite literally a myth, one comparable to the belief that priests are holier, or scientists smarter, than the run of humanity. Collins shows in painstaking cross-cultural detail that depth is a function of the networks that sustain the philosophical community in a given time and space. These interaction ritual chains set the standard for what counts as a good answer to a question at a given time. The formation and dissolution of such chains help to explain why perceptions of depth have varied so much across history.

Consider an example of philosophical 'deepening' from our own time that Collins does not discuss. The nature of consciousness is once again taken to be a philosophically deep problem, perhaps the one that figures most prominently in the literature of science popularization. Yet, a little over a generation ago – under the influence of Gilbert Ryle and Ludwig Wittgenstein – it was fashionable to hold that consciousness was a pseudo-problem. What changed in the interim were the criteria of a good answer. Philosophers have become much more accountable to the findings of experimental science, on the one hand, and the experiences of diversely situated cultures, on the other. From Collins's sociological standpoint, a solution to the problem of consciousness will be difficult because, while suffering through a period of diminished cognitive authority, philosophy must reconcile the largely opposed interests and standards of groups whose natural academic homes these days are psychology and anthropology departments.

However, philosophical depth is more than just the complexity one might expect as the long-term cumulative effect of argumentation. A striking feature of pedagogy in philosophy, when compared with other academic disciplines, is that the depth of its current problems is routinely conveyed in introductory courses that invoke centuries-old texts (in the Western tradition) by Plato, Aristotle, Descartes, Hume and Kant. Here Collins draws on cognitive psychology's definition of working memory as limited attention space to introduce the 'law of small numbers', a sociological version of Hegel's world-historic spirit. The 'numbers' here refer to the 3–6 positions that can be entertained in a given debate at a given moment by the philosophical community. Philosophers become exemplary by standing for these positions, in virtue of their ability to recombine interests of already existing networks. Typically they draw on cultural capital from having participated in those networks. This point is often obscured in canonical histories of philosophy, which, like other legitimatory accounts of 'genius', neglect the privileged backgrounds of creative intellects and the often self-imposed character of the marginality they supposedly 'endured' in their day. This point applies equally to Galileo, Spinoza, Schopenhauer, Peirce and Wittgenstein – who struck quite different poses as 'marginals'.

Finally, one difference between Goldman's and Collins's orientations to social epistemology explains all their other differences. Goldman takes for granted that epistemic virtue – 'truth' – can be distinguished, not only analytically, but also substantively, from other normative virtues such as 'goodness', 'justice', 'beauty', 'efficacy' and 'power'. Consequently, he sees the social epistemologist as designing institutions for the reliable production of knowledge, assuming that any such institution would have a knock-on effect for the promotion of the other virtues. In effect, he raises the legendarily 'autonomous' character of organized inquiry to a policy imperative. But from Collins's standpoint, Goldman is simply reifying the distinction between epistemology and ethics, which only emerged once philosophy became a specialized academic field in the late nineteenth century. However, Goldman's move involves more than forgetting the past: it also adumbrates a range of possible futures for the relationship between systematic knowledge and the social practices that constitute it.

As mentioned earlier, Goldman appears willing to let the need to preserve autonomous inquiry justify a paternalistic attitude to those members of the larger society who are unable to assimilate new knowledge in a duly 'rational' fashion. However, with the weakening of the nation-state in these neo-liberal days, it is more likely that purportedly reliable knowledge processes will be codified as computer algorithms, subject to patents and traded on the stock market. After all, the value of the bids that speculators make on particular stocks rests ultimately on the performance of the companies that sold them the stocks. Indeed, this is a reasonable extension of Goldman's own tendency to reformulate classic epistemological issues in terms of problems in rational choice theory and cognitive science.

But there is also a dystopic future implicit in Collins's social epistemology, which results from knowledge systems becoming victims of their own success. As the number of people participating in organized inquiry increases and the knowledge they produce figures more prominently in the larger processes of social reproduction, the possibilities for intellectual innovation are pushed to the margins. Those who cannot make it in a highly competitive and bureaucratized knowledge system must seek support in the less official arenas of freelance writing, business and political activism. Thus, Collins recounts that Europe's original 'knowledge society' was late sixteenth-century Spain, which contained 32 universities that were attended by 3 per cent of the country's male population. (That figure was only matched by the USA in the early twentieth century.) Spain was then reaching the limit of its imperial reach. It also fostered a 'Golden Age' in literature, epitomized by the work of Lopé de Vega, Calderon and Cervantes. However, this literary activity existed outside, and largely in opposition to, academia. Indeed, when Bacon, Descartes and other leaders of the Scientific Revolution wished to refer to the scholastic orthodoxy, they typically turned to Spanish tracts. Collins periodically intimates that we in the West currently live in just such a society; hence, innovation flourishes in such academically marginal fields as computer programming and science-fiction writing. If history is to be believed, these para-academic pursuits are sowing the seeds of the next intellectual revolution.

Goldman and Collins epitomize the rather divergent directions in which philosophers and sociologists have taken the research programme of social epistemology. Goldman stresses the efficient production of knowledge at the expense of querying who participates in the process and the extent to which a given epistemic community represents the interests of the society that sustains it. Collins illustrates the complementary case of defining the conditions of participation in the knowledge system, while downplaying the efficacy that the system's products have on the larger society. Since Goldman and Collins generally presume that the community of knowledge producers is a well-defined subset of any given society, they are unable to address how the nature of knowledge would change, were more and different people officially involved in its production. In both cases, this is largely a result of the simplifying assumptions they have had to make to bring their heroic projects to fruition. Nevertheless, the promise of social epistemology will only be realized once a theorist is able to connect questions about participation and production in the knowledge system without supposing the optimality of the prevailing linkages.

From Social Epistemology to the Sociology of Philosophy: The Codification of Professional Prejudices?

The Sociology of Philosophies (Collins 1998) is a treatise not only in social epistemology but also more explicitly in the sociology of philosophical knowledge. However, he sticks rather closely to the professional self-understanding of the dominant analytic school in the English-speaking philosophical world. This ultimately serves to undercut the critical role that the sociology of knowledge has traditionally played in exposing the reflexive implications of belief systems. And while Collins's work is the most impressive exercise in the sociology of philosophical knowledge, it is by no means the first. At least three precursors are worth noting in the English-speaking world, all thoroughly familiar with analytic philosophy's professional self-understanding. Nevertheless they remained aloof and typically critical of that self-understanding, much more in the spirit of Mannheim than Collins. All held prestigious professorships in their respective countries. All wrote many books that received considerable publicity in their day. Yet all were promptly forgotten once they died, and none appear in the index of the book that claims to have canonised the 'sociology of philosophical knowledge' as a field of serious inquiry (Kusch 2000). I refer here to the American Morton White (1957), the British Ernest Gellner (1992) and the Australian John Passmore (1966).

The great strength of Collins's (1998) work is that it lays bare the sociology implicit in the historical narratives through which academic philosophy presents its official face to students and lay readers of philosophy. More circumspect versions of these narratives provide the basic terms of reference for histories of philosophy written by philosophers and, of course, professional philosophers looking for distinguished precursors to legitimize their current pursuits. In short, Collins holds up a sociological mirror to philosophy. If philosophers do not like the reflected image, they really have only themselves to blame. Unsurprisingly, however, philosophers have found the image flattering (e.g. Quinton 1999). This suggests the great weakness of Collins's method. Extending the optical metaphor, his preferred instrument of theoretical vision is a mere mirror rather than, say, a more probing X-ray. Consequently, Collins's project is a rather uncharacteristic exercise in the sociology of knowledge, the results of which normally leave the reader uneasy that the top dogs in a field have nothing more in their favour than a monopoly of force or some other scarce resource. Yet, all seems to be well with philosophy in Collins's account. The 'good guys' are winning: Western philosophy is the most progressive philosophical culture the world has ever seen; logic, epistemology and metaphysics have been its vanguard fields; and analytic philosophy the most successful of its contemporary schools. If you doubt any of these three propositions, then you will not find much comfort in Collins. At the risk of committing the dreaded sin of Eurocentrism, let me confess at the outset that I accept the first proposition but not the other two.

The main sense in which Collins does not challenge philosophy's self-representation is his acceptance that philosophical activity is most naturally related to the work of other school-based intellectuals. In practice, this assumption enables Collins to sweep up many – though by no means all – of the developments in the natural and social sciences, religion and literature. But the walks of life represented by this approach are still narrower than in, say, Wuthnow (1989), which examines how the Reformation, the Enlightenment and Socialism metamorphosed from internecine philosophical disputes to fully fledged social movements. Just armed with Collins's account, it would be hard to see how people outside academic life, such as professional writers, journalists, lawyers, entrepreneurs, priests and ideologues, could ever be major forces of intellectual change – except through whatever umbilical ties they retained to where they were trained. Otherwise, they are fated to provide either external stimulus for internal developments in philosophical discourse or inchoate expressions of such developments.

The fact that academics are the premier producers of intellectual histories means that sociologists of knowledge need to take extra care to ensure that the ultimate contributions of non-academic intellectuals are not underestimated. That Collins so closely associates intellectual creativity with long-term peer reputation creates some cause for concern here. He may not have sufficiently distanced the goal of explaining how philosophical intellectuals have come to acquire their current significance from the fact that his evidence base consists mainly of intellectual histories written about people whom the historians regard as their own progenitors. This can lead to some striking omissions, such as the absence of any discussion of Islam once it completed its contribution to European philosophy in the thirteenth century, though Islam continued to sustain philosophically significant discourses, even according to contemporary Western historians of 'world philosophy' (Cooper 1996a: 386–396). Consequently, those familiar with the history of philosophy from conventional disciplinary sources will be surprised only by the closeness of fit between the development of philosophical ideas and the exfoliation of network affiliations, not by the actual network members or the relative significance Collins assigns to them.

This is strange. If sociological categories are prima facie alien to the subject matter of philosophy, then it would be reasonable to expect a revisionist account of the plot structure of philosophical discourse, once it had been explained sociologically. Failing that, someone of an uncharitable disposition might conclude that Collins's law of small numbers merely re-inscribes on the stage of world history the process by which intellectual historians prune the past for the purpose of focusing their fields for the future. To his credit, Collins realizes that this process is itself very much part of ongoing intellectual debate, and he periodically shows how forward movement involves reinterpreting the significance of past figures and events. However, because this not done systematically, it is unclear how the boundaries dividing philosophy from other academic disciplines and non-academic forms of intellectual life have been reflexively constructed by historical agents over time.

Consider again the case of the Scientific Revolution. Collins upends the received philosophical wisdom that the sciences spun off as specialized branches of philosophy by showing that philosophy itself was forced into more abstract and specialized formulations, as natural knowledge claims, even ones of universal scope, came to be pursued and settled by technological means. Collins dates this development to the seventeenth-century Scientific Revolution in Europe, which should surprise no one these days. What we do not learn is why this is *our* response to Collins's account. After all, at least another two centuries had to pass after this so-called Scientific Revolution before philosophy and science started to be treated as having separate histories. Indeed, the very usage of 'Scientific Revolution' to encompass the intellectual ferment from Copernicus to Newton dates only from the 1940s (Cohen 1985). In that case, how, when, and why did the historical agents themselves – the philosophers, scientists, etc. from the seventeenth century onwards – gradually come to see that philosophy and science deserved largely separate histories? Moreover, what was at stake in the struggle to distinguish these histories, and what was gained and lost (by whom?) with the institutionalization of this distinction? Instead of answering these questions, Collins simply provides some sociological legitimation for maintaining the boundary between science and philosophy. For my own part, I have addressed these matters in terms of the origins of 'philosophy of science' as a separate field from science, even though the same people practised both until at least the early twentieth century (e.g. Fuller 2003: especially chap. 9).

Let me point out two significant implications of Collins's general strategy of taking professional histories of philosophy largely at face value. The first is that Collins's normative stance remains obscure, needlessly exposing his account to the uncharitable interpretations of defensive philosophers. Some will say it merely rewrites conventional history in sociological jargon, while others will suspect that this jargon serves to desecrate the history. Even if

Collins could not have revealed all the possibly superior philosophical trajectories that were preempted by the paths the history actually took, he might have made some sociologically inspired arguments for revaluing the significance of various figures, movements, or debates. In that case, the critical side of his project would have become clearer. For example, on Collins's own account (and here I defer to his method of counting pages), Kant's student Fichte, and idealism more generally, would seem to merit a boost in fortunes for making philosophy the intellectual anchor of the modern university. Some explicit engagement with when, how, and why professional histories of philosophy came to minimize this point – and the costs incurred – could have formed the basis for some useful polemics with a philosophical community that has struggled throughout the twentieth century to appear as something more than an atavism.

The second implication of Collins's strategy is that metaphysics and epistemology, rather than value theory, appear as the foundational philosophical disciplines. This accords well with the academic presumption that philosophy flourishes most – in the sense of pursuing higher levels of abstractness and reflexivity – when it is autonomous from the concerete concerns of religion and politics. In terms of Collins's own practice, it means, inter alia, that Machiavelli is discussed only once in the book, and then in order to make sense of a Japanese philosopher. Collins does not seem especially alive to the idea that metaphysical discourse constitutes a rhetoric that masks uncomfortable truths in politically difficult times. This thesis, most often tied to the provenance of Plato's *Republic*, has been a productive historiographical tool in the hands of Leo Strauss and Quentin Skinner, who hail from opposite sides of the political spectrum without either being an unreconstructed Marxist theorist of ideology. Indeed, an important strand of this thinking persists in modern philosophical histories of science, especially when support for science has been tied to national security concerns (Fuller 2000b: chaps 1–2).

Of course, Collins cannot be faulted for not having pursued a hypothesis other than his own, especially given its manifest fecundity. However, let me just mention the potential benefits of developing in comparable detail the alternative hypothesis that philosophy is ultimately politics in exile. First, the significance of some of the figures and debates might appear differently, especially once the concept of 'attention space' is adjusted to reflect a wider rhetorical horizon. Second, the account would avoid the whiff of the 'external–internal' distinction familiar in the history of science, which suggests that social factors can do little more than constrain or distort the free flow of ideas. Third, it would be easier to see when internecine philosophical disputes are vehicles for swaying spectators with the power to put the philosopher's words into action. Indeed, the philosophers themselves may want to have their views implemented by 'political technologies' analogous to the material practices that were required to transform natural philosophy into natural science – but an important preparatory stage may be the collegial jousting matches that Collins chronicles.

Let us focus on Collins's privileging of metaphysics and epistemology over value theory as driving the history of philosophy – a thesis made explicit in a follow-up essay to his *magnum opus* (Collins 2000). By 'value theory' I mean the range of philosophical sub-disciplines – including aesthetics, ethics, economics, politics, law – that define rationality as a disciplining of one's desires rather than beliefs. Rudolf Hermann Lotze, the influential nineteenth-century German medical doctor turned philosopher, named the field of value theory 'axiology', implying that knowledge is based on a foundational orientation to the world, what the Neo-Kantians (up to the early Habermas) called 'knowledge interests' (Schnädelbach 1984: chap. 6). A good example of a philosopher who in our own day saw the entire history of his discipline from the standpoint of value theory (i.e. as a theory of the objects of desire) was Michel Foucault. Instead of seeing value theory as the mere application of metaphysics and epistemology, I shall argue that a more critical perspective would see metaphysics and epistemology as coded versions of value positions that can have, and have had, serious consequences for those who take philosophy seriously – that is, as a guide to life.

Collins's sociology of philosophy reinforces philosophers' professional prejudices most clearly in his discussion of the cognitive superiority of epistemology and metaphysics to value theory. Thus, Collins (2000) stresses value theory's relative lack of intellectual adventurousness. However, he could have equally mentioned the gendered character of the dichotomy, as women are much more prominent in value theory than in epistemology and metaphysics. In other professions, this would be read as a mark of the field's relatively low status. This point is perhaps not unrelated to informal views about value theory being sloppier, less substantive (as in: 'Ethics is the mere codification of folk attitudes, not the result of logically compelling argument'), and more susceptible to the influence of other disciplines, not to mention ambient political pressures.

Intentionally or not, Collins spins the history of value theory to keep these prejudices afloat. For example, he says that the 'Great Philosophers' typically saw value theory as an application of carefully forged arguments in metaphysics and epistemology. However, this ignores the fact that many, if not most, of them saw their ethical philosophies as the ultimate pay-off – the alimentary proof that the metaphysical pudding was worth baking, so to speak. Moreover, if Leo Strauss and Quentin Skinner are even partly right, metaphysics and epistemology may provide a politically safer ground to carry on arguments with serious, but largely implicit, value implications. In other words, metaphysics and epistemology may themselves be encrypted ways of saying things about how we should live our lives and distribute our allegiances that, said more straightforwardly (e.g. as an explicit moral prescription), would have jeopardized the author's own well-being.

A watered-down version of this disguised practice occurs nowadays when a philosopher of science expresses her distaste for religious education to a hostile audience by attempting to exclude Creationist teaching on grounds relating to the 'definition' of science, as opposed to the anticipated anti-scientific or anti-liberal attitudes that an exposure to Creationism is likely to foster (cf. Fuller 2007c: chap. 5; Fuller 2008: chap. 4). Hence, an essentially moral objection is rendered a matter of epistemic adjudication. To be sure, two can play this game, as witnessed in the metaphysically inspired 'definitions' of life that enable Catholic advocates to make 'principled' objections to abortion, a practice they find morally abhorrent.

Indeed, given the pervasiveness of this use of epistemic arguments to moral ends, I am tempted to claim that the stock-in-trade appeals that metaphysicians and epistemologists make to foundations, presuppositions and definitions are just a high-grade form of conflict resolution (or sublimation?), a way to decide between often radically different judgements concerning the consequences of holding certain beliefs without having to confront openly the value preferences that these judgments imply. Is it mere coincidence, then, that general-purpose philosophies with a strong consequentialist (usually teleological) orientation – Aristotelianism, Hegelianism, Pragmatism – have tended to place values at the very centre of their metaphysics, thereby conflating the distinction in branches of philosophy that Collins wishes to draw?

It is worth pointing out the sense of 'reflexivity' involved in the above three paragraphs is *not* Collins's. Collins appeals to what I earlier identified as the 'narrow' sense of reflexivity that is close to the logician's or linguist's interest in the consistency of self-applied statements. In contrast, I mean here the 'wider' sense traditionally associated with the sociology of knowledge's interest in the existential implications of making a statement for the statement-maker given his or her place in the larger culture. In terms of my sense of reflexivity, there is nothing especially 'puzzling' that philosophers who express their ethical philosophies openly tend to keep close to the normative bounds of their day.

One by-product of the relatively abstract terms in which metaphysical and epistemological statements are expressed is that they are appropriable by many different parties with many different value orientations for many different ends. From a standpoint of the sociology of philosophy that accorded value theory a privilege denied by Collins, the ready-to-hand character of this discourse would probably be subject to critical scrutiny and maybe even labelled opportunistic. But given Collins's own sympathy with the metaphysicians and epistemologists, such ease of appropriation would seem to be a plus, not a minus.

So far I have been taking Collins's expression 'metaphysics and epistemology' at face value, since it still captures something recognizable in the philosophy curriculum. However, much of the boldness that he ascribes to these branches of philosophy – especially when compared with value theory – is no more than nostalgic when projected onto the contemporary anglophone scene, where metaphysics and epistemology have become at least as specialized and restricted in focus as the various branches of value theory. For example, consider the 'big names' in contemporary epistemology: Alvin Goldman, Keith Lehrer, John Pollock, Isaac Levi, Henry Kyburg. Are any of these likely to be elevated even to Collins's second tier of Great Philosophers? Indeed, what is usually taught as 'metaphysics and epistemology' in today's anglophone courses (barring the ones explicitly devoted to the Great Philosophers) is just playing out an endgame begun by Wilfrid Sellars and Roderick Chisholm after the latter discovered the works of Brentano while doing military service for the USA in Austria during World War II (Chisholm and Sellars 1957).

Perhaps logical positivism's most lasting institutional legacy to philosophy has been to shift the locus of 'bold' philosophizing from metaphysics and epistemology to the philosophy of language and the philosophy of science, respectively. That is really where the sort of intellectual adventurousness that Collins valorizes can be found in the English-speaking world in the second half of the twentieth century. And here one finds the normative aroma of value theory much more clearly in the air, be it in the various Oxbridge injunctions concerning language use or the Popperian strictures on scientific rationality that would rule out most 'normal science' as irrational.

A possible reason why value theorists do not appear very high on Collins's list of Great Philosophers is that they were typically more than just philosophers – at least that is how they look to us today. And for us, steeped in philosophy as a technical discipline, to be more than a philosopher is always to be *less* than one. Admittedly, this is a tricky historiographical issue: to what extent do our intuitive judgements about the status of these figures reflect how they lived their lives, as opposed to the contribution (or not) we take them to have made to legitimizing our current intellectual pursuits?

A striking version of the problem can be found far from the centre of value theory, namely, in the origins of modern philosophy of science. Virtually all the nineteenth-century founding fathers – William Whewell, Pierre Duhem, Ernst Mach, etc. – were on the losing side of the major scientific disputes of their day, often spectacularly so; whereas we tend to regard the major scientists as indifferent or flawed philosophers. (The difference becomes more pronounced the farther back we go, as in, say, the scientific versus philosophical merit of Hobbes and Boyle or, for that matter, Descartes and Newton.) If in all these cases, the parties did not detect the hard line between science and philosophy we observe today, was it because they were confused about what they were up to (mixing science and philosophy indiscriminately) – or rather, that we are letting our retrospectively applied categories colour our judgement of how the history actually transpired? Indeed, I have examined the 1908–1913 public debates between Mach and Max Planck as a highly visible attempt to resolve this issue (Fuller 2000b: chap. 2).

Collins's main database is a set of professional histories of philosophy taken from various points in the twentieth century. This is a period when the relationship between philosophy and the other disciplines has not only changed, but more importantly has been subject to intense disagreement and variation. Perhaps Collins was too impressed by the relatively airbrushed version of history conveyed in these philosophy texts and hence may have been a bit too quick in assuming closure has been reached on where, say, philosophy ends and something else begins. For, an interesting feature of the twentieth century has been the number of academically based thinkers who either explicitly or implicitly challenged the overall trend of increased professionalization in philosophy: Popper, Hayek, Kuhn, and Chomsky each did this in their own inimitable way. (Of course, a list of Marx-inspired thinkers could be given as well.) Needless to say, all have been accused of being sub-philosophical performers by one or another academic philosopher. Unfortunately, Collins's sociological approach may only to serve to bolster this sort of 'establishment' judgement because of the relatively uncritical way with which he deals with the evidence provided by philosophers' histories of philosophy.

It is striking just how close Collins's account of philosophical change is to Kuhn's account of scientific change. As in normal science, philosophers deal in ever higher levels of abstraction and reflexivity, except during the relatively brief periods when 'external' concerns intervene, only to be then erased from the reformed historical record as the next cycle of abstraction and reflexivity is set in motion. Here I am especially struck by the highly circumscribed role Collins assigns to rational life-conduct advice in the development of value theory. I wonder, however, whether the story would be so neat, had he not focussed so much on ethics *strictu sensu*, but had instead ranged a bit more widely to cover not only political theory but especially jurisprudence and aesthetics – two areas where philosophical discourse has probably played a more constitutive role in the activities of lawyers and artists, respectively.

One disturbing feature of Collins's implicit sense of philosophical progress is that – again like Kuhn's – it seems to favour the single-minded pursuit of pedigreed irrelevance. Thus, the history of ethics acquires a sense of progress only with the rise of meta-ethics in the twentieth century. Aside from sounding suspiciously like the very same story analytic philosophers would tell, it bears an uncomfortable resemblance to a story sometimes told about the contemporary philosophy of science (again, especially by analytic philosophers). Accordingly, the philosophy of science was a bit of an embarrassment when philosophers were disputing scientists over things the latter knew more about (e.g. Popper on quantum mechanics, evolutionary theory and his general contempt for 'normal science'). But once the smoke had cleared from the Kuhn–Popper debates in the 1970s, philosophers finally found their rightful place in going tit-for-tat in the second-order realism-instrumentalism debate (Fuller 2003).

Although they are allegedly trying to explain 'the success of science', the two sides of this debate would largely give the same positively disposed first-order narrative of the history of science but offer different second-order accounts of why the narrative is as it is. Neither side is particularly critical of science as it is actually practised; indeed, scientists can easily go about their business without paying attention to either camp. To be sure, the philosophical debate becomes more sophisticated as it is played out, and even the use of history becomes more detailed to illustrate the major claims. Yet, in the end, this sounds very much like the relationship between meta-ethics and the conduct of life. As such, it jars with my intuitive sense of progress in an intellectual endeavour, which admittedly is influenced by the 'wide' sense of reflexivity.

Related to this last point is what may be Collins's misleading causal talk that meta-ethics, be it starting with Prichard or Nietzsche, constitutes an intellectual 'breakthrough'. This would seem to imply that value theorists had been *trying* to make a semantic ascent but failed to do so, for whatever reason – lack of incentive, lack of intellect? In contrast, there may simply be something much less edifying going on here. It could be that over the twentieth century, moral philosophers have increasingly found themselves talking only to each other as they have gradually lost their traditional pedagogical charges, aspirant priests and civil servants. The intellectually challenging discourse about rational life-conduct in the secular era has been transferred from theology to the liberal professions, largely bypassing professional philosophy altogether.

In a sense, then, Collins is right that philosophy has had little of its own to say about first-order moral issues. But that is not because these issues are incapable of interesting intellectual development. (Collins's remarks about the 'conservative' nature of ethics sometimes suggest that he holds such a view.) Rather, the development is occurring offstage. Here I think Collins underrates the significance of business, medical, legal, engineering, research – and all the other species of 'professional ethics' that have arisen in the past generation. Although these fields initially tried to apply standard ethical philosophies 'off the shelf' (and hence were seen as 'applied philosophy'), it became clear that judgements reached in this fashion did not do justice to the specificity and complexity of the cases, which demanded a more 'bottom-up' conceptualization.

Indeed, Stephen Toulmin (2001) has gone so far as to claim that this realization marks the resurgence of a countercurrent in the history of value theory – the casuistic tradition – which has been historically associated with the cultivation of rhetoric and the need to provide explicit justifications for actions in situations where trust in the relevant experts has broken down. In other words, rather than gradually transcend the society in which it is embedded, progress in philosophical ethics would consist in its ability to suture together the torn social fabric. However, as suggested by the disparate institutional pattern of professional ethics programmes, it would be difficult to do a Collins-like streamlined sociology of philosophy for this tradition. Nevertheless, it would be a task worth undertaking as a test run for a wide reflexivity account of philosophical progress.

Interlude: Seeds of an Alternative Sociology of Philosophy

How does one begin to lay the groundwork for a more critical sociology of philosophy? We can summarily get the measure of this project by posing a set of questions affording multiple answers, which together constitute a menu of possibilities for how to proceed:

I *How is 'philosophy' defined for sociological purposes?*

    1 Public definitions (e.g. through surveys of intellectuals, citizens).
    2 Symptomatic definitions (e.g. through references in philosophical works).
    3 Self-definitions (e.g. through affiliation in philosophical schools).
    4 Official definitions (e.g. through disciplinary histories).

II *What is it about philosophy that needs to be sociologically explained?*

    1 Its (dis)continuity as an activity over time and space.
    2 Its influence on/by society.
    3 Its autonomy (or lack) from society.
    4 Its progress (or lack) as an activity.

III *'Reflexivity' as a measure of progress in philosophy*

    1 *Narrow reflexivity*: philosophy reflects on the logical presuppositions of its claims.

       • *Progress*: philosophy rises to levels of generality, articulation and consistency that transcend the demands of its social context.
       • *Regress*: philosophy becomes either so alienated from its socieity that it appears irrelevant or so useful to various social interests that it becomes 'too relevant'.

    2 *Wide reflexivity*: philosophy reflects on the social conditions of its practice.

       • *Progress*: philosophy challenges the society that houses it by realizing (and perhaps resolving) latent contradictions.
       • *Regress*: philosophy reproduces the society that houses it by refusing to probe hidden tensions.

Collins's project can be seen as having opted for the following possibilities on this menu. For (I), option (4) is chosen, in part as a means of getting at (3) and less directly (2), while (1) is largely ignored. For (II), (4) is of principal interest, with (3) being used as the main indirect indicator (i.e. progress and autonomy are presumed to be positively correlated). For (III), Collins opts for (1) but, as I have suggested, perhaps without having seriously considered the regressive side of the equation. The result is a view of philosophy as a self-determining and largely self-regarding enterprise.

    An important lesson of Popper's (1972) account of the origins of objective knowledge is that autonomous inquiry arises as a by-product of practical activity. Thus, mathematics as a body of knowledge emerged from people taking counting and measuring procedures as ends in themselves rather than as mere means for the determination of taxes, architectural foundations and horoscopes. In that sense, a reflection on tools as objects in their own right may provide the evolutionary basis for an *Ur*-sense of reflexivity as the basic capacity for second-order thought. This principle can be easily generalized to the origin of philosophical concerns: to wit, philosophy may be said to begin when particular arguments used to influence public debate are treated as belonging to a specific class of arguments, which is then itself treated as a focus of discussion.

This helps explain why it is relatively easy to get an initial fix on the sociology of philosophical knowledge: almost all the canonical positions have their origins in more ordinary forms of social legitimation. Consider Table 2.1, a list of standard philosophical positions that can be historically motivated as attempts to universalize types of arguments, instances of which are commonly found in public debate.

Table 2.1 The origins of philosophical positions in projects of social legitimation

Philosophical position	Legitimatory origins
Kantianism (in ethics)	How to legislate so as to respect the integrity of each individual
Utilitarianism (in ethics)	How to legislate so as to advance society as a whole
Rationalism (in epistemology)	How to pre-empt an irresolvable religious dispute
Empiricism (in epistemology)	How to secure minimal agreement in an irresolvable religious dispute
Realism (in philosophy of science)	What replaces religion in secular society
Instrumentalism (in philosophy of science)	Why secular society does not need a replacement for religion
Objectivism (in philosophy of social science)	What enables the ultimate success of the imperialist project
Relativism (in philosophy of social science)	What enables resistance to the imperialist project

A striking feature of the history of modern philosophy is the infrequency with which philosophers have tried to reintroduce these philosophical extrapolations to practical decision-making. A notable effort in this respect was Henry Sidgwick's *The Methods of Ethics* (1966), which canonized the opposition between Kantianism and utilitarianism by stressing the situations in which trade-offs had to be made between the two positions. Of course, in most cases, the two positions affirm the same decisions. Perhaps this is because philosophy flourishes on the margins, the extreme cases where differences in reasoning finally make a palpable difference for action. The construction of such hypothetical cases would therefore constitute a distinctly philosophical art.

The only problem with this characterization is that fully articulated philosophical positions of the sort valorized by Collins in the name of narrow reflexivity do not merely concur in the main and diverge at the margins: they can even be invoked to support policies diametrically opposed to the spirit of their original conception. Thus, a dash of ingenuity coupled with diabolical intent has enabled Kantianism to legitimize blind obedience to dictators and utilitarianism to justify impoverishing the majority in many nations. What this shows is that the dogged pursuit of philosophical inquiry detached from specific practical concerns can render the resulting positions ideological wild cards available to the highest bidder. Since Collins places such great store on Western philosophy's ability to develop relatively insulated from ambient social concerns, it is incumbent upon him to explain (and perhaps excuse?) such significant unintended consequences.

In the end, even a wide reflexivist like myself must account for the motivation of those who pursue the narrow reflexivist route, since admittedly this is what empirically distinguishes philosophy from other organized intellectual pursuits. In a nutshell, I take my cue from Plato's attempt to protect reason from the public corruption exhibited in his lifetime, beginning with the rise of the Sophists, the trial of Socrates, and finally the fall of Athens at the hands of Sparta (Fuller 2000b: chap. 1). The relevant emotions here are disappointment, frustration and, to some extent, resentment. A definitive experience of failure can heighten one's sense of the distance between the ideal and the actual, as well as decrease the likelihood that the distinction will be subsequently blurred by feats of cognitive accommodation, or what social psychologists call 'adaptive preference formation' (Elster 1983). I regard this alternative vision of the sociology of philosophy as itself a post-Nietzschean position, at least insofar as, for Nietzsche, the transcendental power of the afterlife was ultimately grounded in slaves realizing that they could not appreciably improve their lot by ordinary secular means. In this respect, there may be some truth to the idea that philosophy trades off knowledge against power.

Prolegomena to a Critical Sociology of Twentieth-century Anglophone Philosophy

In the twentieth century, philosophy came to be dominated by the English-speaking world, first Britain and then the United States. Accompanying this development was an unprecedented professionalization and specialization of the discipline. The most general result has been a decline in philosophy's normative mission, which roughly corresponds to the increasing pursuit of philosophy in isolation from public life and especially other forms of inquiry, including ultimately its own history. This is how I explain the increasing tendency, over the past quarter-century, for philosophy to embrace the role of 'underlabourer' for the special sciences. Indicative of this attitude is the long-term popularity of *The Structure of Scientific Revolutions* (Kuhn 1970), which argues that fields reach maturity when they forget their past and focus on highly specialized problems. The chapter concludes by recalling the history of philosophy that following Kuhn's advice has caused us to forget, namely, the fate of Neo-Kantianism in the early twentieth century.

Some features of twentieth-century philosophy will strike future sociologists of knowledge as distinctive of this period. First, is that English became the undisputed *lingua franca* of academic philosophy. Second, is that philosophy became more professionalized and specialized than ever before, especially in the United States, which over the course of the century came to dominate virtually every area of the discipline. Third, is that a mark of philosophy's professionalization and specialization was its retreat from public affairs and normative pronouncements, more generally.

To be sure, not all philosophers eschewed prescriptions, but by the end of the century they had come to be seen as more eccentric and even troublesome, certainly when compared with the start of the century. A more controversial judgement of this period, one associated with Collins (1998), is that most of the original insights had been made in the first quarter of the century, and that the remaining years had been devoted to extending and elaborating these insights. Thus, the 'decadence' often associated with contemporary postmodern thought may be seen as a sublimated form of world-weariness. In what follows, the reader will sense that I largely concur with Collins on this point. However, my aim here is to show how developments that, in many respects, testified to the success and resilience of philosophy in the twentieth-century English-speaking world at the same time reveal the blindspots in that enterprise, which we may be able to overcome in the twenty-first century.

At the start of the twentieth century, philosophy in the English-speaking world was a thoroughly normative discipline. I do not mean that the branches of philosophy devoted to value theory – ethics, politics, jurisprudence and aesthetics – dominated the discipline. On the contrary, the traditional mainstays of philosophy – logic, metaphysics and epistemology – were themselves already normative pursuits. Before Russell and Whitehead's *Principia Mathematica* (1910), 'logic' was generally seen as rules for the conduct of mental life, a kind of normative psychology focused on concrete judgements, not abstract propositions. Metaphysics was centrally concerned with the meaning of life and sometimes divine purpose. Even debates in epistemology, the most recent and technical of the philosophical fields, revolved around the correct 'attitude' one should have toward human and non-human domains of inquiry.

To get a good sense of how far we have retreated from that original normative sensibility, consider the current status of the debate over 'theories of truth' in the anglophone world. If we exclude the silent majority of philosophers who follow Dewey and Rorty in holding that 'truth' is merely an honorific title bestowed on statements we are willing to assert, or predict that we will eventually assert, the partisans of *coherence* and *correspondence* theories of truth appear to have reached a compromise, courtesy of Wilfrid Sellars (Delaney 1977). Whereas truth is defined as the correspondence between a statement and reality, the criterion that a given statement corresponds to reality is that it coheres with other similarly oriented statements. This neat solution, which assigns correspondence to ontology and coherence to epistemology, may satisfy professional metaphysicians and philosophers of language; however, it fails to do justice to the intuitions that motivated the promotion of coherence and correspondence as *opposing* images of validation. As we shall see, eliminated in this compromise has been the explicit normative orientations of the two positions.

The correspondence image of validation has been shared by a wide variety of philosophers: empiricists, inductivists and some positivists. Many of them – like, say, John Stuart Mill and Bertrand Russell – disagreed over the truth of many substantive philosophical theses. However, the image has been traditionally motivated by the idea that our beliefs and desires are ultimately disciplined by whatever happens to escape them, otherwise known as 'the external world'. The final phase of philosophy's secularization in the twentieth century has consisted of re-specifying this sense in which reality exceeds our grasp from (metaphysical) *transcendence* to (linguistic) *reference*. (Here attention might be paid to the theological residues in both Husserl's and Frege's thought, something to which Michael Dummett has been intermittently sensitive.) Thus, the correspondence of a statement with reality has been associated with the fact that people continue to assert it over large expanses of space and time, however much their other statements contradict or disagree with each other. This supposedly testifies to the statement's survival value independent of the various discourses in which it appears. In this respect, any focus on the statement's coherence with others is gratuitous and misleading to any genuine 'reality check'.

In contrast, the coherence image of validation has generally supposed that the point of inquiry is provided by us, not a world that stands outside us. Such a vision united idealists with pragmatists and other process philosophers, who otherwise disagreed on many substantive philosophical points. For the coherence theorist, 'the pursuit of truth' is a radically underdetermined activity, absent of any clear sense of overall purpose, in terms of which the search for particular truths can be motivated. In this context, 'survival' is little more than a default position adopted by inquirers who have lost their sense of direction and need something or someone else to provide it for them.

Thus, the relevant opposition between the correspondence and coherence mentality is not, as is often portrayed, *atomism vs. holism* (i.e. the correspondence of particular statements to bits of reality versus the overall coherence of a body of statements in the face of all of reality), but rather *passivism vs. activism* (i.e. the passive attitude of inquirers who wait to see if reality corresponds to their statements versus the active attitude of inquirers who organize their environment so that reality acquires the shape of their mind). In the early twentieth century, this latter dichotomy was often portrayed as *determinism vs. voluntarism*, although arguably that reified what was essentially a difference in fundamental life attitudes.

In its original strong normative form, philosophy had a very secure place in the US and UK university curriculum, and in both cases it was dominated by the coherence image of validation (Hylton 1990). It dealt with substantive concerns relevant to both personal and civil life. One work in this vein whose influence in the UK extended from the 1880s to the 1930s was F.H. Bradley's *Ethical Studies*, which included the famous essay, 'My Station and Its Duties' (1876). Despite its title, Bradley's work was less a work in philosophical ethics than an exploration of the implications of his absolute idealist metaphysics for the conduct of life. A comparable work in the US context was William James's *Essays in Pragmatism* (1910), which in the guise of metaphysical argument expressed a general world-view, which one of James's admirers, President Theodore Roosevelt, called 'rugged individualism'. This conception of philosophy was largely a function of the student market for the topic, of which philosophy majors constituted only a small fraction (White 1957).

In the case of Britain, the 'moral sciences' curriculum at Oxford and Cambridge was primarily oriented to the training of clergymen and, by the end of the nineteenth century, civil servants. The emphasis was on the teaching of the 'pagan' (Greco-Roman) and Christian classics, as well as such 'modern' classics of political philosophy as Machiavelli, Hobbes and Locke. The official aim of this curriculum was to instill in students the values they needed to administer to an increasingly complex society (read: empire) that was at the same time increasing the scope of public participation. However, like imperial China and Japan, which trained bureaucrats in much the same way, the content of this curriculum was less important than the skills in writing and speaking it imparted, which helped perpetuate the existing social hierarchy. In the twentieth century, this role would be carried on by ordinary language philosophy.

In the case of America, until at least World War I, the mission of the major private universities resembled that of the original medieval universities in their devotion to the training of lawyers and clerics, the principal source of political and academic leaders, respectively. This medieval vestige remains today in the organization of American 'liberal arts colleges', which see themselves as training the nation's future leaders rather than pushing the frontiers of knowledge in specialized fields. Consequently, these institutions have devoted relatively few resources to the development of graduate programmes, outside the context of professional training. However, the liberal-arts mentality still characterizes the British academic system as a whole, although it has seriously eroded over the last two decades, as the polytechnic sector was rapidly incorporated into the university system. Nowadays, in Britain, we say that the system has become 'Americanized', though that really only refers to the American adoption and perfection of the German research-driven model of the university, which had already begun by 1900 (Metzger 1955).

This difference in the development of British and American academic life is reflected in the tendency for the history of American philosophy to be told as a story of its institutionalization as an academic subject (e.g. Kuklick 2001). Thus, the origins of a distinctively 'American' philosophy are traced to the founding of the pragmatist movement by William James at Harvard, usually infused with the spirit of his childhood friend Charles Sanders Peirce. According to this narrative, earlier residents of Massachusetts who worked outside the university, such as Jonathan Edwards, Ralph Waldo Emerson and Henry David Thoreau, were seen as derivative – perhaps even colonial – figures, whose substantive intellectual sources were to be found in Britain or Germany. When cast in a less romantic and ethnocentric light, this sense of America's cultural distinctiveness is sometimes described as philosophy's disciplinary release from the grip of theology, with Darwin depicted as a catalyst (e.g. Menand 2001).

This assessment of the American philosophical tradition has been creatively challenged in recent years from two opposing quarters, one aiming to reintegrate the pre-pragmatist Americans and thereby deepen a sense of America's uniqueness, the other aiming to foster cross-border intellectual affiliations that would render pragmatism the human face of America's global hegemony. On the one hand, we have Stanley Cavell, the Harvard aesthetician whose own interests have turned to the critique of film and other popular genres traditionally beyond the pale of academic philosophy. For Cavell (1992), the fact that Edwards, Emerson and Thoreau communicated via sermons and poems – as well as treatises – suggests a nascent multimedia sensibility that speaks well to the spontaneous tendency of Americans to integrate philosophy into the stuff of life. On the other hand, the most internationally visible standard-bearer of 'American philosophy' in recent times, Richard Rorty (1982), still begins the story with James and sees its culmination in the work of John Dewey. But Rorty's America is a Baudrillardian 'hyperrealist' entity that suits the nation's late twentieth-century superpower status. Thus, rather than engage in James or Dewey exegesis, Rorty tries to show that the early Heidegger and the later Wittgenstein were really 'always already' pragmatists.

In contrast to this search for academic legitimation, the non-academic roots of the most distinctive streams of nineteenth-century British philosophical thought are generally acknowledged. Of course, the famous Scottish Enlightenment of the mid-to-late eighteenth century that included David Hume, Adam Smith and Adam Ferguson had been a university-based movement centred in Edinburgh and Glasgow. However, these Scots were largely Anglophiles in an educational system that was still heavily dominated by the Church of Scotland. (For example, Adam Smith, holder of the Chair in Rhetoric at Glasgow, had encouraged educated Scots to adopt an 'English' accent.) The characteristic Church-based philosophy, represented by Thomas Reid and an early acceptance of Kant, drew close ties between the mental faculty of common sense and a natural propensity toward faith. The Scottish Enlightenment figures thus had little academic influence in the first half of the nineteenth century. Hume was rediscovered as a proto-Darwinist by T.H. Huxley in the wave of anti-clericalism that followed the publication of Darwin's On the Origin of Species (Passmore 1966: 40).

Smith and Ferguson were absorbed more quickly into the public intellectual scene of nineteenth-century England through emerging movements in what eventually became political economy and sociology. I say 'movements' because these fields came into existence not through academic initiatives but political platforms of 'philosophical radicalism', most notably utilitarianism. Here I refer to the journalism and pamphlets of such London-based intellectuals as Jeremy Bentham, John Stuart Mill and Herbert Spencer – and, of course, the German expatriate Karl Marx. However, these contributors were met by significant institutional resistance from Oxford and Cambridge. Indeed, the 'revolution' spawned by G.E. Moore's *Principia Ethica* (1903), which eventuated in the dominance of the analytic tradition in all of anglophone philosophy, can be seen as a reactionary move by British academics who felt their authority challenged by these 'outsiders' who often represented 'radical' viewpoints that would threaten their livelihood, not only as representatives of the philosophical profession but also as teachers of the next generation's elites.

These concerns were crystallized in the institution that provided the most explicit challenge to the Oxbridge hegemony in the twentieth century – the London School of Economics (LSE), which Sidney and Beatrice Webb founded in 1895 to provide a Fabian Socialist alternative to the conservative teaching of value theory at Oxbridge (Dahrendorf 1995). Out went religion and aesthetics and in came politics and economics – and, controversially, eugenics – as the relevant normative disciplines. Once established, the LSE completed London's secular counterbalance to lingering Oxbridge clericalism – a path originally charted with Bentham's endowment of University College London and continued with Huxley's promotion of Imperial College from polytechnic to university. During the twentieth century, the LSE has been the natural home of major social theorists who have not fitted comfortably within the emerging analytic philosophical consensus: e.g. L.T. Hobhouse, R.H. Tawney, Harold Laski, Karl Mannheim, Michael Oakeshott, Friedrich von Hayek, Karl Popper and Ernest Gellner. To be sure, few of these thinkers could be counted as true socialists. Many were liberals, and some even conservatives. However, they all shared a broadly consequentialist approach to philosophy that invariably opened the door to empirical considerations in the determination of value questions that spanned disciplinary boundaries.

A good way to encapsulate the difference between the Oxbridge and LSE approaches to value theory is to examine the positions of the leading philosophers of the respective schools – Ludwig Wittgenstein and Karl Popper – on the relationship between the empirical and normative elements of knowledge producing communities. To be sure, there are certain similarities of viewpoint. Both were hostile to attempts at providing *a priori* normative closure to such communities, be it in terms of appeals to laws of history, functionalist sociology or theories of human nature. Both were committed to a broadly 'constructivist' understanding of social life whereby the past always underdetermines future practice. However, Popper held these shared views almost entirely on normative philosophical grounds, having to do with the value of 'open societies' as vehicles for maximizing the exploration of human potential, which in turn are tied to the idea of endless experimentation: hence, the axiological roots of the falsificationist method and the Popperian penchant for market-based solutions to social problems, which typically presuppose indefinitely plastic individuals operating in a constantly changing environment. Nothing could be further from Wittgenstein's sensibility: where Popperians see their perspective as having a critical leverage on particular 'closed societies', Wittgensteinians regard such a perspective as having no purchase beyond those willing to play the Popperian language game.

While Popper's view has enjoyed some enduring support within the natural and social sciences, Wittgenstein's view remains triumphant in both philosophy and the more relativistic precincts of social science, such as cultural anthropology and the sociology of knowledge. The names of Peter Winch, John Searle and David Bloor conjure up the wide scope of this Wittgensteinian consensus. All three thinkers hold that 'ought' can be, in an important sense, derived from 'is': namely, once the norms of a community have been empirically determined, all the relevant criteria for evaluating knowledge claims have been given. For the most part, however, twentieth-century anglophone philosophers have believed that their field is better served by sticking to G.E. Moore's invocation of the naturalistic fallacy – which would sever all ties between 'ought' and 'is' – than by embracing the naturalized normativity implied in the Wittgensteinian formulation. It is to this studied philosophical avoidance of empirical argument that we now turn.

Analytic Philosophy's Ambivalence Toward the Empirical Sciences

A key to understanding the development of analytic philosophy in the twentieth century has been its studied aversion to empirically based arguments, usually out of fear that philosophy would be absorbed into the natural and social scientific disciplines that were gradually proving their worth in society at large: utilitarianism had strong ties to economics; pragmatism to psychology and sociology; and other more generalized forms of naturalism to physics and biology. All of these movements have been subject to resistance from the academic philosophical establishment, especially in the United Kingdom, where the divide between the 'two cultures' of science and humanities has been sharpest.

Philosophy remained, with history, the bastion of a distinctly humanist mentality in twentieth-century British academia. For example, the history of analytic ethics has favoured emotivist or deontological interpretations of moral obligation over utilitarian ones that would open the door to scientific arguments. Even more telling is the case of analytic epistemology, which has tended toward the analysis of commonsense, not scientific, conceptions of knowledge. Thus, epistemologists tend to worry about how we know that there is a chair in this room, as opposed to, say, quarks in all of space. For the latter, one needs to turn to the philosophy of science, which is quite distinct from epistemology in the anglophone – though not the Continental European – philosophical tradition.

An interesting way of understanding the history of analytic philosophy is as a particular realization of what would have happened, if over the course of the nineteenth century the humanities had not relinquished their status as the exemplar of scientific inquiry, or *Wissenschaft*, to the natural sciences. The distinctive feature of this shift is that the natural sciences (and most of the social sciences, which broke away from the humanities on precisely these grounds) do not limit their evidence base to documents; rather they rely on non-written sources for most of their data (i.e. spontaneous speech and behaviour). Indeed, an important function of natural and social scientific inquiry is to record phenomena that would otherwise remain without documentation, since rocks, plants, animals and, of course, most people do not normally write down their own histories. In that sense, the natural and social sciences extend their epistemic aspiration from interpreting texts that have been already written to writing texts that would otherwise not be written. A recent sociology of scientific knowledge has referred to this difference as 'the turn to practice', thereby drawing attention to the work in which the *Naturwissenschaften* and their emulators engage when 'inscribing' various features of reality.

This point also goes some way toward explaining why the expatriate Austrian philosopher Ludwig Wittgenstein commanded the authority he did in British academic philosophy in the twentieth century. Wittgenstein argued that philosophical inquiry 'leaves the world alone', which appealed to the implicit epistemology of humanist inquiry. Like the classical humanist, the Wittgensteinian philosopher adds nothing substantial to what has been already said by others, but rather opens the space that enables them to speak in a clearer voice. Thus, despite Wittgenstein's location at Cambridge, the Oxford philosophers most sympathetic to his viewpoint were trained in the oldest branch of the humanities, the Greek classics: Gilbert Ryle specialized in Plato, and J.L. Austin in Aristotle. Together they cultivated a style of 'ordinary language' that encouraged philosophers to reduce classical philosophical problems to matters of attentiveness to the semantics of word use, as might be expected of someone who comes to philosophy from philology.

The British promotion of linguistic chauvinism was enhanced by the ascendancy of English at the expense of German as the universal language of scholarship in the twentieth century – initially for political rather than strictly scientific reasons, namely, Germany's defeat in two world wars. In a rhetorically deflated way, the fixation of virtuosity in English, so well critiqued in Gellner (1959), bears comparison with what had transpired much more grandiosely in Germany for more than a century. Starting with Hegel and the Romantics, and culminating in the thought of that great renegade philologist Friedrich Nietzsche, German thinkers have regularly held that their language is the only modern one that is truly conducive to philosophical thought based on its fidelity to Greek sources. Indeed, in the second half of the twentieth century, the French arguably took the Germans even more seriously on this point than the Germans themselves had – even as the polestar of French philosophy shifted between Hegel, Husserl and Heidegger (Descombes 1980).

Given their common background in the classics, it should come as no surprise that Ryle wrote a favourable review in *Mind* of Martin Heidegger's *Sein und Zeit* shortly after it was published in 1927 (Murray, 1973). The main difference between classically trained twentieth-century British and

German philosophers was over how language was supposed to unlock the secrets of philosophy: whereas the British believed that the key lay in aspects of word usage that had survived the centuries, the Germans held that it lay in the meanings and uses that had been lost. This reflects, in turn, a profound difference in sensibility as to what requires philosophical explanation: the British presumed the continued and even increasing success of our communicative and expressive capacities, whereas the Germans presumed a discontinuity and decline in such capacities. Has philosophy made progress on the questions first asked by the Greeks, or have we forgotten what they were asking about? This encapsulates the difference between the British and German language-based approaches to philosophy.

The general strategy that analytic philosophers have used to protect their discipline from scientific encroachment has been to argue that philosophy uses *a priori* means to capture intuitions that are common to all rational beings. This was certainly Moore's original orientation, and it was the one revived by L. Jonathan Cohen in *The Dialogue of Reason* (1986), in response to Richard Rorty's charge, in *Philosophy and the Mirror of Nature* (1979), that analytic philosophy had lost all its subject matter to the special disciplines.

It is rarely observed that Moore's strategy owed more to Plato than the great modern rationalist, Descartes, who actually allowed a much wider berth for empirical reasoning than Moore permitted. Moore generally endorsed the ancient Greek vision of the philosophical life as a leisured pursuit. He was a typical Oxbridge humanist of his day, trained in classical philology. Moore's ethos was embodied in the 'Bloomsbury Circle' of intellectuals and aesthetes who followed his work in the first decades of the twentieth century.

Moore canonized the antipathy between analytic philosophy and the empirical scientific mindset as the 'naturalistic fallacy', that is, the logical invalidity of deriving an ought-statement from an is-statement. Moore's original targets were Mill and Spencer because they held that 'goodness' was nothing more than a consequence of what people either freely decided (Mill) or were hardwired (Spencer) to do. Although Moore meant his argument to establish a distinct domain of reality corresponding to moral knowledge, nowadays it is taken merely to have proven a negative point, namely, that what is, is not necessarily what ought to be. And until recently, the generally noncognitivist strain in twentieth-century ethics interpreted Moore's point as implicitly opening the door to more of a subjective than a Platonic version of idealism.

Plato's status as the standard-bearer of anglophone rationalism began to change once the Nazis forced the logical positivists to flee Germany and Austria. The extended Austro-German network that included not only the logical positivists but also, among others, Popper and Hayek had been keepers of the anglophone flame in the germanophone world. This flame had been first ignited with the translation of Mill's expression 'moral sciences' as *Geisteswissenschaften* in the mid-nineteenth century (Kolakowski 1972). But the positivist cultivation of 'English' attitudes went beyond an absorption in the empiricism of Hume and Mill and, later the adoption of Russell and Whitehead's logic. It also involved an appreciation for the centre-left of the British political spectrum, which disavowed violence as a vehicle for major social change. The term 'social democracy' was often used in this context, which ranged from Eduard Bernstein's evolutionary socialism to Ernst Mach's parliamentary liberalism.

The logical positivists and their fellow travellers were thus sensitive to the value of procedurally based, incremental change that learns from experience and is not simply dictated from the top down. A legacy of this sensibility is what Carl Hempel canonized as the 'symmetry' between explanation and prediction in scientific inference, which implies that a theoretical framework is only as good as the range of empirical phenomena it captures. This may be regarded as the epistemological equivalent of the democratic principle that a representative is only as powerful as the support she receives from the people on whose behalf she speaks. In other words, there must be, in some sense, a mutual calibration between representatives and the represented that does not involve subordinating one to the other.

When the logical positivists became US philosophy's establishment in the 1950s, Descartes replaced Plato as the founding father of the analytic point of view, a position he continues to enjoy as the cornerstone for most 'modern' philosophy courses in the English-speaking world. Given the logical positivists' affinities with empiricism, the choice of Descartes may seem strange. Of course, like the positivists, Descartes was preoccupied with the foundations of physics, in which he argued that sound empirical inquiry was impossible without a secure conceptual starting point. But before the ascendancy of logical positivism, Descartes would not have been the most obvious exemplar of the seventeenth-century scientific attitude. Rather, it would have been someone of a more empirical or even applied turn of mind, such as Galileo, Bacon or Newton – the very antithesis of the armchair intuitionist exemplified by Moore.

At this point, we need to explain the plausibility of Descartes as the logical positivists' historical bridge between the apriorism of analytic philosophy and the scientific naturalism that Moore so strongly detested. Closest to the institutional surface and perhaps of most lasting significance was the educational context of philosophy in the United States. From the beginning of the twentieth century, Descartes had been seen as providing the challenge to which empiricists, pragmatists, idealists and realists all saw themselves as responding: namely, an account of knowledge that does not ultimately resort to an unconditional commitment to the truth of certain propositions (Kuklick 1984). The positivists would already have been familiar with this challenge from Bertrand Russell's formulation of 'the problem of knowledge' in *The Problems of Philosophy* (1912). Russell, in turn, had been influenced by Husserl, Meinong and Brentano, all of whom had given the Cartesian challenge a broadly psychologistic interpretation (Kusch 1995).

Russell's innovation, partly influenced by Moore and partly by his work on logic with Whitehead, was to cast the problem as concerning propositions rather than propositional attitudes. This served to simplify the account of the human mind needed to conduct epistemological inquiry – basically reducing cognition to the assertion and denial of propositions (a.k.a. 'beliefs') – and hence insulate philosophy from the encroachment of experimental psychology. The legacy of these boundary manoeuvres is Roderick Chisholm's redefinition of the problem of knowledge as the justification of our true beliefs.

In the case of the positivists' own lives, two formative events stand out in enabling their acceptance of the Cartesian starting point to modern philosophy. Both occurred in the first two decades of the twentieth century: Einstein's revolution in physics and Germany's loss in World War I. The positivists generally credited Einstein with having reconceptualized scientific foundations by reinterpreting the results of some problematic experiments – not by conducting new experiments or producing new data. Einstein was thus seen as having engaged in a recognizably philosophical activity. At the same time, however, the German scientific community was staunchly behind the Kaiser in World War I, but only managed in the end to unleash new weapons of mass destruction in the course of losing the war. This defeat, in turn, spurred a backlash against the natural sciences in the ensuing Weimar Republic. In light of these two events, the logical positivists wished to cultivate an image of science that was at once conceptually foundational yet technologically neutral. Ultimately, Descartes' unique brand of apriorism fitted the bill.

In short, then, the openness of philosophers of science to empirical arguments is largely explained by the dominance of expatriate German and Austrian philosophers in the USA and UK for whom the two cultures divide was seen as a parochially English problem. To be sure, debates over the *Geistes-* and *Natur- Wissenschaften* captured the German philosophical imagination for the hundred years following the translation of Mill's *System of Logic*, and continue to live on in discussions of the philosophical foundations of the social sciences, both in the anglophone and germanophone worlds. However, the German debates were mainly concerned with the *relationship*, not the *choice* one needs to make, between the two cultures (Schnädelbach 1984: chaps 1–4). Behind this difference was the quicker acceptance of Darwinism by German rather than British academics, which reflects a larger pattern in nineteenth-century scientific influence: what is originated in Britain is institutionalized in Germany. (To be sure, philosophy tended to exhibit the reverse flow of influence: witness Russell's flirtation with virtually every strand of German idealism, including Leibniz's, Hegel's and Frege's.) By assuming the biological unity of *homo sapiens*, germanophone philosophers could argue that we are predisposed to sympathize with the life problems faced by all humans, regardless of cultural differences. Thus, Wilhelm Dilthey and Max Weber had no problem grounding the quintessentially *geisteswissenschaftlich* method of *Verstehen* in the Darwinian world-view.

Not surprisingly, in the post-World War II era, the only anglophones who have advanced influential visions of philosophical inquiry that attempt to unite the normative concerns of both politics and epistemology have been such emigrant philosophers of science as Karl Popper and Paul Feyerabend. For all their differences with the logical positivists, Popper and Feyerabend shared with them a normative conception of 'Science', which was treated as the standard bearer of all forms of collective rationality, even though it was only partly (if at all, in Feyerabend's view) achieved by contemporary scientific practices (Notturno 2000). My own project of 'social epistemology' has followed up their initiative, taking into account the increasingly interdisciplinary environment in which a general philosophical vision must be forged in the English-speaking world.

Professionalism as Differentiating American and British Philosophy

The most obvious feature of American philosophy from the British stand-point is the former's 'professionalism', in both its positive and negative senses. As suggested earlier, what historically made the difference was the influence of the German conception of the research university on the USA, especially the use of the doctoral degree as the measure of ultimate acade-mic distinction. This conception did not find favour in Britain until the 1980s, when under Margaret Thatcher's influence, the relative lack of uni-versity graduates in the population was implicated in the nation's alleged economic decline on the international stage. This induced a degree of pro-fessionalism hitherto unseen in British academic life, sometimes as a col-lective defence against encroaching market forces, other times as a means of catering to them.

In the USA, the German model made its first impression with the rise of pragmatism. Despite William James's avowed attempts to navigate a distinct course between what he regarded as the German excesses of idealism and positivism, his own background as a student of medicine made him a kindred spirit of Hermann von Helmholtz and Wilhelm Wundt, the great German research professors who endeavoured to solve the mind–body problem by experimental means in the late nineteenth century. Thus, while James himself remained a 'public philosopher', he sponsored a great deal of rather technical and even esoteric research at Harvard that aimed to make metaphysical points by experimental means. The results constitute the early history of experimental psychology in the USA, as demonstrated by the pattern followed by other early philosophy graduate programmes, including Johns Hopkins, Clark and Chicago universities (the last under the influence of John Dewey).

However, it was really the migration of the logical positivists from Central Europe with the rise of Nazism that crystallized the current professional ethos of American philosophy. At that point, the public character of philosophy that had characterized pragmatism and other indigenous American movements began to disappear. This shift can be explained in terms of a major – though largely unnoticed – difference in emphasis between positivism and pragmatism. Whereas pragmatists regard science as little more than commonsense rendered self-conscious, positivists regard common sense as an inchoate and hence imperfect expression of the scientific mindset. W.V.O. Quine, the US student-observer at the original Vienna Circle meetings, is usually credited with smoothing over this difference. In particular, he translated pragmatism's open-ended view of inquiry into the logical principle of the underdetermination of theory choice by the available evidence (Thayer 1968). Yet, at least as important here was the person who chaired the Harvard philosophy department in Quine's student days, C.I. Lewis. Lewis was a student of James who became one of the earliest American innovators in symbolic logic. He resurrected the corpus of Charles Sanders Peirce, the Harvard eccentric whose interest and competence in formal scientific matters provided the 'missing link' between pragmatism and logical positivism.

Prior to the arrival of the logical positivists, the public face of American philosophy was historically tied to the Christian, typically liberal Protestant, foundations of most US colleges and universities. It was a secular version of the pastoral ministry. Even a figure as overtly secular as John Dewey continued to evoke the air of a Protestant minister in his public performances. The contrast here with the modern German university system is noteworthy. From its renaissance in the early nineteenth century, German academia drew a sharp distinction between the pastoral and critical sides of theology, with the former seen as compromising the intellectual integrity of the latter as a form of inquiry. (Michael Polanyi [1957] updated this distinction for the twentieth-century natural sciences in terms of the 'priestly' attitude of the ideologue and the 'monastic' one of genuine scientists.) To be sure, this distinction was easier to observe in theory than practice, as evidenced by the expulsion of radical theologians like Ludwig Feuerbach and David Friedrich Strauss in the 1840s, and the prevention of Karl Marx from ever pursuing an academic career (Toews 1985).

By the rise of Hitler, the exclusion of pastoral matters from education had radically polarized German academia. Germany's ignominious defeat in the First World War was widely diagnosed as the result of an arrogant scientific materialism that had been allowed a free rein in politics without proper moral guidance (Herf 1984). Some like Heidegger wanted to return to a pastoral mission that harked back to Martin Luther himself. For a while, the Nazis hid behind the promise of a neo-Lutheran revival, especially Luther's valorization of immediate experience at the expense of intellectual mediation. Nevertheless, devout Lutherans like Dietrich Bonhoeffer saw through this and paid with their lives. Partly in response to the Nazi manipulation of religious sentiment, more positivistic academics became militant atheists and generally suspicious of the cognitive content of emotional appeals. Once the positivists were ensconced in the USA, their anti-Nazi ethos effectively drove out the traditional American concern with philosophizing about morals and the 'good life'.

The conventional mark of intellectual integrity in the German university system was the use of technical language and (in the case of, say, Frege) even symbolic notation. As the logical positivists famously stressed, if terms are defined very carefully, then stray semantic associations would be minimized and hence one would not invite the discussion of so-called 'lifestyle' considerations that could compromise the single-minded pursuit of truth, as well as inhibit students from freely deliberating over how they might conduct their own lives (Dummett 1993). Indeed, many German defenders of this conception of academic freedom at the dawn of the twentieth century, such as Ernst Mach and Max Weber, had made a point of stressing the latter: that is, by making inquiry appear very technical and hence self-contained, students would not be pressured into thinking that science had 'proven' the truth or falsity of their fundamental value commitments (Proctor 1991: chap. 10). An interesting reinvention of this line of thought – one tailored to the pluralistic US context of the late twentieth century – was the 'anything goes' philosophy of Paul Feyerabend, the Austrian student of Popper and Wittgenstein who eventually settled in California. Whereas Mach and Weber preached academic self-restraint on value issues, Feyerabend called for 'letting a thousand flowers bloom', but the motivation was much the same.

While most British philosophers are not familiar with the impact of German academia on American philosophy, they have no problem detecting its effects. American philosophical writing is jargon-laden, gratuitously technical and symbolized, and overspecialized. The most philosophically interesting manifestation of this overspecialization is that Americans are often so impressed by the results of the latest scientific achievement that they make the Kantian move of turning it into a synthetic *a priori* truth. For, just as Kant tried to make Newton appear to have discovered the fundamental categories by which we make sense of the world, American philosophers of psychology and biology, such as Daniel Dennett and the husband-and-wife team of Paul and Patricia Churchland, try to construct their theories so as to render the relevant scientific achievements as near-deductive consequences of vaguely reasonable assumptions of how the world works. In a more Marx-friendly time, we would call this 'ideology'; logicians still call it '*post hoc* rationalization'. Of course, philosophers have been taught to dignify this move as 'naturalism' (Callebaut 1993).

Once such homegrown Oxford-based logical positivists as A.J. Ayer and T.D. Weldon declared in the 1940s that moral and political discourse consisted of barely disguised appeals to emotion, anglophone philosophers also began to declare the death of politics as a philosophically interesting subject. That these death knells were taken seriously in both the USA and the UK in the two decades following World War II is telling. The logical positivists had reduced political discourse to ideological differences that could not be resolved by strictly empirical means, as they involved appeals to the fears and hopes of the audiences to whom they were directed. From the standpoint of the Cold War, such discourse was therefore best 'contained', since the only foreseeable alternative was violent conflict. Politics left philosophy when it was no longer seen as something that could be reasoned about. Moreover, many postwar societies instantiated this depoliticized sensibility by shifting the job requirements of their civil servants, encouraging those trained in the 'technocratic' sciences of engineering and economics, while discouraging those trained in the more traditional humanistic fields. Just this shift enabled C.P. Snow's (1956) lecture on the 'two cultures' to acquire the iconic status it has held over the past half-century.

Alasdair MacIntyre (1984[1891]) had an interesting but damning way of referring to these developments, which continue to a large extent in the anglophone world today. MacIntyre argued that moral discourse had lost its moorings from concrete conceptions of the good life, and consequently morality had come to be reduced to *mere* discourse, that is, an analysis of the conditions that licence 'ought-statements'. For MacIntyre this attitude was akin to Martian archaeologists who come to earth after a nuclear holocaust and treat morality as an elaborate but ultimately alien language-game performed by the former earthly inhabitants. Lost in the translation is any sense of the cultural meaning that humans invested in these linguistic manoeuvres. MacIntyre's own account of the degraded state of contemporary moral and political philosophy presupposed some controversial, quasi-Heideggerian views about how Western philosophy lost touch with its Greek and Christian roots. However, it would be a mistake to suppose that this decontextualized sense of morals and politics terminated anglophone philosophical thinking on these topics. Indeed, the most sophisticated expression of this approach may be found in the work of the Harvard philosopher John Rawls.

Rawls began his career in the late 1950s commenting on the work of Stephen Toulmin and Nelson Goodman, advocating the need for a decision procedure to determine whether and how current normative practices should be continued into the indefinite future. Evident in these early writings was the original influence of the logical positivist commitment to verificationism, as inflected through the later Wittgenstein's concern for the openness of the lifeworld, whereby variously interested people manage to resolve their differences in common social practices. However, Rawls did not model his decision procedure on the 'crucial experiments' and 'operationalizations' favoured by the positivists. Instead, he retreated from any direct empirical tests to a counterfactual situation that was more in the spirit of Wittgenstein, which by *A Theory of Justice* (Rawls 1971) he had dubbed 'The Original Position'. Here a person decides in isolation the principles of justice that she would have govern her own society, imagining that she is ignorant of which socio-economic position she herself actually occupies.

It is tempting to argue that Rawls's dominance of anglophone moral and political philosophy in the last quarter of the twentieth century has reflected the alienation of theory from practice in the political sphere of Western democracies, especially in the USA, the most notorious site of voter apathy. For, even at the level of theory, Rawls's stance does not presuppose any interaction among the people taking decisions on the principles of justice. It is here that Rawls reveals most clearly his dissatisfaction with the utilitarian tradition, which takes for granted a parliamentary setting where legislators argue about the means and ends of policies, take votes and change their minds once they observe the consequences of their policies. Rawls's obvious precedent here is Kant's categorical imperative, which would have *anyone* hypothetically imagine what *everyone* would accept as a collectively binding judgement for action. To be sure, Rawls's and Kant's political backdrops were different: Kant was more directly concerned with censorship and repression by the Prussian King than the disaffection and cynicism of the American citizenry. Nevertheless, the basic philosophical message is the same: one can do politics without ever having to deal with people.

In what will no doubt appear a curiosity to future historians, Rawls's position – and the vast literature spawned by it – is called 'contractarian'. While the term clearly alludes to Hobbes's original formulation of social contract theory, it is worth recalling that Hobbesian agents, in their pre-social state, are more in the business of second-guessing each other's actions than actual face-to-face negotiation, as would take place in, say, the framing of a national constitution. For Hobbes, the original parties to the social contract do not trust each other sufficiently to engage in the democratic art of rhetoric. In Kant's hands, this frightened atomized individual was transformed into a confident universal subject, as each person came to be presumed capable of deciding for all without consultation. To be sure, both Hobbes and Kant were contending with absolute monarchy: Hobbes legitimizing it, Kant adapting to it. However, one can only explain Rawls's elision of his Hobbesian and Kantian sources as the work of an American who is impressed by the resilience of his nation's constitution but disaffected with the day-to-day politics that it has enabled. In any case, Rawls is no different from Hobbes and Kant in abstracting something salient in his own socio-political situation and projecting it on a universal plane.

Of course, even in the USA, there has been a much more vibrant tradition of political philosophical debate that moved back and forth between the academy and the mass media. However, that precedent would return us to the 1920s, when John Dewey and Walter Lippman contested the terms of democratic governance in large complex societies in the pages of such centre-left weekly magazines as *The New Republic* and *The Nation* (Diggins 1994). The principal difference between the way American philosophers contested political issues then and now (when they do) is that the philosopher now appears less a discussant in a public conversation than a kind of higher-order judge who pronounces on issues of public import, but without allowing much scope for disagreement. Here I have in mind the persona of the contemporary Anglo-American legal philosopher Ronald Dworkin that regularly comes through in the pages of *The New York Review of Books*. It would be hard to imagine a journalist or other policy pundit challenging his dicta. Whether that would be out of reverence or irrelevance is an open question of no small significance.

It may be argued, however, that the public face of contemporary American philosophy is better seen in the burgeoning field of 'professional ethics', which includes business ethics, legal ethics, engineering ethics, research ethics and, most notably, biomedical ethics. If there is a 'growth area' for jobseekers in anglophone philosophy today, it is in these fields, which are increasingly pursued, not in philosophy departments but professional schools. Moreover, these are the fields most likely to attract day-to-day media attention, as measured in terms of soundbites and interviews (as opposed to longer written pieces). Nevertheless, in keeping with American philosophy's own sense of professionalism, the people who gravitate towards professional ethics tend to be accorded relatively low status as philosophers and, indeed, are sometimes regarded as mere sophists who provide legitimation on demand. One name likely to stir up strong opinions on this score is that of the media-friendly Arthur Caplan.

As might be expected, the less professionalized state of British philosophy offers brighter prospects for public impact. This is epitomized by the influence of Jonathan Glover's *What Kind of People Should There Be?* (1984), which introduced a generation of philosophy students to debates concerning newly emerging techniques of genetic engineering and other areas of biotechnology. The result has been to make biomedical ethics in the UK much more a field devoted to scholarly research than clinical judgement. Moreover, following the example set by the great public philosopher, Bertrand Russell, Britain has enjoyed a relatively long tradition of well-recognized philosophers chairing 'blue ribbon' panels designed to set the normative parameters within which long-term social policy should be made. Anthony Kenny, Gary Runciman, Bernard Williams and Mary Warnock have been prominent here. To be sure, this practice typically capitalizes on the continuing close ties between Oxbridge and Parliament, which testifies to the residual elitism of British democracy.

Conclusion: Anglophone Philosophy as a Victim of Its Own Success

Professionalism in philosophy clearly has its costs and benefits, as the contrast between the USA and the UK in the twentieth century amply makes clear. In the most general terms, American philosophy has flourished in an institutional environment that has been relatively impermeable (or impervious?) to extra-mural political and economic concerns. This level of autonomy in teaching and research has resulted in an unprecedented level of technical sophistication and specialization. But it has also meant that US philosophers have generally found it more difficult than their British and especially Continental European counterparts to justify the distinct pursuit of philosophy to increasingly budget-conscious legislators and ideologically discriminating citizens. Indeed, the success of Continental European philosophers on this score is that they are more popular than US or UK philosophers among anglophone non-philosophers (e.g. literary critics, sociologists) in search of philosophical guidance.

The intensification of analytic philosophy in the United States from the end of World War II to the end of the Cold War may have unwittingly instilled what the social critic Thorstein Veblen would have called a 'learned incapacity' to reflect on the social conditions of philosophical knowledge production. In terms that evolutionary biologists would appreciate, US analytic philosophers may be 'overadapted' to their 'ecological niche', and so cannot respond adequately to the changing political and economic environment in which they find themselves at the end of the twentieth century. Even a philosopher as reflective as Richard Rorty (1982) ultimately resorts to an appeal to 'tradition' – the distinctive history of the United States as a nation – to explain his commitment to philosophy as the pursuit of free critical inquiry. But perhaps more disturbing is that recent graduates of US philosophy programmes are less likely to justify the pursuit of philosophy as having intrinsic merit (say, in terms of its ability to provide an overarching world-view or a rigorous critical perspective from which to comment on the social order) than as instrumental in the pursuit of some other, presumably more worthy, subject.

A natural interpretation of this situation is that young philosophers believe that if they are unable to pursue careers in the narrow technical puzzles in which they were formally trained, the only alternative is to work as a technical puzzle-solver in someone else's project. Little thought is given to the possibility that philosophy may justify its autonomous pursuit even as a non-specialist subject.

In the previous section, I observed that the philosophical 'growth area' of professional ethics is easily regarded as a field that offers legitimation to whomever happens to be paying the philosopher's salary. However, a somewhat rarefied version of the same phenomenon is found in all normative branches of late twentieth-century anglophone philosophy. For example, when utilitarians and deontologists debate the merits of their respective ethical theories, they typically do so by accounting for case-based judgements that are already presumed to be moral. In other words, the arguments are about *why* a judgement is moral, not *whether* it is moral. Similarly, when realists and instrumentalists in the philosophy of science engage in debate, they want to decide why a theory choice (say, preferring Einstein to Newton in 1920) was the right one to make, not if it was the right one. The realist and instrumentalist are largely in agreement about which moments in the history of science succeed and fail in conforming to the norms of scientific rationality. The issue dividing them is what those norms are.

In light of the above, it would seem that the normative horizons of philosophers have been reduced from being *legislators* to being *evaluators*. In Fuller (2000b: chap. 6), I compared this downgraded status to being an accountant of someone else's books. Philosophers do not prescribe the norms governing moral life or scientific practice: they merely judge whether the norms are being followed in particular cases and offer alternative accounts of what make those norms distinctly 'normative' – as opposed to accidentally reinforced social regularities.

The book most responsible for promoting this diminished normative role for philosophy in the anglophone world is Thomas Kuhn's *The Structure of*

Scientific Revolutions (1970). Based on sales, translations and citations, it may turn out to be the most influential single work on the nature of science in the twentieth century. In any case, *Structure*'s impact has encouraged philosophers to embrace the role of *underlabourer*, a term that John Locke originally used to describe his relationship to Newton (Locke 1959, Callebaut 1993). Locke lacked the mathematical training needed to understand the details of Newton's *Principia Mathematica*. Nevertheless, he functioned as a 'detached' but able publicist for Newton's views, once personally instructed on the philosophical implications of the arcane calculations that constitute the core of Newtonian mechanics.

Despite their initial protests, philosophers have come to accept the underlabouring vision of philosophy as their own, as illustrated in the proliferation of philosophies of the special sciences, such as the 'philosophy of physics' or 'philosophy of biology', in which the philosopher may actually know more about physics or biology than philosophy. And the more philosophers immerse themselves in the details of a particular science, which increasingly includes an apprenticeship in a laboratory, the less likely they are to be critical of the science in question.

Philosophers who spend time in such scientific apprenticeships often think they are continuing the project of the logical positivists and their Popperian cousins. The positivists are credited with good intentions in wanting to model philosophical practices on scientific ones. But they are faulted for not mastering the details of particular sciences, with the partial exception of physics. Yet how, then, for all their technical deficiencies, did the positivists nevertheless managed to exert so much influence over scientific methodology and the public image of science? The answer is that perhaps the logical positivists were *not* trying to be underlabourers at all, but rather were using science to promote certain philosophical ends of larger societal import. Take the symbolic function of the natural sciences in the project of 'Enlightenment' promoted most consistently in our own time by Karl Popper. The idea here was *not* one of philosophers paving the way for a mounting body of esoteric knowledge; rather, it was of extending to all spheres of life the critical attitude that had motivated scientists to challenge traditional beliefs in the first place. As science comes to be materially committed to particular lines of inquiry, such that the costs of reversing them become prohibitive, this spirit of criticism is increasingly difficult to sustain.

Some have followed Paul Feyerabend (1979) in suggesting that scientific research programmes need to be cut down to a size that enables criticism to flourish (Fuller 2000a: chap. 2). Thus, when Feyerabend argued that Creationism should be taught alongside evolutionary theory in the US public schools, he was primarily offering an opinion, not on the probative value of Creationism per se but on the social contexts in which its probative value should be determined: namely, that it should rest with local educational authorities rather than the professional scientific community. This distinction between one's personal judgements and the framework within which they should be evaluated is subtle but crucial for understanding the politics of science implied by the underlabourer model. Feyerabend intervened in the Creationist controversy as someone who wanted to square the imperatives of science and democracy. This is a classically philosophical interest that requires sustained thinking about science, but without being beholden to particular scientific research programmes. Indeed, it may even involve supporting decision-making conditions that would issue in judgements counter to one's own personal preferences.

In contrast, the underlabourer's identification of philosophical and specialized scientific interests is by no means unprecedented in the history of philosophy. However, making such an identification typically requires forgetting that history. As Kuhn (1970) realized from his study of scientific textbooks, a field of inquiry gives the appearance of progress by making it seem that its current state is the inevitable outcome of its past. Alternative possible futures based on 'the path not taken' are airbrushed from the official history and left to historians, whose esoteric pursuits are autonomous from the everyday practice of the science in question. This is no less true in philosophy. Thus, we find no concern about the precedent for the underlabouring orientation of contemporary philosophy in early twentieth-century Neo-Kantianism, against which both logical positivism and existential phenomenology eventually revolted by the 1930s (Fuller 2000b: chap. 6).

Neo-Kantianism was the main adaptive response by academic philosophers in Germany to the discrediting of Hegel's normative synthesis (Collins, 1998: chap. 13). It was largely a defensive posture to protect the university from external interference, given the rather divisive ways in which Hegel's vision had been harnessed to political action by his younger followers in the 1840s – including Karl Marx, whose atheistic reading of Hegel's philosophy of history ensured he would never get a job in academia. Thus, the next three generations of academic philosophers reverted to underlabouring for the emerging special sciences that were beginning to occupy departments in an increasingly complex university system.

Like today's underlabourers, the philosophical tasks undertaken by the Neo-Kantians involved disentangling disciplinary foundations, streamlining their histories and adjudicating boundary disputes. Wilhelm Windelband, Wilhelm Dilthey, Heinrich Rickert and Ernst Cassirer are prominent names from this period. Their perspective is captured by the slogan: 'epistemology recapitulates bureaucracy'. Moreover, as is common today, Neo-Kantians jealously guarded their 'academic freedom' by allowing their knowledge claims to be filtered by 'peers' before being unleashed to policymakers and the larger public, for whom they claimed no responsibility. Even at the time, this appeal to specialization was seen as a strategy to distance controversial knowledge claims generated in the academic environment from similar ones routinely promoted by social movements, such as socialism, feminism and Aryanism. Considering the recent performance of philosophers and sociologists of science in the 'Science Wars', it would seem that nothing much has changed here (Proctor 1991: Part 2; cf. Fuller 2000b: chap. 7).

As I mentioned earlier, in connection with the rise of logical positivism, the defeat of a scientifically backed Germany in World War I generated an irrationalist backlash. It was crystallized in the popularity of Oswald Spengler's *The Decline of the West* (1918–22). The Neo-Kantians had no effective response to this backlash, since they had divided the forces of 'Reason' and 'Truth' into specialized 'reasons' and 'truths' that together failed to address Spengler's looming question: what precisely gives meaning and direction to the pursuit of knowledge? Despite their profound differences, the followers of logical positivism and existential phenomenology took this question seriously, leading them to trawl through the history of philosophy to find lost insights into the unity of inquiry, even if it made them appear 'reductive' and even 'reactionary' to academics who treated the current array of disciplines as normatively acceptable (Schnädelbach 1984: chaps 5–8).

Much can be learned from the failure of Neo-Kantianism to meet Spengler's challenge. Neo-Kantianism is itself dead, but its spirit lives on in the current spate of 'disunificationists' in the philosophy and sociology of science (Galison and Stump 1996). To be sure, some of the substance has changed. Instead of epistemology recapitulating academic bureaucracy, today ontology recapitulates laboratory technology. (For a more thorough contextualization and critique of this development, see Fuller 2007b: 60ff.) Nevertheless, the disunificationists follow the Neo-Kantians on the larger philosophical point that there is no perspective from which to judge the value of science other than the sciences themselves. The abdication of philosophy's prescriptive function has rarely been as complete and learned as it is today, but those with a long institutional memory can take comfort in the prospect that it too will eventually come to pass once the next cycle of radical thinkers find their voice.

3

The People of Intellectual Life
Intellectuals

Can Intellectuals Survive if the Academy Is a No-fool Zone?

One of the shrewdest short essays ever written on the social role of the intellectual is a meditation on some remarks of Otto von Bismarck's, under whose regime German universities became the envy of the world. Ralf Dahrendorf quotes Bismarck, who observed that if the sovereign 'in his idealism is not to become a public danger, he needs the critical sting with the help of which he is able to find his way when he is in danger of losing it' (Dahrendorf 1970: 54). It is easy to see in this insight the seeds of Max Weber's sense of the complementary world-views of the politician and the scientist. For his part, Dahrendorf specifically identifies the sovereign's critical foil with the *fool*, someone whose openness is tolerated because he exerts no power and performs purely at the pleasure of the sovereign. The fool can say things that the sovereign's rivals dare not utter because their remarks might be taken seriously, given the means at their disposal to do something about them. The fool's periodic unpleasantness is thus worth enduring in this diminished capacity because he can effectively warn the sovereign against the truly serious threat potentially posed by such rivals. In short, the fool strengthens the sovereign's ideological immune system.

Academics could be reasonably counted as fools in Bismarck's time because their salaries were paid exclusively by the state (or with state approval) and their 'academic freedom' was specifically tied to their job as academics and not part of some generalized legal right to free speech. The situation of academics, and the university more generally today, is not so clearly like that of the fool. On the one hand, this seems to be for the good, reflecting academia's increasing financial independence from the state and, in some cases, the acquisition of functions previously performed by the state. By this enhanced power and relevance has not necessarily translated into enhanced autonomy. Precisely because the university has become so much more integral to the reproduction of the social order, it has arguably lost its freedom to speak and act in its own name – the luxury afforded to the powerless yet protected fool. For this reason, those who value intellectual autonomy above all other academic virtues are nowadays tempted to migrate from the campus to the riskier environments afforded by the mass media and even the business world.

To the naïve observer, intellectuals and academics look very much alike. Both talk a lot, gesture wildly and wear bad clothes. The big difference, however, is that intellectuals actually care about ideas and know how to deal with them effectively. Ideas can be conveyed in many media to many audiences in whatever time and space is allowed. If you can't convey things in this fashion, then either you're not much of an intellectual or what you're trying to convey isn't much of an idea. Instead you may be a flack flogging a policy, an entrepreneur marketing a product or an academic advancing your career.

Of course, some academics are intellectuals. They are the ones who are not panic stricken when told their presentation time has been halved or, better still, when they forget to bring a prepared text or Powerpoint. They have no trouble making an impact because they can always go beyond the words they've written. If they know nothing else, which is always a possibility, intellectuals know their own minds. When they speak, they don't sound like they're miming, an impression one often gets from what passes as academic 'talks' today. Ask even a distinguished professor something related to but slightly off his official topic and you might as well have flashed your headlights at an innocent deer.

How to explain this peculiar state-of-affairs? Perhaps the cult of research productivity prevents academics from devoting the time needed to fully grasp all the ideas their work contains. In that sense, they know less than they say. This then leaves lots of room for intellectuals to borrow and steal, use and abuse, their ideas for their own more broadly gauged purposes. When academics complain about journalists and politicians mishandling their ideas, they should ask themselves why they hadn't gone public sooner: Grant application deadlines? Too many essays to mark? Too many meetings to attend? An intellectual needs to get her priorities straight. I shall return to this point in Chapter 4 as speaking to 'the improvisational nature of intellectual life'.

Interestingly the only academics who have made a concerted effort to act like intellectuals are natural scientists. In many countries, there is an institutionalized 'public understanding of science' movement but no comparable 'public understanding of the humanities' or 'public understanding of the social sciences'. Little surprise, then, that Richard 'Selfish Gene' Dawkins topped *Prospect* magazine's 2004 poll of Britain's leading intellectuals and was placed third in the world as a whole in a 2005 survey that *Prospect* conducted with the US journal *Foreign Policy*. While this generated consternation in that bastion of US conservative high culture, *The New Criterion* (Johnson 2005), the result should not be surprising. Only science popularizations like *A Brief History of Time* (Hawking 1988), *The Selfish Gene* (Dawkins 1976), *The Mismeasure of Man* (Gould 1981) and *The Blank Slate* (Pinker 2002) – four transatlantic best sellers that epitomize the genre's heterogeneity – can compete in sales with pop psychology, New Age mysticism and the latest wheeze from the management gurus.

Among the branches of higher learning, the natural sciences are the least wedded to a specific expressive medium. Journal articles and popular books are typically afterthoughts to knowledge initially embodied in field observations, laboratory experiments and, increasingly, computer simulations. Not surprisingly, then, natural scientists are comfortable delivering papers without reading them, chunking their theses into media soundbites, and otherwise adapting to the Powerpoint generation. Moreover, the research costs of the natural sciences exceed those of the other disciplines, and so scientists have become accustomed to sing for their supper. Of course, I generalize, and what I generalize about has not come without some tears. Nevertheless, natural scientists do not display the 'principled hesitation' about multimedia translation one so often finds among humanists and social scientists. When people complain about 'jargon' in the latter fields, this is usually what they mean – and it is often accompanied by relatively uncommunicative text-bound behaviour. We academics outside the natural sciences must ask a hard question at this point: do we hesitate because we truly fear that our knowledge claims might be distorted or merely that their implications might be made sufficiently clear to render us accountable to more people than we would like?

Of course, academics themselves should be capable of performing the requisite translations to extend access to their linguistic and technical cartels. This is what pedagogy and curriculum design are supposed to accomplish. However, we inhabit an academic culture that disproportionately values what is uncritically called 'research' over teaching, so that the latter needs to be informed by the former but not vice versa. This is bound to discourage any general 'intellectualization' of society that does not at the same time stratify people into the 'knows' and the 'know nots'. I place 'research' in scare quotes to recall that the tendency to subject the production of novel findings and counter-intuitive insights to the discipline of 'peer review' invariably contains their subversive potential. I don't mean to condemn this tendency out of hand. But what is gained in the insurance policy effectively underwritten by a peer-reviewed journal must be weighed against the exaggerated authority that publication under such a regime tends to command both inside and outside the peer community.

Dawkins's best efforts notwithstanding, one taken-for-granted feature of contemporary academic life routinely undermines our ability to be proper intellectuals. It is a fundamental assumption of the periodic evaluations of individual research outputs known as the 'Research Assessment Exercise (RAE)' that the UK has pioneered and exported throughout the world – namely, that we are in the business of 'knowledge production'. Intellectuals may destroy dogmas but they most certainly do not produce knowledge. The latter implies the alienation of ideas from the thinker to such 'outputs' as publications and patents, the value of which is determined in a market consisting of either other similarly alienated knowledge producers or, increasingly, a class of grateful parasites euphemistically called 'users and beneficiaries'. An apt target of intellectual loathing, then, is the practice of profligate citation that currently blights academic writing and is increasingly favoured as an indicator of 'impact' in the RAE. The basic idea is that the more often your work is cited, the more important it is taken to be (Fuller 1997: chap. 4; Fuller 2000a: chap. 5). To the intellectual, the problem with this practice is not what it says about the relatively few who receive the lion's share of citations – but the many more who prop up these market leaders by citing them so much. It fosters a dependency culture whereby academics are rewarded for feats of ventriloquism, that is, an ability to speak through the authority of others. The result is institutionalized cowardice.

In contrast to all this, intellectuals demand to take personal responsibility for their ideas and enjoy nothing more than to have them contested by others equally willing to expose themselves in public. The great intellectuals from Socrates and Jesus to Galileo, Voltaire, Zola and Russell all stood trial, and most of the rest courted lawsuits. When intellectuals mention people's names in print, it is to praise or attack them, not to be excused for transiting through a bit of intellectual property bearing their name. The latter situation conjures up words like 'toll', 'rent' and even 'protection money' – especially if one thinks about the need for academic writing to undergo a 'peer review' process before publication. In that case, 'argument by name-check' simply becomes a prudent strategy for surviving in an academic culture that values indebtedness over solvency in the life of the mind.

At this point, a scandalized academic will observe that all this name-checking really does serve a proper intellectual function. It helps to orient the reader around a complex field. Unfortunately the number of citations in an academic article is usually surplus to requirements. The curious reader with a limited tolerance for false leads is better served by consulting a good web-based search engine for what she does not understand than dutifully following up an article's list of references. Of course, the list may provide a reliable guide to whose opinion the author thinks she needs to take seriously.

Being an intellectual is about thinking for yourself, not second-guessing who might pass judgement on you. Academics suffer the consequences of failing to tell the difference. Professional training in academic life involves learning where the research frontier lies and how to push it forward – not how to challenge the field inside the frontier. Consequently most academics carry on producing more sophisticated versions of the kind of research they were taught. Solutions to problems of significant intellectual and social import can be easily ignored simply because they do not conform to what academics have been trained and rewarded to see. A library scientist at the University of Chicago, Don Swanson (1986), coined the phrase 'undiscovered public knowledge' to capture this phenomenon. Swanson himself had hit upon the cure for a puzzling medical condition not by obtaining a large grant that required prior peer approval but simply by combining insights he had gathered from reading across academic specialities.

Management gurus like to speak of Swanson's discovery as 'lateral thinking' or 'thinking outside the box'. It was certainly thinking outside the academic box. He supposed it might be more worthwhile to read old research in several fields than conduct new research that promised a breakthrough in a single field. Re-examining what the thundering herd has left behind is a time-honoured strategy for cultivating the independent-mindedness that marks a true intellectual. Too bad there are no academic grants for it. Nevertheless if there is a recipe, it may go something like this:

1 Read lots of books that cut across existing categories of thought.
2 Do not take any of these books as the final word on anything but instead take them all as offering nuggets of insight. After all, you do not want to be reduced to someone else but you do not want to be disrespectful either.
3 Combine the insights so derived in ways that are strange yet also traceable at least by some future historian.
4 Background condition: to ensure that future historians find you, make certain that you are sufficiently prominent so that you are at least seen as an 'also ran' in the intellectual brilliance sweepstakes.
5 In the venerable tradition of 'he who cannot do teaches', Friedrich Nietzsche is a 'virtual model' of the fearless academic intellectual. Unfortunately the real Nietzsche lost his nerve early on in his career after a devastating review of his first book. The trick is to be a Nietzsche with staying power who lives up to his own motto, 'What does not kill me makes me stronger'. (That Nietzsche is venerated rather than derided reveals a normally hidden empathic capacity in academics.)
6 Taking the Nietzschean turn means, among other things, taking tenure seriously as a basis for what might be called *intellectual venture capitalism* – that is, the risking of some of your reputation and institutional security on ideas whose pursuit would easily bankrupt more poorly placed souls.

Intellectuals differ from ordinary academics in holding that the truth is best approached not by producing new knowledge, but by destroying old beliefs. When the Enlightenment philosophers renovated the old Christian slogan 'The truth shall set you free', they imagined a process of opening doors, not building barricades. In short, intellectuals want their audiences to think for themselves, not simply shift allegiances from one expert to another. The intellectual's ethic is both exhilarating and harsh, for it places the responsibility for thinking squarely on the thinker's shoulders. Every act of deference thus becomes an abdication of one's own intellectual authority. Only intellectuals see the full implications of the familiar slogan, 'Knowledge is power'. Obviously, greater knowledge enhances our capacity to act. What is much less obvious is that such empowerment requires the destruction of socially sanctioned knowledge. Only then is a society's space for decision opened up, enabling its members to move in many more directions than previously deemed possible.

This implies a studied sort of unconventionality that characterizes the great intellectuals down through the ages. Consider Peter Abelard in the twelfth century, Desiderius Erasmus in the sixteenth century, Galileo

Galilei in the seventeenth century, Voltaire in the eighteenth century, Emile Zola in the nineteenth century and Bertrand Russell in the twentieth century – each challenged the pieties of his era, and we now regard their success as a good thing. But most of us are likely to recoil at the methods they used in their work as intellectuals: caricature, deception and even fabrication. Consider each in turn:

1 Abelard is credited with the introduction of theology as a critical discipline in Christianity. Yet, he did so by juxtaposing contradictory quotes taken out of context, and showing that neither the Bible nor the Church fathers spoke in one voice and that readers had to decide for themselves.
2 Erasmus claimed that the 'true faith' had nothing to fear from a knowledge of Christianity's past, though in practice a critical-historical reading of the Bible invalidated the metaphysical claims that divided Catholics and Protestants. Perhaps not surprisingly, Erasmus came to be fully rehabilitated only once 'humanism' was taken to be, contrary to his own intentions, a fully secular position.
3 Galileo is now known to have committed what we now call 'research fraud' in his famed physical experiments. Assuming he conducted the experiments at all, they probably did not produce the neat results that he used to assail his opponents. Yet, the consequent appearance of persecution bought time for sympathizers to follow up Galileo's leads.
4 Voltaire resorted to hyperbole and ridicule to destabilize clerical opponents, whose own rhetorical strength lay in the solemn moderation of their self-expression (Goldgar 1995). It helped that Voltaire's middle-class audience already had doubts about the secular advice that clerics were giving to the monarchy about how to manage domestic and foreign affairs.
5 Zola famously declared '*J'Accuse!*' in defence of Captain Alfred Dreyfus from charges of treason fuelled by anti-Semitism yet was easily convicted of libel because he merely questioned the motives of witnesses without offering any new evidence.
6 Russell pioneered the role of the elite academic radical nowadays exemplified by Noam Chomsky, especially when it comes to pronouncing well beyond his formal training. However, Russell lacked the institutional security of today's 'tenured radicals' (Kimball 1990), and so found himself committing acts of 'civil disobedience' in defence of, say, sexual freedom and nuclear disarmament.

All were subsequently vindicated – sometimes in their lifetimes, sometimes not. What they shared is a paradoxical ethic common to all intellectuals: *the end cause of truth justifies whatever means happen to be at your disposal.* This is because the whole truth is rarely what passes for the truth at any moment. Such an ethic is abhorrent in today's world, where knowledge is parceled out to academic disciplines like bits of real estate. To academics, intellectuals look like ramblers freely trespassing on other people's property, picking the fruits and despoiling the soil. But to an intellectual, an academic often looks like someone who mistakes the means of inquiry for its end.

Five years ago, I wrote a book defending the intellectual in this broadest, most anti-academic and least fashionable sense, what under the influence of Michel Foucault continues to be derided as the 'universal intellectual'. This book, *The Intellectual* (Fuller 2005), was intended as an analogue of Machiavelli's *The Prince*. I assumed that the performance of the role of intellectual is such a hit-and-miss affair, especially among academics, that a manual offering some guidance in this matter would not be amiss. However, Machiavelli also inspired me to keep my eye on the ball. Machiavelli's 'ball' was statecraft. A prince may genuflect to all the relevant pieties, but if he cannot manage his own court or pre-empt the causes of civil unrest, then he doesn't deserve to rule: end of story. My 'ball' might be called *idea-craft*. Intellectuals are mainly in the business of promoting ideas. This means, among other things, that they must assume the existence of ideas. As we shall see in the next section, this is a tall order in postmodern academia, which tends to regard ideas as annoying remnants of the dreaded 'metaphysics of (spiritual) presence'. Without denying the centrality of academics to the certification, elaboration and reproduction of the disciplinary discourses and techniques that carry the authority of 'knowledge' in the wider society, this by itself is merely 'knowledge work', to recall management guru Peter Drucker's brutal but accurate expression. Without the additional ontological commitment to ideas, such knowledge work as academics normally perform is not intellectual activity, notwithstanding the wishful thinking promoted by Alvin Gouldner's (1979) 'culture of critical discourse'.

I insist on a sharp distinction between academics and intellectuals for much the same reason that Machiavelli wanted to make the grounds of political legitimacy forward- rather than backward-looking. In Machiavelli's terms, the prince is never justified by the power on which he draws – be it noble ancestors or papal blessing – but only by the power he makes available to his constituency, which may be as basic as living in peace and prosperity with one's fellows. (This was the point on which Hobbes subsequently insisted.) There is also a more robust interpretation of this task that charts the scary course from Machiavelli to Mussolini, namely, that the ruler must enable the ruled to see their own intentions realized in his actions. Whatever else one wishes to say about this as a vision of politics, it assumes that the exercise of power is a creative process that compels the ruler to continually translate the hopes and fears of his people into a whole greater than the sum of the parts. To be sure, it can result in a contempt for the rule of law – as in the case of Carl Schmitt, the Weimar jurist who did the most to legitimate the Nazi regime. However, even if Machiavelli cannot be said to offer an adequate normative theory of politics, he may nevertheless provide *malgré lui* the elements for a normative theory of that pre-, proto-, meta-, crypto- (if not pseudo-) form of political existence we call intellectual life.

In that case, academics who trade on their discipline-based authority are like the backward-looking rulers derided by Machiavelli. They try to compel obedience by reminding the audience of the distance they stand above them by virtue of their distinctive lineage, which for academics pertains to their degrees rather than, say, their heredity. Public-choice economists bring together the two sides of this analogy in the concept of 'rent-seeking behaviour', whereby exclusive possession of a factor of production, such as land, is a source of value regardless of its actual productivity. Without wishing to contribute to the cynicism that often accompanies such appeals to economics, there is no denying that often there is not much more to the 'ideas' of academics and other knowledge workers than the restricted access their discourses provide to spheres of action that, assuming their larger relevance, could be accessed by other means – if not in simpler words, then in some form of non-verbal imagery. In this respect, a testimony to the intellectualist aspirations of the logical positivists is that, in their incarnation as the 'Red' Vienna Circle of the 1920s and 1930s, they tried to design a universally applicable iconic language of thought – what Otto Neurath dubbed 'ISOTYPE' – for representing complex socio-economic data on public newsboards to inform political debate.

Some general conditions are necessary for a world fit for the existence of ideas and intellectuals:

1 Ideas must be capable of multiple forms of realization, i.e. they are eligible for multimedia transmission. Anything worth saying can always be said in other words and maybe even by other media.
2 Ideas must open up a sphere of potential action that would be otherwise absent, i.e. they must expand the collective imagination in certain directions (even if that means contracting it in others).
3 The material conditions must exist for realizing a 'collective mind', nowadays de-ontologized and democratized as the 'public sphere', into which one can reasonably speak of ideas as being introduced, contested and variably influential.
4 Ideas are *shared* in the strict sense, i.e. an idea does not spring full-blown from an original genius who then imprints it on the masses; rather an idea comes to be realized gradually as more people participate in its production.

Historically speaking, the realization of these conditions has required two transitions. On the one hand, the origin of ideas had to be pulled out of the Platonic heaven and relocated in human psychology. On the other, human psychology had to be seen, not as irreducibly private, but as beholden to common intellectual property. France became the spiritual home of intellectuals with the establishment of the Third Republic in 1870 because both conditions were very self-consciously put in place. The educational system was explicitly secularized, and prior affective attachments to the Church were transferred to the 'Republic' as the common heritage (i.e. *res publica*) of French citizens, in which they were invited, if not obliged, to participate through a free press. This heritage is symbolized in the Panthéon, a cruciform neo-classical structure resembling the US Capitol located near the Sorbonne. It contains the remains of the great French citizens, many of whom are reasonably classed as intellectuals. Although these figures typically operated with a universalist normative orientation, it was always articulated in relation to the nation's pressing concerns. Consequently, a genealogy of French intellectuals – and the same could be said of intellectuals from other nations – would not form a neat self-contained network of teachers and students (as, say, Collins 1998 does for the history of philosophy), but a more centrifugal system of dissenters vis-à-vis core political tendencies in the nation's history. This alone continues to undermine any attempt to write a coherent narrative about the place of the intellectual in modern society.

How Intellectuals Became an Endangered Species in Our Times: The Trail of Psychologism

In this section, I survey the problems facing the existence of intellectuals in the twenty-first century by reflecting on the historical and conceptual conditions that have enabled them to flourish in the past but less so in recent times. First I consider several strands of contemporary philosophical and social thought that, despite their progressive veneer, have served to undermine the legitimacy of the intellectual's role. This delegitimation is largely traceable to a scepticism about the existence of ideas that are simultaneously normative and manipulable. Next I deal with the rise of anti-intellectualism in philosophy and psychology in the twentieth century, focussing especially on the debates surrounding 'psychologism'. In the section after this one I will examine what remains of the most attractive expression of anti-intellectualism, namely, invisible thinking and its late nineteenth-century transformation through the influence of statistics, evolution and epidemiology. In the conclusion, I provide one strategy for stemming the current tide of anti-intellectualism by a reinterpretation of the currently popular concept of 'heuristics'.

It will not be easy to justify the existence of intellectuals in the twenty-first century. Ideas do not seem to exist in just the right way for intellectuals to be possible. Consider some general attitudes toward ideas that are prevalent in contemporary philosophy. Most generally, there is what may be called the 'Platonic residue' of ideas. Accordingly, ideas are not the same as beliefs; rather, they enjoy a second-order status as the framework within which beliefs are forged. This ideational framework is often called a 'conceptual scheme'. Nowadays it tends to function as a necessarily taken-for-granted (a.k.a. 'transcendental') condition for our beliefs, and hence is not easily open to manipulation. To be sure, the original pragmatists and logical positivists (including the Popperians) treated a conceptual scheme as a pure convention whose fate was to be decided by its consequences for whatever matters to those bound by the convention. However, more recent discussions of conceptual schemes – influenced by thinkers as varied as Martin Heidegger, Thomas Kuhn, Michel Foucault and Donald Davidson – have stressed our captivity to the decisions taken by our predecessors (often glossed as 'contingencies'), such that our conceptual scheme appears an inheritance that is no less durable simply because its medium of transmission is cultural rather than strictly biological. In that case, ideas are not things we use, but things that use us. Although there is more to being an intellectual than simply being able to use ideas, the manipulability of ideas is an essential ingredient of intellectual life. In that respect, the 'historicized Platonism' that is currently fashionable in both analytic and continental philosophy (e.g. Hacking 2002) undermines the legitimacy of the intellectual.

Two other current philosophical attitudes that make intellectual life difficult are normally seen within philosophy as 'progressive' and even 'radical'. The first is the tendency to reduce ideas to their linguistic or, more generally, behavioural expression. Gilbert Ryle (1949) famously spoke of concepts as 'inference-tickets', which is to say, a set of conditions that licence a range of responses. This view remains influential among philosophical antirealists and discourse analysts in the social sciences. It has had the admirable aim of rendering publicly accountable a class of entity – ideas – that would otherwise be shrouded in mystery, either in people's heads or Plato's heaven. But how then does one capture the classic intellectual's task of speaking truth to power, which often requires 'saying the unsayable', if ideas do not exist beyond the sentences expressing them? Especially after Theodor Adorno and Jacques Derrida, this problem is often tackled by stressing the strategic significance of 'difficult writing', which capitalizes on indirect modes of expression like irony and paradox that partially subvert, or at least confront, the standing communicative conventions. However, as even proponents of this strategy concede, it consigns the critical intellectual to the margins of discourse, a voice in the wilderness in search of an audience capable of making sense of what is, strictly speaking, meaningless.

The second philosophical attitude is evidenced in the popularity of Bruno Latour's concept of 'technoscience' as the proper object of science and technology studies (Latour 1987). Technoscience is the culmination of a set of tendencies traceable to Heidegger, Wittgenstein and Gaston Bachelard that, broadly speaking, embed normative ideals into the architecture of the life-world. In effect, technoscience introduces a measure of both relativism and materialism into the historicized Platonism raised at the start of this discussion. To be sure, unlike the seemingly fixed and totalizing character of a conceptual scheme, technoscience is subject to considerable construction, reconstruction and deconstruction – as artifacts and agents (or 'actants') make their way in and out of a networked ecology. However, all of this activity is described relative to the actor–network ecology; hence, Latour's methodological maxim, 'Always follow the actors!' There is no legitimate standpoint from which, say, a philosopher might defend an ideal of science that is not already being realized by actual scientists. Indeed, on closer inspection, a philosopher's normative ideal of science turns out to be an obsolete, oversimplified, or simply misinformed account of scientific practice – which unfortunately sometimes infects scientists' self-understanding. Accordingly, intellectuals share the most objectionable features of philosophers who pontificate on practices in which they do not participate. In that case, students of technoscience constitute a phalanx of 'counter-intellectuals', if not anti-intellectuals, whose job is to undermine the legitimacy of those who think they can teach about what they do not do themselves. Not surprisingly, Latour (1997) himself has targeted 'critique' as a gratuitous activity in much the same way as followers of Wittgenstein two generations earlier had urged applying 'language therapy' to the philosophical impulse to 'theorize'.

It would seem, then, that the existence of intellectuals requires not only that certain social conditions be in place but certain conceptual conditions as well. Ideas need to exist in a particular way. For example, Plato's Ideas exist in an independent realm from which they affect us without yielding to our designs. Such ideas behave like de-personalized gods. Not surprisingly, then, Plato's bugbears, the Sophists, who resemble modern intellectuals in many respects, did not think of themselves as dealing in ideas. They claimed to be purveyors in instruments for achieving specific ends. Plato demonized those instruments as 'rhetoric'. Although intellectuals typically display considerable rhetorical skill, the moral high ground to which they aspire cannot be attained without a credible claim to espousing ideas they believe to be correct.

The bridge between Plato's detached ideas and the intellectual's manipulable ones was made possible with early Christianity's attribution of a distinctive character of the human soul, known as *the will*. The will was designed to capture the human capacity to resist the inertial tendencies of the soul's material embodiment. Subsequently, philosophers often identified rationality with the exertion of maximum resistance. However, as the Christian God receded from the public arena, it became increasingly difficult to justify so much resistance. Kant's solution – the self-legislating will of the categorical imperative – has been the most influential in academic philosophy. It makes morality an intensely private struggle. An alternative, more publicly oriented solution was proposed in Kant's own day. It has been dominant outside of academic circles and, indeed, provides an adequate metaphysical basis for the work of intellectuals. I refer here to the conversion of ideas to *ideology* by Marie-François-Pierre Maine de Biran (1766–1824).

For Maine de Biran, an aristocrat whose life spanned the *Ancien Régime*, the French Revolution, Napoleon and the Bourbon Restoration, ideologies are produced by psychologizing philosophical ideas to make them easier to appropriate for political purposes. So far this sounds like the Sophist's trade, and it may even capture the client-driven market for ideas that propel the proposals that flow from 'think tanks' today. However, the predominance of the will in Maine de Biran's moral psychology makes all the difference in converting someone with a knack for selling ideas into a proper intellectual. The will enables Plato's ideas to be 'personalized', so that ideas do not simply inhabit a level of reality distinct from material things; rather, they struggle to assert themselves against a recalcitrant materiality – that is, in the bodies of particular ideologues. The job of the intellectual then is to enact this personal struggle in public.

Hegel's younger followers, especially Karl Marx, realized that Maine de Biran had not only secularized the Christian struggle of good against evil but had also relativized it so much as to invite perpetual conflict among competing ideologies. To recall the great Manichaean dualism to come out of the French Revolution, material resistance to realizing 'leftist' ideas may constitute the very conditions for realizing 'rightist' ideas – and vice versa. Take the existence of social inequality: for the one, a disruptive social problem; for the other, the basis of social order. In that respect, the Comtean, Hegelian and Marxist projects may be seen as having advanced a universalist version of the ideational dynamism that Maine de Biran's personalized Platonism had introduced. For them, intellectual conflict is contained, subsumed and focussed – in Hegel's word, 'sublated' – as dialectical progress. However, this process transpires in no ordinary ideologue but a member of the political or scientific (or preferably both) vanguard whose socio-cognitive horizons are somewhat wider and clearer than those of a the normal member of society.

Moreover, this vanguard do not simply live exemplary lives that are admired from afar and to which lesser mortals aspire in a future incarnation. Rather, the vanguard assume responsibility for raising those mortals to their own lofty heights – if possible, in the same lifetime. This quintessentially modernist sensibility presupposes that ideas possess sufficient power to overturn generations of presumption, prejudice and habit. But why might someone invest so much power in ideas? Perhaps because she had already caught a glimpse of a realized ideal shortly before, say, political corruption or economic collapse forced reality to retreat from the ideal. In short, what social movement theorists call 'relative deprivation' may help to explain that peculiar amalgam of the diagnostic and the utopian that characterizes the mentality of intellectuals in full bloom.

The default tendency in the history of philosophy and the social sciences has been to conceptualize the social order as a kind of ideational order – if not necessarily vice versa. This tendency unites thinkers as otherwise different as Plato and Durkheim, Comte and Hegel, Adorno and Popper. My own social epistemology also assumes this starting point (Fuller 1988). The Young Hegelians, notably Ludwig Feuerbach and Karl Marx, tried – with mixed success – to interrogate the closeness of fit between the social and the ideational. They correctly sensed that it has been historically underwritten by a conception of ultimate reality as a community of souls, one traceable to Stoicism's original efforts to personalize Platonism and culminating in the millenarian Christian ideal of 'heaven on earth' (Toews 1985). Moreover, thanks to Maine de Biran, ideas turn out to be more than pure forms that subsist independently in Plato's heaven. They are also relational principles that extend beyond their specific embodiments to be enriched by other ideas. Indeed, ideas would seem to be inherently fugitive, always trying to escape their socially sanctioned representations.

The most distinctive forms of human relations involve an engagement of ideas. These have presupposed some kind of 'meeting of minds', though the exact forum for this meeting has ranged from interpretation, often at a considerable spatio-temporal distance, to face-to-face encounters, in which the impact of the meeting may be immediately felt on the body. In most general terms, the meeting of minds includes acts of identification, association, adaptation, differentiation and confrontation. Ian Hacking (1975: chaps 2–5) originally spoke of 'the way of ideas'. Actually, there are two ways, or alternative *intellectual epidemiologies*. They correspond to some familiar distinctions but are now seen in a rather different light. According to the first epidemiology, good ideas spread naturally, while bad ideas spread only through forced application. According to the second version, bad ideas spread naturally, while good ideas require sustained resistance. (Compare Fuller 1993: 59–66, which distinguishes between rationality as 'released' and 'imposed', respectively.) I wish to call the first *anti-intellectualist* and the latter *intellectualist*, fully aware of the polemical import of these labels. For the former, intellectuals are, at best, a nuisance and, at worst, the source of value-destruction. For the latter, intellectuals are necessary correctives, even moral heroes, in a world where people accept their plight all too willingly.

Philosophers of science are already familiar with the most abstract version of this distinction in intellectual epidemiologies. *Inductivism* and *deductivism* correspond to anti-intellectualism and intellectualism, respectively. Inductivists hold that ideas normally track experience without reaching beyond it. They follow the path of least empirical resistance. In Latour's personification, the analyst always follows the agents around, which is to say, she never gets ahead of them with her own conception of what they might be up to. (Methodologically, this is often called 'grounded theory', the inductivist roots of which are explicitly discussed in Glaser and Strauss 1967.) Experience transcended at best means experience unrecognized. Thus, Kant's transcendental philosophy is symptomatic of someone living in a regime where experience is routinely discounted and hence needs to be reasserted, say, by generating a level of reality metaphysically superior to the official one. For inductivists, this situation is understandable, albeit regrettable, given the circumstances. In contrast, deductivists believe that Kant's situation is more the rule than the exception – namely, that our experience is normally so unreliable as a guide to action that an alternative standard of conduct must be established that can serve as either a hypothesis to be measured up against experience (i.e. scientific experimentation) or a norm against which to measure experience (i.e. political criticism). Whereas the inductivist trusts default epistemic and social institutions like common sense and family lore, the deductivist designs counter-intuitive checks and correctives to these biased orders, such as academic disciplines and written constitutions. For the inductivist, the ethical inquirer is an honest reporter of the facts; whereas for the deductivist she is a publicly accountable decision-maker.

Perhaps the most lasting modern impression of the conflict between our two intellectual epidemiologies was made in the debates over 'psychologism' among German-speaking philosophers from 1866 to 1930 (Kusch 1995). Psychologism was invoked pejoratively, if not always consistently, by philosophers against their own colleagues and empirical psychologists who adopted an anti-intellectualist approach to ideas. In the more recent euphemism of cognitive psychologists, those suffering from psychologism were diligent subscribers to the 'availability heuristic' (Tversky and Kahneman 1974). The availability heuristic is the mental tendency to take the immediacy or vividness of a thought as indicative of its representativeness of reality. In a sense, the heuristic merely restates the fundamental premise of classical empiricism and associationism. It presupposes that an idea would not stick in one's mind, especially as a response to a specific stimulus or problem, unless it was grounded in the reality of the situation. The supposed general reliability of the heuristic inspired the early experimental psychologists to develop the method of trained introspection. Later psychologists, following Egon Brunswik, a deductivist among inductivists, hypothesized that we are 'intuitive statisticians' who refine our thoughts by acquiring better samples of the environment.

Among recent philosophers of science who have followed developments in experimental psychology, Thomas Kuhn stood with and Karl Popper against those wedded to 'psychologism'. Popper, whose doctorate was in educational psychology, believed that a philosopher was an anti-psychologistic psychologist (Berkson and Wettersten 1984). More exactly, a philosopher conceptualizes the human mind as consisting of at least two independent and potentially countervailing tendencies: one that relies on the availability heuristic and another that overrides the heuristic in various ways – e.g. by discounting or avoiding first impressions, by distinguishing one's own viewpoint from what one perceives to be prevalent or expected (even given one's own experience), and more generally by hesitating before responding to a stimulus.

Popper's mentor, Karl Bühler, had been trained by Oswald Külpe, whose Würzburg School deliberately broke from mainstream introspective psychology by claiming to have demonstrated just such a second tier of 'imageless thought' responsible for 'judgement', a mental function that cannot be reduced to induction from past experience (Kusch 1999: Part I). This tendency provided the subject with what Bühler (1930) called 'degrees of freedom' in theorizing an inherently underdetermined world. To be sure, external media for the expression of thought – language most generally but writing especially – have historically helped to stabilize the contexts in which certain stimuli have elicited certain responses. But these are ultimately social conventions whose cognitive focus is purchased by limiting the subject's degrees of freedom. Thus, for Bühler's student Popper, the acquisition of a scientific discipline amounts to an act of self-restraint that always involves lost opportunities that may create blind spots that are only much later revealed through the confounding of an expectation. In contrast, for Kuhn, the very same act of self-restraint does not carry the same sense of regret and so unsurprisingly anomalies are deferred until the last possible moment and then quickly resolved with an eye towards erasing their occurrence from the discipline's collective memory.

Popper would have the scientist brood over alternative theories and encourage changes in perspective in light of experience. Kuhn, in contrast, would have the scientists maximize their problem-solving effectiveness, in accordance with the dominant paradigm. One might say that, in terms of a classic 'gestalt switch' experiment, Popper adopted the standpoint of the *experimenter* who can alter the stimulus conditions to facilitate one or another response, whereas Kuhn adopted that of the *subject* who is presented with the stimulus already framed toward eliciting a particular response (Fuller 2000b: 273, fn. 25). This distinction in standpoint recalls my remarks at the start of this section about the decidedly anti-intellectualist cast of post-Kuhnian discussions of conceptual schemes. It is probably more fundamental for understanding the history of scientific psychology than, say, the difference between the use of 'introspective' and 'extraspective' methods to study the human mind. It reflects what may be the most fundamental distinction for understanding the history of psychology – more fundamental than divide separating 'introspective' and 'extrapsective' methods: whether *deliberation* (and its behavioural correlate, hesitancy) or *automation* (and its behavioural correlate, efficiency) is taken to be the paradigm of thought, in terms of which the other is regarded as defective and hence in need of remediation. The historical ascendancy of automation over deliberation as the paradigm of thought has been a triumph for anti-intellectualism.

But exactly how did response times come to be the basis for judgements of ignorance or intelligence? Among the animal psychologists who are often regarded as proto-behaviourists – perhaps most notably T.H. Huxley's student C. Lloyd Morgan – there was concern that turning automaticity into an unqualified virtue would obscure the distinctive virtues of deliberative thought (a.k.a. 'rationality') that rendered *homo* fully *sapiens*. Nevertheless, this did not prevent the development and mass administration of timed intelligence tests, for which students predictably would be trained to complete as quickly and accurately as possible. Moreover, it is often overlooked that a parallel version of the same issue plagued the more 'mentalistic' side of psychology. Specifically, the Würzburg School criticized the Gestalt psychologists for reducing cognition to 'problem-solving' in the simple sense of arriving at an appropriate means for achieving pre-existent ends. The subject would not select the problem herself. Instead the Gestaltists focused on whether the subject already had what, after Kuhn, would be called a 'paradigm' for solving the problem. The main Gestaltist targeted in this criticism, Otto Selz, explicitly modelled the process of 'completing the Gestalt' on solving the value of a variable in a mathematical equation (Berkson and Wettersten 1984: chaps 1, 5). This move turned out to be quite influential in analytic philosophy, via Rudolf Carnap and W.V.O. Quine, and especially enabled Herbert Simon in the 1950s to construct his distinctive approach to the 'logic of scientific discovery'. However, it removed the subject from any responsibility for the second-order task of setting the problem. That remained squarely in the experimenter's hands, a product of the division of labour between subject and experimenter about which Würzburgers, as autopsychologists, always had misgivings. To what extent, then, could the experimental subject be considered a fully fledged intellectual agent, as opposed to a mere recipient and transmitter of ideas?

The Würzburgers were not alone in their concern for experimental psychology to encourage subjects to express their distinctly human natures, and not simply elicit default animal responses. Although not normally regarded as a defender of intellectualism, William James's advocacy of 'the will to believe' in the face of ambiguous or contrary evidence should be understood in this light.

In James's day, 'intellectualism' referred to *a priori* rationalism, an epistemology typically associated with Descartes but sometimes also Kant and Hegel, committed to the doctrine of innate ideas. For a pragmatist like James the main offence of intellectualism was its dogmatism in the face of experience. Nevertheless, the pragmatists, like the logical positivists and the Popperians in the twentieth century, retained a key feature of this dogmatism, namely, a principled resistance to default patterns of experience. However, the source of this resistance differed radically between James and the demonized 'intellectualists': for James it lay in a personal decision ('the will to believe' or 'by convention', as the Viennese preferred) rather than the mind's pre-programming. This difference clearly has profound consequences for assigning the fault for mismatches between the mind and reality: James (and the positivists and the Popperians) assigns it to the decision-maker who is then burdened with arriving at a more effective means to achieve her ends, as opposed to simply saying that the facts are a corrupt version of the truth that can be idealized away. At the risk of paradox, James's self-declared anti-intellectualism thus upheld an intellectualist approach to ideas.

A background consideration that weighed on James's mind was that some philosophers – following the lead of mathematician W.K. Clifford's 'ethics of belief' – had begun to argue, on evolutionary grounds, that people should not assert more than what was compelled by the evidence, lest they might not survive (Passmore 1966: chaps 5, 14). The James–Clifford debate is nowadays taken to be about making room for religion in a world of science. However, it is better seen as a general defence of hypothesis-making as a mark of humanity that can be too easily obscured by a Darwinian world-view that reduces cognition to adaptive responses to proximal stimuli that are then methodologically glorified as 'induction'.

Jerome Bruner provides the linchpin between Clifford and Kuhn in the 'de-deliberation' of cognition. In many respects, Bruner et al. (1956), which so influenced Kuhn's account of scientific change, was Gestalt psychology carried to an anti-intellectualist extreme. Bruner had reduced 'conceptualization' to quick and subliminal responses to ambiguous stimuli in the environment (e.g. anomalous features of playing cards like the wrong colours on card suits). 'Decisions' was a fancy word for responses that presupposed a fixed range of options over which the subject had no control. 'Theory-laden observation' was nothing more than pattern recognition, which is to say, the reduction of theorizing to sheer observation (Fuller 2003: chap. 11). The only methodological difference between Bruner and a radical behaviourist like his Harvard colleague B.F. Skinner was that the latter would simply try to eliminate, through conditioning, whatever hesitation, confusion, or anxiety subjects experience in the face of ambiguous stimuli, whereas Bruner would first speculate about the source of such inefficiencies. However, both would treat these signature qualities of deliberative thought as worthy of elimination over time.

In effect, Bruner treated his human subjects as less intelligent than one of the original Gestalt psychologists, Wolfgang Koehler, had treated the apes of the Canary Islands in his famed insight experiments. Whereas Koehler's apes had to discover the problem he had set for them, Bruner simply informed his subjects of the task that lay before them. A 'smart environment' consisting of an informative experimenter thus pre-empted the subjects' ability to demonstrate what might be otherwise regarded as a distinctly human form of intelligence, the kind epitomized by intellectuals. As it turns out, in addition to his Gestalt roots, Bruner had been influenced by the ethologist Niko Tinbergen and his teacher, Jakob von Uexküll, both of whom had promoted – under the rubric of *Umwelt* – the idea that organisms were born pre-adapted to their likely environments (Bruner 1983: chap. 6). Humans differ only in that the relevant front-loading (a.k.a paradigm acquisition) typically occurs after birth through indoctrination, the only sociological process to which Kuhn ever gave any serious attention. In the next section, we shall encounter another intellectual offspring of Tinbergen and von Uexküll, Richard Dawkins, who also – under the rubric of 'memetics' – places great store on the role of indoctrination in thought.

A Genealogy of Anti-intellectualism: From Invisible Hand to Social Contagion

Perhaps the most attractive expression of the anti-intellectualist strand in the way of ideas is the 'invisible hand'. According to this image, a spontaneously generated division of labour in a society facilitates the free exchange of goods and services, which thereby enables each individual to maximize her own interests in the course of maximizing the interests of everyone else. The process is not planned from the outset but allowed to evolve through chained associations that emerge from contingent origins. This 'evolution' is made possible by presuming that all individuals are fundamentally self-interested but also capable of learning from others. Our learning is, in turn, based on a second-order capacity for imitation, or what is nowadays sometimes called 'cognitive simulation'. (Adam Smith himself preferred the word 'sympathy'.) In other words, the invisible hand does not work by everyone mindlessly copying the behaviour of an innovator but rather by everyone reproducing the strategy that (one hypothesises) led to the innovative behaviour. According to invisible hand theorists, the strategy involves each individual doing something that will be recognized by everyone else as better than they could do themselves, thereby creating a market niche for the individual.

Despite its rather attractive picture of the flow of ideas, the invisible hand is resolutely anti-intellectualist by virtue of its studied refusal to subject that flow to a normative ideal on whose behalf an 'intellectual' might speak. To be sure, in the eighteenth-century context that spawned the invisible hand, the relevant 'intellectuals' were clerics who wished to constrain free trade in the name of various religiously inspired ideas that enhanced the legitimacy of royal dynasties whose authority would be otherwise based on little more than force. These constraints included the granting of monopolies to politically compliant producers, which had the effect of restricting the productivity and hence the wealth of those outside the royal circuit. Much of this original sentiment remains in the law's inherent hostility to the idea of 'intellectual property' (Kitch 1980).

Two assumptions have historically contributed to the attractiveness of this particular species of anti-intellectualism. The first is that individuals naturally comport themselves with the confidence of free and equal citizens, even in societies where the political reality would seem to be quite different. The arguments leading to the American Revolution made this point most forcefully. The complaints lodged by the colonists behind the revolution, the 'founding fathers' of the United States, presupposed that the Crown and its agents were glorified service providers within the existing division of labour in North America – not some privileged second-order presence unilaterally entitled to dictate the terms of exchange.

The second assumption is that the kind of order spontaneously generated by the invisible hand will be at least as – if not more – stable than an order imposed by the state. This assumption reveals the invisible hand's normative grounding in a world where financial speculation is kept firmly to the margins of the economy. In effect, the invisible hand presupposes a late medieval fantasy consisting of rural freeholders and urban tradesmen with equal stakes in maintaining a 'commonwealth' through their patterns of exchange. Such a world perhaps existed briefly somewhere at the dawn of industrial capitalism, before the consolidated nation-state and its creation of currencies that can be accumulated and deployed to influence – and typically to destabilize – future production without themselves producing anything useful. (Thus, the invisible hand already had a nostalgic feel when proposed at the height of *dirigiste* mercantile capitalism.) Not surprisingly, modern 'true believers' in the invisible hand – that is, the Austrian rather than the neo-classical economists – are fond of distinguishing *kinds* of capital, so as to consign the financier, as a parasite on production, to a circle of hell not far above that of the commissar.

Behind these assumptions are still deeper assumptions that carry forward into more modern expressions of anti-intellectualism. Especially significant have been the following two presuppositions: (1) that our cognitive equipment is normally well adapted to serve our interests; (2) that we normally possess a roughly equal ability to realize our own interests. In short, anti-intellectualists presuppose that, once unjust or otherwise unnatural constraints are removed from the free exchange of ideas (and goods and services), our already existing capacities will deliver what self-proclaimed intellectuals claim can only be provided by design and hence force. From the eighteenth century onward, there have been two different interpretations of this rather sanguine resolution of the problem of knowledge and power. Both require a conception of collective memory but their respective modes of intergenerational transmission differ substantially. In retrospect, we would say that the original invisible hand theorists operated with a view of culture and nature as 'co-produced' in historical narratives, whereas the collective psychologists of the next century saw culture as an extended by-product of nature made possible by the grammar of our genetic code, what Richard Dawkins (1983) has called the 'extended phenotype'.

The first view establishes a line of descent from the Calvinist conception of Providence to Darwinian natural selection without directly confronting matters of genetic transmission. It argues that ideas (and practices) that have flourished in the same place for a long time *ipso facto* constitute a successful adaptation strategy, regardless of the strange or even repulsive character of the ideas or the fates of those who fail to abide by them. Clearly, this view breeds a sense of political tolerance and moral relativism that may verge on complacency by countenancing 'whatever is, ought to be'. Not surprisingly, for an invisible hand theorist like David Hume, the *universal* abolition of slavery was the typical example of an intellectualist movement, since by refusing to budge from a principle of human equality (often on biblical grounds), abolitionists ignored the apparent stability of slave-holding societies prior to European colonial expansion. To be sure, invisible hand theorists opposed slavery in their own societies, but that was only because they understood Europe as having undergone a unique pattern of development, in which earlier generations of its inhabitants had enjoyed the freedom and equality to which they once again aspired against the dictates of tyrants. The transmitted memories in that case would seem to be more cultural than biological – something inscribed in narratives retold through the ages (about, say, the noble Athenians, Romans, Venetians, etc.) rather than directly on the genetic code of the society's current membership.

A good sense of the mentality that informs invisible hand thinking can be gained from Adam Ferguson's article on 'History' in the 1780 edition of the *Encyclopaedia Britannica*. The article is regaled with one of the earliest pull-out timelines to represent the overall course of human history. In a manner reminiscent of twentieth-century philosophers of history like Arnold

Toynbee, Ferguson depicted history as a series of geographically distinct cultures, each with its own internal trajectory, proceeding in parallel with respect to time. According to Ferguson, 'revolutions' are caused by the interaction of peoples with inherently different characters. While Ferguson did not regard revolutions as necessarily destructive, he found them disruptive and capable of positive long-term effect only if their results are normalized within the revolutionized culture, as in the new paradigm that results from a Kuhnian scientific revolution. What Ferguson did not seem to envisage was that the persistent diffusion and migration of individuals and ideas could radically reconfigure the boundaries that physically separate cultures. In this respect, contrary to the universalized free-trade doctrine that would become the cornerstone of liberal imperialism by the end of the following century, the original purveyors of the invisible hand appeared to believe that the natural flow of good ideas presupposed equally natural borders within which those ideas could flow to good effect.

In the nineteenth century, progress in two areas of scientific research helped to clarify the process of idea transmission. One occurred in probability theory, much of it triggered by the collection of statistical data in consolidating the authority of nation-states; the other in developmental biology, ranging across organic levels from species evolution and embryological growth to cell division. These trends added to the anti-intellectualist's arsenal the notion that imitation is itself never the simple multiplication of identical events but a process of imperfect replication that is tantamount to differentiation, whereby each imitator naturally deviates from the imitated. Usually such deviations occur within a fixed range that in the long run these will cancel each other out. But occasionally these 'errors' accumulate until they acquire a global magnitude that effectively re-calibrates the norms of the social or biological system in which they occur. Nowadays this state is popularized as the 'tipping point' (Gladwell 2000). In the early twentieth century, as biologists came to incorporate Mendelian genetics into the causal substructure of Darwinian evolution, errors in genetic re-inscription initiated during the reproductive cycle that eventually shift population patterns so as to re-define species boundaries came to be called 'mutations'. Typically a mutation flourished because of a change in the ecology that accidentally favoured its somewhat deviant range of traits.

However, even before biologists came to agree on the concept of mutation, social scientists of an anti-intellectualist bent had already accounted for the periodic emergence of a 'genius' or 'inventor' (or Joseph Schumpeter's 'creative destroyer', the entrepreneur) in similar terms. Such distinctive individuals serve as what complexity theorists nowadays call 'strong attractors' whose presence alters the selection environment for behaviour sufficiently to appear to draw others toward its own distinctive behavioural patterns (Sperber 1996). The overall character of a group may change over time as its members are effectively offered new paths of least resistance for their natural tendencies. On this model, features of individual cognition that would be otherwise considered liabilities are treated as virtues, especially the natural erosion of memory, whose traces are shaped to facilitate an association with the impression recently left by a strong attractor, what I earlier identified as the 'availability heuristic'.

Foremost among the early social scientists promoting this line of thought was Gabriel Tarde (1843–1904), an early statistical director at the French Ministry of Justice in the Third Republic, Durkheim's main rival as the French founder of sociology (albeit as 'interpsychology'), and ultimately Professor of Modern Philosophy at the College de France (Gane 1988: chap. 8). After many years of neglect, Tarde has been recently revived in France by Gilles Deleuze and Bruno Latour, the latter especially drawn to Tarde's minimalist view of society as a patchwork of overlapping associations (Latour 2002). Tarde embraced the new scientifically enhanced anti-intellectualism with an enthusiasm that was much more influential in the United States than France itself (Ross 1991: chap. 7), where considerable ambivalence was shown towards the 'hopeful monsters', as Donna Haraway (1990), after the geneticist Richard Goldschmidt, nowadays calls mutations. Most *fin-de-siècle* French psychologists regarded the mind as a collective entity – the soul corresponding to the body politic – into which individuals are introduced through education and may subsequently need to be remediated through psychiatry. For them the perils entailed by the spread of ideas through strong attractors was epitomized in the term 'suggestibility', which covered everything from hypnotic states to collective hysteria (Valsiner and van der Veer 2000: chap. 2). It implied that humanity existed as *homo duplex*, a being whose mind is divided against itself. By 1892 the French pioneer of intelligence testing, Alfred Binet, had begun to speak of our 'double consciousness', an expression shortly thereafter adopted by W.E.B. DuBois and Antonio Gramsci to characterize the ongoing struggle of 'organic intellectuals' against the material conditions that both enable and constrain their activities.

The mutation approach to idea transmission, currently popularized as 'memetics' by Richard Dawkins (1976), intensifies anti-intellectualism. In political terms, the model justifies people gravitating spontaneously towards a charismatic leader who stands out to focus the crowd's hazy beliefs and desires into a dynamic course of action. Such a leader, a strong attractor, enables a flow of deep-seated sentiment that had previously been blocked. To be sure, the century-long metamorphosis of anti-intellectualism from the invisible hand to the herd mentality would have scandalized the Scottish Enlightenment figures Hume, Smith and Ferguson. For them unrepressed Europeans would be equal in their pursuit of enlightened self-interest, not in their surrender to base animal impulses. To be sure, there was an intellectualist residue in the Scots' thinking. They clung to the medieval scholastic conception – again traceable to Plato – that ideas spread through the 'communication of forms', a process envisaged as the transmission of a common spirit across multiple bodies that 'instantiate' the forms. For the invisible-hand theorists, this medieval residue did not appear in the formation of agents' first-order mental states, which indeed differed according to one's personal experience and position in society's division of labour. Rather, it appeared in the formation of agents' second-order beliefs, especially the sympathy that enables a strategic reflection on how individuals manage to benefit both themselves and others by means of the same set of actions. Such sympathy presupposed a robust innate psychology – the secular residue of the Christian soul – common to all humans.

Absent from the herd mentality promoted by memeticists is precisely this capacity for second-order reflection, a relatively protected mental space dedicated to passing an independent, normatively appropriate judgement on the deliveries of first-order experience. At the turn of the last century, three kinds of responses were generated to deal with this excess of anti-intellectualism that threatened to reduce *homo sapiens* to a glorified pack animal. The first was to institutionalize second-order reflection in the role of the public intellectual as the conscience of society, with Emile Zola serving unofficially as France's first 'intellectual laureate'. The second response moved in the exact opposite direction: Freud's introduction of the 'superego' as each individual's internalized parent. In a profound concession to anti-intellectualism, the superego does not appeal to a special faculty of reason to invalidate first-order impulses, but rather deploys emotions like guilt, shame and disgust to neutralize and channel the worst effects of our impulses. The surface composure of rationality thus depends on endless sublimation. The third response, Emile Durkheim's 'moral education', prescribed a role for the state as the ultimate 'loyal opposition' to the default tendencies in human experience – that is, our 'impressionableness'. Durkheim founded sociology to train future teachers in norms, especially those involving responsibility at both the individual and the collective levels, that would enable secular France to emerge from its decadent malaise (including a net decline in population), a persistent hangover of the nation's easy loss to Germany in the Franco-Prussian War of 1870–1 (Jones 1994).

Durkheim's response is especially interesting because his conception of a society's well-being was partly based on an analogy with the individual organism as an 'internal milieu', as advanced by the great French methodologist of experimental medicine, Claude Bernard (Hirst 1975: chap. 4). For Bernard, health amounts to the maintenance of equilibrium in the face of changes in the external environment. Illness is only proximally, but not ultimately, caused by particular germs or other alien bodies. Rather, it is the result of an organism's own failure to resume an equilibrium in response to such externally driven changes. What is striking here – and was not lost on medical scientists at the time – is that health requires a normative commitment that is independent, proactive and even resistant vis-à-vis normal biological tendencies. Indeed, as early as 1855, the founder of the modern science of pathology Rudolf Virchow had declared medicine the profoundest social science – one much superior to the law – because it was not content simply to draw a boundary between spontaneously occurring behaviour that was permissible (i.e. trade) and that which was prohibited (i.e. crime), which may itself change to follow the fashions of behaviour. Rather, the medical scientist aimed to strengthen the body politic by improving its collective immunity (Saracci 2001). A key strategy for cultivating immunity is inoculation, as modelled on Edward Jenner's smallpox vaccine, whereby a mitigated introduction of an external threat – in this case, a virus – enables the body to absorb the novelty of the threat without succumbing to its will, as, would be the case in, say, an epidemic. The classic role of the intellectual as 'loyal opposition' or even 'devil's advocate' vis-à-vis society's prevailing views may be seen as immunizing the body politic in just this fashion.

Interestingly, this process of collective immunity through inoculation was taken most seriously as a research topic at the height of US anti-propaganda research during the Cold War (e.g. McGuire and Papageorgis 1961). Perhaps that timing alone explains its unpopularity today. Nevertheless, there is something in this idea from which latter-day intellectuals may learn – especially if we extend 'external threats' to include market-driven tendencies as the ideational equivalent of epidemics. In that case, intellectuals may construct immune systems by setting up the terms in which a wave of virulent new ideas are assimilated into the body politic. Within the history of political economy there have been precedents for this 'protectionist' role. The domestic precedents include consumer collectives whose united front gives them the capacity to rebuff and shape the shape of market forces away from the path of least resistance for producers. International precedents include Japan's defensive modernization strategy, which involved a strategic introduction of Western products (and ideas), just enough to learn to reverse engineer and supply them themselves but not so much as to become exclusively dependent on Western producers.

At the most basic level, today's scientifically informed anti-intellectualism is largely about *heuristics*, i.e. cognitive strategies that, while deficient by classical standards of rationality, nevertheless have proven themselves over time to be adaptive responses to the environment (Gigerenzer 1999). Yet sophisticated evolutionary psychologists (e.g. Boyd and Richerson 1985) have been forced to concede that most individuals do not prove the heuristic value of these strategies in their own life experiences but rather presume their value as part of ordinary social learning. The spirit informing the transmission of these heuristics then is not that of a useful but fallible hypothesis; rather it is of an auxiliary but necessary piece of one's mental architecture. It is justified by counterfactually suggesting the potential cost that would be incurred by an agent who violated the heuristic. In other words, agents are actively discouraged from testing the limits of the heuristic's efficacy and instead simply encouraged to operate within its limits. Of course, precisely because of their wide applicability, heuristics cannot automatically dictate an adaptive response in particular situations. Agents must thus supplement the heuristics with their own 'constructions'. This means that agents must come to see the world in a way that enables the heuristics to work, regardless of whether their own or anyone else's interests are served in the process. In other words, the agent collects evidence only until her experience starts to conform to one of the expectations provided by the heuristic. To an intellectual's ears, this sounds like a socially distributed and empirically administered version of dogmatism.

Numerous mental shortcuts pass for heuristics these days, many claiming some quasi-evolutionary provenance, if their presence can be detected over a sufficiently wide expanse of space and time and bears some analogical resemblance to patterns found in other species. Even one's manner of dress (sometimes as a 'second skin') may function as a heuristic for social class, knowledge of which then enables agents equipped with the heuristic to deal with each other in an appropriate fashion. Validation of the heuristic has nothing to do with general issues of fairness or social justice but simply with whether the heuristic allows agents to make similar judgements in the future. The Jesuits offered an interesting antidote to this entire line of thought in the seventeenth century (Franklin 2001). They too recognized that we often make stereotyped judgements based on insufficient evidence that nevertheless end up enabling us to flourish. However, the Jesuits refused to interpret this phenomenon providentially as implying that we possess more knowledge than we realize. Rather, it meant that we stake our souls to close the epistemic gap – that is, a heuristic is at bottom a moral judgement of how we would prefer the world to be, given that we lack a perfect knowledge of how it is. Thus, the Jesuits invented the idea of 'moral certainty' frequently invoked in trials. What is unfortunately often lost from the original Jesuit conception is that conditions of ignorance are relieved not by default beliefs but by assertions of personal responsibility, even if – as with heuristics – these assertions have been made repeatedly. To fail to see heuristics in the full light of moral certainty is to succumb to prejudice, the worst sin and the easiest vice facing the intellectual in the twenty-first century.

Re-defining the Intellectual as an Agent of Distributive Justice

The public intellectual is ultimately an agent of distributive justice. This sounds strange only if we conceive of justice as pertaining exclusively to relationships among people and things. However, the public intellectual's *raison d'être* comes into view once our sense of distributive justice is expanded to cover relationships among ideas and actions. Just as some people enjoy an unearned advantage over others with respect to their access to material goods, so too do some ideas enjoy an unearned advantage with respect to their capacity to motivate action. In the latter case, this advantage usually results from the accumulation of time and resources to develop ideas sufficiently to render their practical implications apparent. The advantage is 'unearned' because it has been acquired at the expense of other ideas whose applicability would become equally apparent, if they were provided with comparable time and resources.

Now this way of seeing things presupposes a robust sense of the public as a unitary 'intellectual ecology' or 'collective attention span', which is subject to the usual economic problems of scarcity. It would be difficult to motivate the public intellectual's instinctive sense of justice – often expressed as righteous indignation – without assuming such scarcity. It forces one to consider which other ideas are marginalized simply by virtue of the fact that only some can receive adequate support. In other words, the public intellectual's animus is born of the view that ideas are never judged on their own merits exclusively but primarily in relation to other ideas. Often these comparative judgements are made implicitly – that is, not by direct reference to the ideas but to those who seem to stand to benefit from their promotion. If we lived in a world of plenty capable of sustaining each worthy idea without others being crowded out in the process, this 'hermeneutics of suspicion' would not be necessary or perhaps even warranted. That we do not live in such a world means that no idea is innocent of the fate of others. What distinguishes the public intellectual from others is that, faced with this situation, she does not become a sceptical fatalist but a sophistic advocate. The relative advantage of ideas is clearly the result of decisions – perhaps many and independently taken – that over time allow a few ideas to dominate over the rest. The task for the public intellectual, then, is clear: to construct situations that enable the balance to be redressed, to re-open cases that for too long have been closed.

In a phrase, the public intellectual is a *professional crisis-monger*. Should she need a patron from Greek mythology, the obvious candidate would be Eris, who provided the prized apple that occasioned Paris's judgement of the most beautiful Greek goddess, thereby unwittingly sparking the Trojan War – which, in turn, set the scene for the first moment in the Western literary canon. The public intellectual becomes a recognizable role once society – operationalized in terms of the nation-state – is envisaged as an organism, a 'body politic', that possesses a collective mind in which a variety of ideas, some long repressed, vie for the forefront of consciousness. As indicated in the previous section, this social ontology was characteristic of France's Third Republic, the period during which Emile Durkheim institutionalized sociology as an academic discipline. This was the context in which the novelist Emile Zola became the icon of public intellectuals in 1898 with the charge of '*J'Accuse!*' to draw attention to the ambient anti-Semitism and an implicit sense of France's declining fortunes on the world stage that led to the framing of Captain Alfred Dreyfus for treason.

Because nearly four years had passed since Dreyfus was consigned to Devil's Island, much of the initial response to Zola's attempt to re-open his case was negative. Indeed, he fled to London to escape imprisonment for libelling the French War Office, as Zola had no new evidence – only a new contextualization – for proclaiming Dreyfus's innocence. Zola was subsequently vindicated as new evidence came to light. As befits the metaphor of the body politic, Zola's intervention functioned as a vaccine to immunize the republic against a more virulent threat. Extremists on both the right and the left were sceptical of the long-term viability of the Third Republic. Zola gave voice to this scepticism, not by staging a coup d'état or supporting acts of terrorism, but by publishing an opinion piece in a newspaper that enabled the literate public to mull over a systematically unflattering portrait of its elected government, so that they might do something about it through the relevant constitutional channels. The result left the republic stronger than ever, with the editor of the newspaper that published Zola's provocation, Georges Clemenceau, going on to serve as the French Premier in the First World War. Unlike the political extremists, Zola genuinely believed that the pen was mightier than the sword – and that made him a true intellectual.

To be sure, the success of Zola's intellectual heroism was predicated on his international literary fame, which allowed him a safe passage to Britain when things started to heat up in France. This is not at all to take away from Zola's achievement. Rather, I mean to draw attention to a crucial element in the cultivation and evaluation of intellectuals: *negative responsibility*. Negative responsibility belongs to the discourse of utilitarian ethics, whereby one always judges the moral worth of an action in relation to the available alternatives not taken by the agent. The implication is that those with a wider scope for action bear a greater responsibility to do good. A failure to do good when one could have easily done so is thus tantamount to doing bad (Fuller 2003: chap. 17; Fuller 2005: 98–100). Zola is a role model for intellectuals because he understood this point well, which I shall elaborate in the next section. While Zola put himself at some risk by 'speaking truth to power' as he did, nevertheless the risk was relatively low, when weighed against the expected benefits of his intervention. Moreover, his fame uniquely positioned him to absorb – via welcomed foreign asylum – whatever flak came his way. It might have been reckless for jobbing writers or untenured academics to speak out against the Dreyfus conviction, but it was feckless for people in secure posts not to have done so.

My counterposition of 'feckless' to 'reckless' intellectuals in the last sentence is meant as a riposte to Mark Lilla 's fashionably conservative history of the failure of intellectuals, *Reckless Minds* (2001). Whereas Lilla queries why intellectuals from Plato onward have so often been attracted by authoritarian politics, I believe we should ask the obverse question: why have intellectuals been so reluctant to speak out against dominant positions in liberal societies, especially when their lives would be put at minimal risk? Such fecklessness goes unnoticed because it does not leave an evidential trace: it simply consists in the refrain from action. I became sensitive to such fecklessness as a failure of negative responsibility from an extensive study of the career of Thomas Kuhn, who remained silent during the Cold War cooptation of the scientific community, even though virtually every other major philosopher of science publicly voiced concern (Fuller 2000b). The problem of feckless minds raises the question of how one might institutionalize the moral courage required of the public intellectual, so that a nation does not need to depend on the heroism of a few famous people.

The German solution has been the most efficacious: *tenured academic appointments*. By 'German', I mean the classical period of the German university, which extended from Wilhelm von Humboldt's rectorship at the University of Berlin in 1810 to the end of the First World War in 1918 (Ringer 1969). The watershed moment was the consolidation of Prussia and most of the German-speaking principalities into the Second German Reich under Otto von Bismarck in 1870. In the ensuing generation, Germany became the world's leading scientific power. Tenure, even divested of its Humboldtian provenance, is very familiar to Americans, yet something got lost in the transatlantic translation (Metzger 1955). Academic tenure in the United States has been traditionally grounded in the 'free speech' guaranteed to all citizens in the First Amendment of the Constitution. Many of the landmark US court challenges to tenure over the last century have had to do with the power of boards of trustees and state legislatures to dismiss academics who wrote or spoke against their interests. The academics were generally vindicated because no form of employment can abrogate the constitutional right to free speech.

In contrast, before 1918, German academics were free to research and teach as a guild privilege in a country without a generalized right to free speech. The period ends in 1918 because then Germany becomes a constitutional democracy for the first time – the so-called Weimar Republic. Thereafter universities were forced to compete with both expanding multimedia outlets and privately funded think-tanks for control of public intellectual life. Thus, Oswald Spengler's influential *The Decline of the West* was a best seller penned by a high-school teacher, Hitler's early career benefited from positive exposure by the media mogul Alfred Hugenburg and among the think-tanks that challenged the authority of the universities was the Institute for Social Research, a.k.a. the Frankfurt School. These developments are easily overlooked because the threat they posed to the universities was short-lived – albeit long enough (15 years) to enable Nazism to ascend by purely democratic means. In the longer term, of course, the academy incorporated virtually all of the Weimar epistemic innovations – airbrushing their potentially offensive bits in ways that would please Hegel and perhaps even Freud (e.g. the academic sublimation of scientific racism as 'ethnic diversity' and the elitist reaction to mass media as 'cultural studies').

Once free inquiry is defined as a guild privilege, it is removed from a Manichean legal universe that recognizes only sheer licence or total prohibition. Rather, it is embedded in a nuanced system of rights and corresponding duties. Thus, in the USA, tenure has protected public intellectual engagement as an option that academics are at liberty to take (or not), whereas in Germany, tenure *compelled* academics to function as public intellectuals to demonstrate that they were worthy of their privileges. One might say that American academics have failed to exploit their abundant opportunities, whereas German academics made the most of their more circumscribed sphere of action – the former marked by widespread complacency punctuated by short-lived controversies, the latter by frequent tests of the limits of self-regulation that were sometimes issued in threats of censorship by government officials. The obvious point of this comparison is that the state of public intellectual life depends on the legal regime in place, and it is not clear that freer is always better.

German academics had a ready-made pretext, a *topos*, for public intellectual engagement. It harked back to the German idealist analogy of nation to state as spirit to matter. In effect, the analogy made academia, as custodians of the nation's spirit, the loyal opposition of whoever held the reins of state power at the time. Thus, every responsible academic was inclined to query the extent to which the state was truly acting for the national interest – *especially* if a likely consequence of state action was the consolidation of its power. But precisely because the state provided the material conditions for the raising of these questions, academics always had to be careful not to bite too hard the hand that fed them. (Keep in mind that German academics were glorified civil servants supported by the taxpayer.) The great sociologist Max Weber was the master of this subtle game: he criticized the Kaiser's needlessly belligerent foreign policy prior to World War I. Yet once the war started, Weber supported German victory but opposed the Kaiser's postwar expansionist ambitions. However, upon Germany's humiliating defeat, which resulted in the Kaiser's removal, Weber enthusiastically helped to draft the constitution of the Weimar Republic.

It would be easy for Americans to read Weber as someone who bobbed and weaved in his publicly expressed opinions to avoid government censorship, and perhaps even to curry government favour: he made the most of a mildly repressive regime that offered a suboptimal setting for intellectual life. However, that would be to shortchange Weber's accomplishment as someone in constant battle – in letters to newspaper editors, journal articles and speeches – defending the intellectual integrity of academia against the German Ministry of Education, which saw the universities as only part – albeit a very important part – of an overall geopolitical strategy (Shils 1974). The premier virtue of public intellectual life is *autonomy*, speaking for oneself in, as the Greek root suggests, a 'self-legislated' fashion. But it is impossible to display this virtue without the presence of external interference, in terms of which autonomy is then defined in terms of one's active resistance, or what used to be called, after György Lukacs, 'oppositional consciousness' (Frisby 1983: 68–106; Fuller 2005: 26–27). In the absence of such pressure, it is unclear whether one's opinions constitute independently taken judgements or simply follow the path of least intellectual resistance. It is not by accident that the most profound discussions of autonomy in the Western philosophical tradition – from the Stoics to Kant, Hegel and Sartre – have been set against a conception of reality that threatens to compromise the efficacy of our intentions at every turn, either by thwarting them outright or producing in us a false sense of their realization.

The latter possibility bears especially in contemporary America, by far the world's most abundant research environment. However, the environment is not uniformly abundant, and the marked differences in prospects for alternative lines of inquiry can easily produce the subtle pathology that social psychologists call 'adaptive preference formation' (Elster 1983).

Accordingly, academics come to prefer more easily funded research, which unsurprisingly results in more rapid intellectual progress and greater professional recognition, which in turn vindicate – at least in the minds of the academics concerned – that the right decision was taken in the first place. This chain of reasoning is pathological because it ignores, first of all, the opportunity costs of going down one rather than another research route but, more importantly, the sophistic point that the attractiveness of the path taken may have depended primarily on properties of the moment of decision. Perhaps *any* line of inquiry, under the right circumstances, would have produced results comparable to those of the chosen path. Moreover, had the key decision been taken earlier or later, or perhaps in some other location by a somewhat different set of people, those alternatives would have come to fruition (Fuller 2005: 7–13).

Our belief in science as the *via regia* to reality rests in mystifying the positive feedback loops just sketched, thereby suppressing the sophistic impulse to always consider alternatives. In that respect, the key to progress is never look back and never regret. I have dubbed this sensibility the 'convenient forgetfulness' that scientists have towards their history (Fuller 1997: 80–105). Thus, the intellectual integrity of academic life is routinely undermined by what may be called a 'higher self-deception', a phrase I originally used to characterize what academics normally experience as 'intellectual autonomy' (Fuller 1993: 208–210). There I observed that the deception is promoted by academics' general indifference – if not hostility – to administrative matters. They fail to see that their autonomy is intimately tied to an understanding of the conditions under which they operate. To be sure, the problem goes both ways, with academic administrators increasingly oblivious to the protection of intellectual autonomy – again not from government censorship but the lure of the market (Fuller 2002a: 196–231).

In the preceding paragraph, I shifted from speaking of the American situation to the academic predicament as such. This elision reflects the sense in which the problems facing intellectuals worldwide have come to resemble those that have routinely challenged Americans: the lure of the market. The great genius of Wilhelm von Humboldt, the founding rector of the University of Berlin, was to construct a state-protected market for intellectual life at the dawn of the nineteenth century by reinventing the university as an institution that integrated teaching and research, which rendered it the most reliable vehicle of social progress in the modern era. Of course, before Humboldt, academics had been central to public intellectual life, but more as the distributors than the producers of ideas. They were more effective in inhibiting or promoting the spread of ideas than coming up with ideas in the first place (Fuller 2000a: 108–112). However, the implied 'non-academic' idea producers were themselves typically well steeped in academic culture. They managed to escape academia's self-limiting strictures – though often with regret, as academia actively marginalized or disowned them.

Take three examples: Galileo's heretical views inevitably led to the loss of his professorial chair, Marx could never apply for any academic posts because of his religious radicalism and Freud failed to secure a professorship because of a reputation for recklessness, having experimented with cocaine, hypnosis, and so on, to treat psychic disorders. However, it would be a mistake to think of these intellectuals as unique in criticizing the status quo of their day. On the contrary, there were other critiques at least as radical in content but embedded within academic writing conventions in which a deference to authority took precedence over the development of an original voice. Thus, these academics were smothered in critical attention by hair-splitting colleagues. Not surprisingly, Galileo, Marx and Freud mastered several genres that circumvented, if not undermined, the authority of the academic voice. Especially in the case of Freud, this has generated charges of intellectual irresponsibility. However, resorting to multiple expressive media marks the true intellectual – that is, someone interested in the conveyance of ideas but sensitive to the demands placed on her by different audiences. This is in contrast to the restricted codes in which academics normally communicate. A sign of the 'academicization' of criticism nowadays is that critiques can be lodged without concern for how – or even whether – the targets are affected, let alone motivated to reorient their course of action.

Notice that the academic strictures relevant to the above alienation of intellectuals concern both the internal 'peer-review' governance structure of academia, which severely regiments intellectual expression, and academia's maintenance of intellectual performance standards in society at large, which inclines it toward conservatism. They relate to the research and the teaching function of the university, respectively. Humboldt's genius was that of the dialectical imagination – the mutual cancellation of these regressive tendencies to produce a progressive whole. I have spoken of his achievement in terms of the 'creative destruction of social capital'. The basic intuition behind the creative destruction of social capital is that whatever initial advantage is enjoyed by those responsible for cutting-edge research is dissipated in the long term as the research is made available in courses of study. The classroom then becomes the natural site for academics to contribute to public intellectual life, as they are forced to translate esoteric ideas into a form that allows students from a variety of backgrounds and interests to be examined on them – a point developed in Chapter I.

The attractiveness of the creative destruction of social capital as an academic ideal presupposes the centrality of the liberal arts curriculum to the university. Only in that context is the value of new knowledge judged primarily in terms of its bearing on the needs of the next generation of citizens, very few – if any – of whom are likely to become specialists in the relevant disciplines. However, as universities have shifted their *raison d'être* from the liberal arts to, first, doctoral training and, more recently, patent generation, the public intellectual's impulse to universally distribute knowledge claims has been eclipsed by a more sectarian and proprietary conception of knowledge. Indeed, this move constitutes a great step back to the original disposition of the medieval universities, before the Masters of Philosophy set the institutional agenda. Originally, academics trained 'doctors' who ministered to the body (medicine), soul (theology) and body politic (law). Knowledge lacked intellectual import as it was applied to exert authority over, and restrict access to, what was already then called 'domains' of reality, not least through the deployment of technical Latin. Thus, the lawyer Peter Drahos's (1995) coining of the neologism 'information feudalism' to capture recent drives towards the privatization of knowledge is much more on the mark than commentators recognize. (For a popular critical account of feudalism as the default position in a de-regulated cyberspace, see Lessig 2001; for the background political economy, see Fuller 2002a: 164–167).

However, even in Humboldt's modern re-invention of the university, cognate feudal tendencies had begun to re-emerge by the end of Hegel's life (1830), a by-product of the civil service status of German academics. As codified by Neo-Kantian philosophy at the end of the nineteenth century, epistemology had come to recapitulate bureaucracy, with each faculty of the university representing a different 'cognitive interest' (Habermas 1971; Collins 1998: 689–696). By the final quarter of the twentieth century, doctorates proliferated, but their value correspondingly declined, as a degree that had been previously awarded for sustained and advanced research now became little more than a licence to enter the academic labour market. The result is the currently diabolical situation in which graduate students who have been rewarded largely for establishing a domain of inquiry as 'their own' through intensive investigation are deposited into a job market that still (rightly) demands the expression of esoteric knowledge in a common tongue.

This situation is masked by euphemisms like 'research-led teaching', which means either that one is competent to teach only that which one has researched or that one organizes teaching so that students end up doing research for the instructor. It is difficult to imagine which theory of pedagogy underwrites this unholy alliance of learned helplessness and rank exploitation, yet its implicit acceptance by the academic community has fostered a scepticism, if not outright hostility, to the forms of knowledge generated by public intellectual life. As we continue to fight the 're-feudalization' of the university on many fronts, one relatively modest proposal to reintegrate academia into public intellectual life would be to put an end to the blurring of the boundary between the Master's and doctoral degrees (i.e. seeing the former as merely a prelude to the latter) and to treat them as distinct programmes, the former to develop a broad teaching competence and the latter a specialized research competence. This should then be coupled with a rolling back of the qualifications required for tenure-stream posts from the doctorate to the Master's degree.

The Critique of Intellectuals in a Time of Pragmatist Captivity

The past twenty years have witnessed the revival of a genre called 'the critique of intellectuals'. Its practitioners are usually American and often, though not always, disappointed leftists. But even when they are not leftists, they are disappointed with the left's obliviousness to some obvious facts, such as the failure of World Communism and the totalitarian sympathies of many thinkers currently fashionable with leftists, notably Martin Heidegger and many of his students and fellow-travellers. Lehman (1991), Judt (1994), Wolin (1990, 2001) and Lilla (2001) are among the more notable names in this genre. These authors manifest the 'Thucydidean virtues', namely, the advantages afforded to an interested non-participant in the events recounted. They typically have a more nuanced sense of the moral complexity of intellectual life than the agents in recounted events. But true to Thucydides, and unlike many professional historians, authors either claim or presuppose that the agents in question could have anticipated, avoided, or pre-empted the disastrous directions in which their ideas led. By failing to think in a sufficiently comprehensive, self-critical and prospective fashion, the agents fail – especially as intellectuals. However, as in Greek tragedy, the critique of intellectuals permits a measure of pity for the agents, as they are diagnosed as victims of some rather deep-seated societal disorder, which overwhelmed even their sense of intellectual responsibility. But in the end, we are meant to learn from the intellectuals' mistakes, at least by trying not to repeat them.

A curious feature of today's critics is that they typically target thinkers who, if not consorted, at least flirted, with world-historic *losers*, as we have now come to regard Hitler and Stalin. This is curious because the most frequently cited precursors of today's critics – Raymond Aron (1957) and his inspiration, Karl Popper (1945) – launched their critiques at times when it was by no means clear whether Nazism (in Popper's case) or Communism (in Aron's case) would turn out to be on the losing side of history. This point is easily obscured because the critical gaze remains firmly fixed on the same people: intellectuals are declared guilty by virtue of having been intellectual associates of Hitler and Stalin. But whereas Popper and Aron had to appeal to values they hoped would be shared by their readers, perhaps a to the point of risking their own lives for their realization, today's critics can quickly presume a common ground with their readers, who easily grant, as a matter of historical fact, that Hitler and Stalin were evil, and that those who sided with them are guilty of facilitating their evil.

Epistemologically speaking, Popper and Aron were testing their values against an unresolved future, whereas, say, Richard Wolin and Tony Judt are using the presumptive verdict of history to confirm their values. Not surprisingly, works by the former pair are read as heroic attempts to speak truth to power, even when they indulged in hyperbole, whereas works by the latter pair, despite their greater respect for the historical record, often strike readers as covert exercises in sour grapes. Popper and Aron are admired for holding intellectual hubris accountable to the ordinary norms of humanity, but Wolin and Judt are chastized for failing to see that genius sometimes requires – or at least excuses – the suspension of just those norms. This asymmetrical reception of the first- and second-generation intellectual critics suggests two points about the temper of our times. The first concerns the latter-day critics' exclusive focus on losers. The second concerns the implication that history eventually brings closure to critical judgement. I shall consider each in turn. Together these points define what I call our 'pragmatist captivity'. For the purposes of this book, 'pragmatism' refers to Richard Rorty's selective appropriation of that tradition.

For Popper and Aron, the very idea of 'winners' and 'losers' in history was immaterial to an intellectual's eligibility for critique. Both were political realists who held that there were no unmitigated goods or unsullied agents in the world: even the most ethical course of action exacts its own costs and casualties. This is sometimes called, after Jean-Paul Sartre, the doctrine of 'dirty hands'. The critique of intellectuals gets its bite from the prospect that one might anticipate consequences that one does not intend: our hands could perhaps have been more or less dirty than they turn out to be. The social responsibility of intellectuals is tied to a heightened sense of circumspection about such counterfactual possibilities. If ideas can be vehicles for launching us into a glorious future, they can equally serve to propel us towards a disastrous fate. A responsible intellectual is mindful of just this Janus-faced potential of ideas. It implies both a cognitive and an ethical burden. From the cognitive standpoint, intellectuals must recognize the two sides of historical contingency: what made the present so dependent on past decisions precisely renders the future open to the decisions that are taken today. From the ethical standpoint, intellectuals must remain sufficiently attached to their ideas to be answerable for them in the public sphere, if only to justify the insulation that intellectuals normally enjoy from whatever substantive impact their ideas manage to have.

There are two versions of the doctrine of dirty hands, both of which refer to negative unintended consequences. The relevant consequences may derive from either well-intentioned acts or simple failures to act. The former, associated with what natural law theorists call the 'doctrine of double effect', has been the subject of much discussion, especially in relation to the ethics of war. But we shall be concerned with the latter situation, which utilitarian moral philosophers have regarded as the basis for 'negative responsibility', that is, a responsibility for what one does not do (Smart and Williams 1973: 93–100). Thus, if your having acted in a certain way would have increased the good of many and the suffering of few, then your failure to act is tantamount to your having acted badly. In this spirit, Sartre blamed the studiously apolitical but well-positioned Gustave Flaubert for the repression of the Paris Commune in 1871 because Flaubert did nothing to prevent it. Clearly the burden of negative responsibility falls more heavily on those whose words and deeds carry authority. More generally, it may be that the toll exacted of world-historic victors is a moral coarseness that makes them blind to the demands of negative responsibility, since the failure to meet its demands typically coincides with a compliance with the vindicated regime. Perhaps unsurprisingly, it is easiest to illustrate this point with respect to the current world-historic victor, the United States, whose national philosophy is pragmatism.

At the height of Cold War tensions in the 1960s and 1970s, when the US and USSR seemed equally poised for world domination, many critiques of the emerging 'military-industrial complex' on university campuses were published by intellectuals living in the USA and its allies. Most of these critiques were written from the standpoint that the excesses of capitalism would be tamed, if not reversed, by socialism in the long run. At the very least, their authors imagined an outcome to the Cold War more favourable to the Soviets than the actual one. However, when it became clear that the USSR's days were numbered, the critiques of the military-industrial complex declined – to such an extent that today the mere utterance of the phrase 'military-industrial complex' marks the utterer as an old-timer, if not a malcontent. Some, like ex-Sovietologist Francis Fukuyama (1992), have turned the old narrative of socialism's inevitability on its head into one of capitalism's inevitability. But such radical reversals are not necessary. Calmer heads graciously concede that the original critiques were not off the mark, but (unfortunately) they are now beside the point, given that only the USA is left standing.

But if, say, analytic philosophers (McCumber 2001), neoclassical economists (Mirowski 2001), computer scientists (Edwards 1996) and cultural anthropologists (Nader 1997) were criticized in the 1950s and 1960s for accepting research funding from the US government – or aligned private foundations – without questioning the uses to which their research might be put, why should that criticism not still be seen as valid today, even though the United States won the Cold War and many of the same researchers still dominate the fields that flourished under this funding regime? In response, it is typical not to deny outright the validity of such critique but to place a greater burden of proof on those who would now reassert the critique's validity. Thus, what would have been apparent to observers in 1968 now needs to be established through archival research, which may be impeded if the researcher plans to put the results to controversial uses (Söderqvist 1997). Moreover, the task of critique is complicated by the written record's bias against revelations of compliance to the established order, since records are normally kept from a standpoint in which compliance is expected and hence not particularly noteworthy. In this respect, diarists and webloggers who envisage an end to the 'American hegemony' would do future critics an enormous service by recording *the image of compliance*, namely, the sorts of things that scholars and other intellectuals have done in order to avoid having to confront the powers that be. (An exemplary precedent is Klemperer 2000, written by a German philologist with an Orwellian ear for Nazi Newspeak.)

However, it would be a mistake to reduce intellectual compliance to thought that is explicitly solicitous of the dominant regime. To be sure, there are clear instances of this practice in the Nazified writings of Martin Heidegger, Paul De Man and Konrad Lorenz, as well as the Stalinized tracts of Gyorgy Lukacs, Jean-Paul Sartre and John Desmond Bernal. However, more intellectually challenging and morally problematic are the cases in which entire bodies of thought appear to be crafted so as to avoid having to acknowledge the regimes that sustain both the legitimacy of what the authors describe and the authors' own legitimacy as describers. The most enduring writings of the previously cited authors would fall under this category. From a sociology of knowledge standpoint, their effect may be regarded as 'obscurantist' in a dual sense. First, they serve to obscure the reader's understanding of the context that led to the decisions that the author took in representing the phenomena formally under investigation. Second, they obscure the background conditions that enabled these works, upon publication, to acquire a prominence beyond that of their competitors. To get a sense of what I mean here, let us consider two Cold War American examples, Thomas Kuhn and Clifford Geertz, not because the extent of their intellectual compliance is uncontroversial, but because a *prima facie* case exists for further investigation.

Kuhn and Geertz are interesting to consider together. Both are somewhat reluctant postmodernists *avant la lettre* who contributed arguments that by the 1970s had led to the downfall of whatever 'positivist' and 'objectivist' hegemony had existed in the social sciences and perhaps science more generally. This much is common knowledge among students of contemporary intellectual life. However, less well known is that Kuhn and Geertz overlapped at Harvard in the early 1950s, just as the university was becoming the intellectual crucible for the US's Cold War strategy. In this period, Kuhn was an instructor in the General Education in Science programme, while Geertz, a graduate student in Talcott Parsons' famed Social Relations Department, worked on a Ford Foundation project focussed on the emerging megastate of post-colonial Southeast Asia, Indonesia (Fuller 2000b: chaps 3–4; Geertz 1995: chap. 5). These experiences were formative for what are now recognized as Kuhn's and Geertz's signature theses.

Kuhn's (1970) work was a substantially reworked version of the lectures he gave in 'Natural Sciences 4', a course designed by Harvard President James Bryant Conant to instruct non-scientists destined for high places on how to secure the integrity of science amidst the hype and pressure of the dawning 'atomic age', which Conant himself was instrumental in bringing about (Fuller 2000b: chaps 3–4). The idea was to reveal a common disciplined mindset (or 'paradigm') within which true scientists have always worked, regardless of the material conditions and dimensions of their enterprise. Meanwhile, Geertz's (1973) ideas about politics as theatre and ideology as cultural expression were developed from fieldwork in a country whose leader, Sukarno, channelled both American and Soviet aid into extravagant public displays of national identity that masked repressive measures against local militants, yet managed to retain the country's political independence.

Kuhn and Geertz are often credited with having demonstrated that 'grand theory' conceptions of, respectively, progressive science and ideological politics are betrayed by actual scientific and political practice. Yet, their alternative visions share a curious characteristic. Although they are routinely understood as operating at the micro-level of social reality, the visions are no less beholden to macro-level developments, which nevertheless remain largely hidden.

In Kuhn's case, his preoccupation with puzzle-solving in paradigm-driven 'normal science' reflects a regimentation and specialization in both training and research that do not exist before the final quarter of the nineteenth century and only come into their own with the emergence of nationalized 'big science' in the twentieth century. Yet, Kuhn's historical examples are restricted to the 300 years of 'little science' prior to the 1920s revolution in quantum physics. Such syncretism leaves the impression that the activities of scientists today are just as self-organizing and self-determining as they arguably were when, say, Priestley and Lavoisier contested the nature of oxygen in the late eighteenth century. As Conant would have his students learn, behind every particle accelerator one sees the hand of Einstein and Bohr instead of the military-industrial complex.

In Geertz's case, the texture of Indonesian political life appears as an eclectic cultural mix focused more on performance than results that serves to defamiliarize the modern Western preoccupation with the exercise of power for the sake of achieving a desired social order. Yet, while Geertz articulates this lesson mainly at the level of, say, the Balinese cockfight, it was also at work – perhaps more clearly – at the level of the geopolitical strategy employed by Sukarno (himself nicknamed the 'Cock') to outfox the superpowers of the First and Second Worlds who thought they could use financial and military incentives to bring Indonesia into their respective orbits. As it turned out, the Communists pushed their ideological politics more strongly and ended up losing more in the process.

Throughout their careers, Kuhn and Geertz have been periodically accused of not being as forthright as they might have been in their attitudes toward the Cold War, especially once they came to occupy privileged positions in their respective fields. (On Kuhn, see Feyerabend 1970, Fuller 2000b: chap. 8; Fuller 2003: chap. 17; on Geertz, see Marcus and Fischer 1986: chap. 6; Nader 1997.) Behind this circumspection lay a normative principle that is central to the politics of intellectual compliance: *you can often accomplish your scientific and political goals with minimum difficulty by not resisting the larger forces in your environment.*

This principle is familiar from the Nazi period. For example, Heidegger's understudy, Hans-Georg Gadamer, never followed his master's example of openly aligning himself with Hitler. Instead, he kept close to classical philology and philosophy, resulting in a steady professional advancement, as Jews were removed from academic posts (Wolin 2000). Compliance became a more pointed matter in occupied France, where the Vichy regime did more than surrender to the Nazis – it actively rounded up Jews for the concentration camps, partly (so it seems) as a perverse expression of their denial that an occupation had actually taken place. Sartre famously condemned France in this period as a 'republic of silence', as most of its *bien pensant* citizens refused to speak out against their government's 'decision' to pursue explicitly anti-Semitic policies. Their silence implied that the state spoke in their name, which meant (for Sartre) that they were 'collaborators' in the Nazi atrocities against which a 'resistance' was morally and politically required. In at least this case, compliance followed the path of least resistance.

As intellectuals who flourished in what turned out to be the winning side of the Cold War, Kuhn's and Geertz's 'path of least resistance' unsurprisingly appears subtler than Heidegger's or even Gadamer's. According to Kuhn (1970), it would seem that scientists are free to pursue their paradigmatic puzzles with impunity as long as they do not question the non-scientific ends to which their work might be put. Otherwise, they risk being mired in that epistemic state of nature that Kuhn calls 'pre-paradigmatic' inquiry, as epitomized by the ideological conflict that marked the Protestant Reformation prior to the establishment of politically neutral scientific bodies like the Royal Society of London. This lesson was renewed in the Faustian bargain struck by German academics at the peak of 'mandarinization' in the Wilhelmine era (Ringer 1969). It also captured the climate of Cold War America, which had begun to inherit Germany's mantle of scientific leadership after World War I, once Conant imported the organizational structure of German chemistry laboratories into academia (Conant 1970: 69–70): scientists enjoy a guild privilege in the fields for which they were trained but, in return, they do not question the political aims of the state that underwrites that privilege, even in relation to the deployment of their expertise. Kuhn reflected this 'heads-down' approach in his only sustained correspondence on the contemporary science-policy climate. Here he maintained that faced with external pressure from either 'the establishment' or 'the movement', true scientists were likely to stick to what they knew best and not contaminate their scientific credibility with political involvement (Bernard and Kuhn 1969–70). Moreover, Kuhn himself applied this principle to condemn others – notably Jerome Ravetz – who attempted to use his theory as the basis for a critique of 'post-normal science', as Ravetz (1971) dubbed organized inquiry's captivity to the military-industrial complex (Kuhn 1977b).

In the case of Geertz, it must be said that he has been openly critical of the US's Cold War strategy – first associated with Eisenhower's Secretary of State John Foster Dulles – of treating the entire world as one big field of engagement against Communism, which has remained the template of US geopolitical thinking in the post-Cold War 'war on terrorism' (Geertz 1995: chap. 4; cf. Fuller 2001). Yet, the critique remains strangely (at least to Geertz's own critics) limited to the conceptual level: Dulles and others committed to the 'containment' of Communist influence misunderstood the complexity and heterogeneity of factors that contributed to, say, the turmoil that has marked Indonesia in its first decades of independence. As a result, they often exacerbated an already confused situation. Nevertheless, Geertz appears to be writing from the standpoint of someone trying to promote American, rather than native, interests in the region. He is studiously agnostic about the propriety of a long-running civil war with a million casualties, given the different sensibility that Indonesians bring to their understanding of politics. It is as if Indonesia's strangeness (to Westerners) partially justifies its abhorrent political climate, perhaps implying that much of what appears abhorrent would remain, even with the cessation of foreign interference. Overall Geertz's message to his US funders and readers would seem to be 'less is more' – a lighter touch in native affairs may ultimately bring more benefit to foreign interests. Without doubting the shrewdness of this advice, it has caused discomfort among Geertz's critics – mostly fellow anthropologists – since it resembles nothing so much as the methodological relativism that characterized the golden age of British social anthropology in the interwar period, only now with the explicit imperial motive and structural-functionalist vision replaced by the image of the 'accidental tourist' conveying to his own society the sense of an alien culture for reasons that are never made entirely clear.

If Kuhn's account of science facilitated the transatlantic migration of the metatheory underwriting German science at its imperial peak, Geertz's account of politics and culture perhaps did something similar for the metatheory underwriting British social anthropology at its imperial peak. In both cases, the cultural translation articulated the new intellectual and policy imperatives posed by Cold War America. Determining whether it constituted compliance in an objectionable sense would have both an epistemic and ethical dimension. It would require comparing Kuhn and Geertz with other similarly placed individuals in their respective fields who dealt with roughly the same situation somewhat differently: What would the alternative accounts reveal and conceal? Would better consequences have resulted from one or more alternatives – and for whom exactly? When the final outcome of the Cold War was in doubt, American intellectuals were very sensitive to the difference that their inaction might make to their government's policies. For example, virtually every philosopher of science who might be considered a rival to Kuhn – Popper, Feyerabend, Lakatos and Toulmin – spoke out against the impact of the military-industrial complex on science; yet Kuhn kept his counsel (Fuller 2003: chap. 17).

But after the fall of the Berlin Wall in 1989, this sensitivity virtually disappeared from public representations of the period. Such a transformation in moral sentiment is captured in two phrases: 'the end justifies the means' and 'sour grapes'. The intellectuals who failed to interfere with US Cold War policy indirectly facilitated an outcome that has turned out to be better than other possible outcomes. Moreover, had the intellectuals interfered with government policy, they might have prevented this outcome and helped to bring about a considerably worse state-of-affairs (e.g. Soviet domination). Therefore, with the 20/20 vision that only hindsight affords, the intellectuals should not feel guilty about their original political inaction because they had been mistaken about the difference their action would have made. Thus, only a small stretch of the historical imagination converts what had been the intellectuals' calculated cowardice into their unconscious wisdom. Meanwhile, the political activists of the period now appear as well intended but, perhaps luckily, ineffectual (Braunstein and Doyle 2001).

At this point, some may argue that the historical elusiveness of negative responsibility merely highlights the inadequacy of a moral theory based exclusively on evaluating the consequences of (actual or possible) actions. In that case, there is no safeguard that the moral significance of particular acts will not change over time, as their consequences interact with those of other acts. Indeed, if the American hegemony should come to an end in the twenty-first century, those prudently inactive intellectuals from the 1960s may come to be judged as duplicitous cowards yet again! But this point tells against negative responsibility only if our moral judgements should be less corrigible than ordinary empirical judgements. For, if we accept that our moral judgements should change as we learn more about what both preceded and followed particular acts, then there is nothing absurd about the presence of significant fluctuations in the moral status of acts and agents over time (Fuller 2002b). In that case, it is *always* a matter for the future to decide whether we are heroes, villains or cowards. That relative agreement can be reached on the interim decisions simply reflects the relative agreement that exists over the causal structure of history, which, as Hegel clearly understood, is normally written from the standpoint of those for whom the past is a legacy they intend to take forward. Thus, the fixity of moral judgements over time requires continuity in what Hegelians call 'the subject of history'. But we need not follow Hegel in envisaging this 'subject' as a nation-state. It may equally involve a succession of intellectual regimes – as defined by canonical texts or scientific paradigms – according to some legitimatory narrative.

Not surprisingly, those who regard themselves as the legatees of such a narrative wish to enforce an historical closure on critical judgement. Specifically, they would keep an intellectual's 'ideas' always officially open to re-evaluation, but her moral and political record is considered only as long as questions remain about the regime housing the intellectual – questions that are eventually closed by the course of history. To be sure, intellectual significance is hard to gauge while the original context of expression continues to influence the reception of the ideas expressed. In that case, the search for an organic unity between life and thought is an understandable interim critical strategy, until history delivers its verdict and it becomes possible to evaluate an intellectual's ideas independent of their original context. This might explain why first-generation intellectual critics like Popper and Aron are held to different standards from those of second-generation critics like Judt and Wolin. But ultimately this argument is unpersuasive as a justification for a long-term restriction on the scope for critical judgement to what is all too loosely called the 'content' of an intellectual's ideas. Moreover, the argument is especially unpersuasive coming from a *pragmatist*, as we shall see in the case of Richard Rorty.

At the outset, it is worth recalling that the major research project of analytic philosophy in the twentieth century – a universal theory of meaning – has produced, to put it charitably, inconclusive results. There remain no agreed upon criteria either for claiming that two or more words, images or actions convey the same content or for distinguishing such content from the words, images and actions expressing it. Content is normally inferred by convention from the partially overlapping media that are alleged to express it – the more diverse the media, the more 'ideational' the content. Here one recalls Russell's 'method of abstraction', according to which *any* group of individuals can be constituted as a class according to some arbitrarily defined relation of similarity. Yet, at the same time, philosophers insist that the material conditions surrounding an idea's transmission (e.g. who said it, when and where it was said, and for what reason and to what end it was said) are immaterial to judgements of its validity. The entire category of informal fallacies in logic known as 'red herrings' – most notably the 'genetic fallacy' – is covered by these strictures, which have served to divide philosophy from sociology and psychology for more than a century (Fuller 2007a: 115–122). Nevertheless, the strict enforcement of this boundary presupposes what has failed to be established, namely, that an idea can be non-arbitrarily distinguished from its material conditions. The default convention perhaps most in favour with philosophers simply identifies intellectual content with a canonical text of the idea's expression. But this convention is applied selectively – a few choice passages are taken to epitomize the meaning of an entire work – and under the influence of a self-serving semantics that permits, say, the introduction of the reader's professional and commonsensical understandings of the text, while restricting what might be reasonably inferred as the author's own original understandings.

A good example of the self-serving character of this convention is the following remarkable quote, made by Rorty in defence of Heidegger from the charge that Nazism had vitiated his thought:

> Karl Popper, in *The Open Society and Its Enemies*, did a good job of showing how passages in Plato, Hegel, and Marx could be taken to justify Hitlerian or Leninist takeovers, but to make his case he had to leave out 90 percent of each man's thought. Such attempts to reduce a philosopher's thought to his possible moral or political influence are as pointless as the attempt to view Socrates as an apologist for Critias, or Jesus as just one more charismatic kook. Jesus was indeed, among other things, a charismatic kook, and Heidegger was, among other things, an egomaniacal, anti-Semitic redneck. But we have gotten a lot out of the Gospels, and I suspect that philosophers for centuries to come will be getting a lot out of Heidegger's original and powerful narrative of the movement of Western thought from Plato to Nietzsche. (Rorty 1988: 33)

What is most striking about this passage is that Rorty is himself routinely guilty of just the charge he lodges against Popper, namely, of strategically omitting most of what philosophers thought. (For example, from reading Rorty, one would have never guessed that the logical positivists considered John Dewey a kindred spirit.) There would seem to be a hidden clause in the principles of interpretive 'charity' and 'humanity' that Rorty periodically cites from Quine and Davidson to justify his philosophical readings: if you interpret people in flattering ways, you need to account for less of what they actually say and do than if you interpret them in unflattering ways. Another, more cynical gloss of this point is that the more 'complex' a thinker is taken to be, the more elusive the accountability of his or her thought, and hence the greater discretion permitted to present thinker and thought as favourably as possible.

To be sure, as a good pragmatist, Rorty officially wants the philosophy canon to be as forward-looking as possible. The ultimate value of the canon lies not in its veneration of the past, but in the utilities it offers those projecting the present into the future. Nevertheless, Rorty's recommended appropriations of dead philosophers continue to invoke their names as markers of respect and authority, while gingerly avoiding any comment on their errors and dangers that might undermine their utility. He thus seems to want both to commit and avoid the genetic fallacy at the same time. Here is an instance of the equivocation, later in the same article:

> … the works of anybody whose mind was complex enough to make his or her books worth reading will not have an 'essence', that those books will admit of a fruitful diversity of interpretations, that the quest for 'an authentic reading' is pointless. One will assume that the author was as mixed-up as the rest of us, and that our job is to pull out, from the tangle we find on the pages, some lines of thought that might turn out to be useful for our own purposes. (Rorty 1988: 34)

While Rorty clearly wants to detach the validity of Heidegger's ideas from Heidegger's Nazi past, he still wants to credit those ideas to that 'complex mind', Heidegger, so that we continue to read *Being and Time*, as opposed to a book with similar content written at roughly the same time by an anti-Nazi. Rorty believes that, Heidegger's Nazi past notwithstanding, no one else wrote a book as profound as *Being and Time*. The profundity of the book thus overrides the despicability of its author. Such special pleading constitutes the main objection against holding intellectuals negatively responsible for their words and deeds. Specifically, the integrity of a life project – say, that of a monomaniacal scientist or artist – may require one to ignore the utilitarian imperative to act always so as to maximize the greatest good for the greatest number (Smart and Williams 1973: 100–118). The critique of intellectuals will not be able to develop unless it can undermine this kind of argument. In the case of Heidegger, then, we should ask if there were other philosophers of roughly the same vintage who said roughly the same things, but were not Nazis. If so, then the dispensation from negative responsibility urged by Heidegger's boosters like Rorty is not justified.

As a student of philosophy twenty-five years ago, it was patently obvious that there were just such non-Nazi alternatives to Heidegger. They would have included Karl Jaspers, Paul Tillich and Jean-Paul Sartre. Back then, Heidegger and they were routinely collected together as 'Existentialists', and Heidegger would not have necessarily received the most respectful treatment. To be sure, there were important differences among these thinkers, but Rortyesque claims to Heidegger's 'striking originality' would certainly need to be tempered, if *Being and Time* continued to be read alongside *Reason and Existenz, The Courage to Be* and *Being and Nothingness*. In that case, one might reasonably query the source of the remaining philosophical nuances that distinguish Heidegger from these contemporaries, and the extent to which those nuances, if not altogether overvalued, might not be indebted to trains of thought that attracted Heidegger – but not Jaspers, Tillich, or Sartre – to Nazism. This would make a good research project in the humanities, even today.

However, it became difficult to pose this question once 'existentialism' disappeared as the name of a philosophical school, along with a sustained study of its major proponents – except, of course, Heidegger. He was renovated as a seminal transition figure: the final deconstructive moment of a larger and older school, 'phenomenology', which seeded the current waves of postmodern continental European thought. Questions about the relative depth of Heidegger's philosophical project are certainly possible, and even desirable, given that a greater recognition of Heidegger's singular 'genius' has historically coincided with a greater awareness of his Nazi past. It is easy to imagine a considered judgement by future intellectual historians that might today be regarded as cynical: 'The status of Heidegger's philosophy was artificially magnified in the late twentieth century to avoid having to face the full normative implications of a "life of the mind" so radically detached from the concerns of ordinary humanity'.

Generally speaking, Rorty capitalizes on the tendency to treat the elusiveness of ideas as agencies of change in ethically asymmetrical terms. Intellectuals are shielded from the bad consequences of their ideas but they are credited with the good consequences. The asymmetry may even occur in the same body of work: philosophers of science chastize self-styled 'Kuhnians' who read too much relativism and political radicalism into his work, as they themselves fixate rather selectively on Kuhn's intermittent discussions of paradigms as conceptual exemplars for high praise and deep interpretation. Moreover, intellectuals are often generously credited for positive developments traceable to their ideas, however unintended, while blame is withheld from them for the negative developments, however intended. For example, scientists are normally given credit for developments that enhance the human condition, even when they occurred several decades after the original intellectual innovation (e.g. Newton's 'responsibility' for the Industrial Revolution), while it is much harder to hold them responsible for developments that diminish the human condition, even when they were brought about by the original intellectual innovators (e.g. the responsibility of the founders of modern atomic physics for nuclear weapons). Even in spheres of life permeated by the postmodern condition, where judgements about the 'correct' application of ideas are bound to be murkier, we still credit, say, Locke with inspiring American democracy, as we continue to chastize those who would blame Nietzsche for seeding Nazism. But *why* this asymmetrical treatment?

A clue to the answer lies in Rorty's curious hostility to the sociology of knowledge, as illustrated by his previous remarks about Popper. *Prima facie* the hostility makes sense, a reflection of a genuine disagreement over the temporal flow of legitimation. The sociology of knowledge wants the material conditions of intellectual life to play a major role in the evaluation of ideas, whereas pragmatism wants to focus entirely on the prospective benefit that ideas might confer on their adopters. The one is past-oriented, the other future-oriented. But underlying this distinction is a more profound difference of opinion about the very detachability of ideas from their material conditions. Sociologists of knowledge are much more sceptical than pragmatists on this point. Rorty simply presumes that philosophers who manage to speak across many contexts are contributors to the 'conversation of mankind', which reflects humanity's perennial concerns, albeit expressed in historically and socially quite specific ways. He does not consider the alternative possibility that we find past figures valuable precisely because aspects of their original contexts remain with us: their prejudices have become our prejudices. In that case, a critique of the social conditions of thought would be required, lest we succumb to an intellectual colonization by the past, what I have elsewhere called 'second-order colonialism' (Fuller 2003: chap. 10). In these postmodern times, we have become so preoccupied with exorcising any hint of teleology from our relationship with history that we run the risk of suffering from the reverse problem of being carried along by the inertia of the past.

It is worth recalling that the genetic fallacy is not designed to prohibit a consideration of an idea's origins from an assessment of its validity. It has a more subtle purpose, namely, to shift the burden of proof to those who would claim – as happened in the 1930s, when the fallacy was first introduced – that Einstein's Jewish origins are *automatically* relevant to an evaluation of relativity theory (Cohen and Nagel 1934; Giere 1996: 344). These origins *may* be somehow relevant, but simply revealing them does not establish the point. One would also have to propose an explanatory narrative of how being Jewish – or being exposed to Jews – could contribute to the spread of ideas that are especially good or bad. Yet, from a logical point of view, the genetic fallacy is often so misrecognized that another fallacy is committed in the process. Thus, Rorty takes the claim 'The origins of an idea need not imply anything about its validity' to mean: 'The origins of an idea *never* imply anything about its validity'. This inferential slide is sometimes called the 'modal fallacy', whereby the modal operator 'not necessarily' (or 'need not') is read to mean 'necessarily not' (or 'never'). The import of committing the modal fallacy in this case is that Rorty enforces a conceptual closure on an issue that should be kept empirically open. To be sure, it is easy to see how the modal fallacy could be committed in this context, given the distrust one might have of the findings of the racialist sociologists who would most likely do the relevant empirical research into the scientific significance of Einstein's Jewishness. But in that case, such an overly strict interpretation of the genetic fallacy is related more to a well-founded sense of 'political correctness' than the possession of a clear procedure for extracting the content of ideas from the material conditions of their expression.

Here it is instructive to consider how the logical positivists thought about this matter when they introduced the distinction on which the genetic fallacy is based – namely, between the 'context of discovery' and the 'context of justification' (Fuller 2000b: 78–92). The positivists claimed that they could rewrite, or 'rationally reconstruct', scientific statements in a 'language of thought' that does not make reference to any potentially incriminating origins that the statement might possess. Once rewritten, the statements could then be properly evaluated. Among the recommended translating languages there were included first-order predicate logic, elementary set theory and the fundamental axioms of probability. Thus, even anti-Semitic physicists could be presented with Einstein's theory of relativity in a way that would force them to accept its validity.

An interesting feature of this strategy is that, unlike Rorty, the positivists did not believe that the distinction between the origins and the validity of an idea could be drawn simply from an ordinary reading of a published statement of the idea. In fact, they believed that we ordinarily import so many preconceptions about the nature of a text's origins into our reading that we blur the distinction, and hence unwittingly commit the genetic fallacy. As a safeguard, we therefore need to engage in some extraordinary activity, be it logical translation (as the positivists themselves thought), dialectical confrontation (as that renegade positivist, Karl Popper, held), or historical idealization (as Popper's student, Imre Lakatos, later argued). Hans Reichenbach, the positivist normally credited with canonizing the distinction between the contexts of discovery and justification, did so while enumerating the tasks of epistemology, which he listed in the following order: *description*, *criticism* and *advice* (Reichenbach 1938: 3–16). In other words, one must first acquire a thorough understanding of the psychological and sociological factors surrounding a knowledge claim in order to see how the claim's manner of presentation might affect the reception of its content. This is then subject to criticism, which then might issue in some policy recommendation as to whether the claim should be believed, followed, and so on.

Positivists like Reichenbach and pragmatists like Rorty assume that the reader starts from rather different cognitive stances when evaluating a text like *Being and Time*. Whereas Rorty regards the insight provided by the psychology of discovery and the sociology of knowledge as little more than *ad hominem* 'reductions' of the complexity of a great mind's work, Reichenbach treated these fields as propaedeutic to (though not replacements for) the logic of scientific justification. In terms of Paul Ricoeur's famous (1970) distinction, positivists presupposed a 'hermeneutics of suspicion' that would have the origins of all such texts scrutinized – and perhaps even laundered – before their messages can be properly identified and evaluated, while pragmatists presuppose a 'hermeneutics of trust' that treats the great philosophical texts as a benign legacy from which we fashion our own self-understandings. Indeed, pragmatists run the risk of succumbing to the panglossian principle that a text would not continue to enjoy canonical status, were it not providing some lasting value to its readers.

In their opposition to positivism, pragmatists have been philosophically aligned with ordinary language philosophy (Austin 1961) and Neo-Darwinism (Dennett 1995). The intuition common to these movements, and opposed by positivism, is that texts prove themselves by having survived many trials in many environments. But this often involves a more pernicious assumption, one used more generally to justify 'the weight of tradition' – and here we should recall Rorty's (1979) debt to the arch-traditionalist Michael Oakeshott for the slogan 'conversation of mankind'. It assumes the unredeemable cognitive limitations of individuals. Thus, the canon – as the collective wisdom of the past – pre-sorts texts into a manageably few exemplars from which we can determine our own intellectual orientations. This justification is 'pernicious' because it implies that the number of texts excluded from the canon is so large that it would now be futile – and perhaps even risky – to reconsider previously discarded alternatives. Yet, today's canonical texts typically did not themselves achieve that status from a careful consideration of all the relevant alternatives with an eye to the various contexts in which the texts might be subsequently read and used. Rather, their selection was 'arbitrary' in that it was the result of decisions taken by many local opinion-makers, for characteristically local reasons, from which then emerged an overall pattern of canonical authors who set the framework for a cultural or disciplinary discussion.

Nevertheless, pragmatists claim that since enough of 'us' have come to benefit from these arbitrary selections then there is *prima facie* little motivation to challenge their legitimacy. Of course, the hermeneutically suspicious may wish to place a less benign spin on this feat of decentralized self-organization – namely, that it simply demonstrates the human capacity to adapt to a wide range of situations that would be considered suboptimal by some independent standard: virtually any set of philosophical texts, suitably institutionalized as a 'canon', would confer some sort of benefit, which in time could be converted into an optimality. But what might be the source of an independent standard that does not succumb to such 'adaptive preference formation', as social psychologists call this phenomenon? The most obvious source would be an unrealized ideal, which 'in exile' sets the terms for judging the actual situation. However, Rorty rejects such situation-transcendent ideals not only because they violate the tenets of his pragmatist philosophy but also because he interprets the philosophical canon as addressed to him and intended for his benefit. Whereas logical positivism was developed in active resistance to a German philosophical culture whose predominance had alienated the positivists' largely Anglophile Enlightenment interests, Rorty enjoys the advantage of being a legatee of the current 'subject of history', the USA and its philosophical culture. As a result, pragmatism lacks the critical acumen of those who believe not only that things can be but also could have been better. The distinction is crucial to the critique of intellectuals, since only the latter counterfactual challenges the legitimacy of history's winners.

In these postmodern times, we tend to assimilate the critical stance to two complementary positions that are better seen as 'acritical', to use Bruno Latour's regrettably apposite (1997) term. One acritical position simply denies the distinguishability of contexts of interpretation – in particular, those of the critic and the criticized. After Gadamer, we might say, 'horizons are always already fused'. (On the provenance of this idea, see Cooper 1996b.) As this view made its way into analytic philosophy, it was originally read as the humanist version of 'theory-laden observation' in science, which implies that we cannot know something except in our own terms. Criticism is thus reduced to a moment in the critic's self-understanding that can be always redressed by making some marginal adjustments to her theory. But thanks to Rorty, Latour and others under the influence of Kuhn, the tables have been turned, and we now speak as if our own minds are colonized by either the thoughts of other people (Rorty) or the actions of other things (Latour). In this respect, the 'turn to the social' has served to objectify what had been seen as rather subjective – or, in Kuhnian terms, to place us inside the paradigms outside of which philosophers previously claimed to stand. From the logical positivists and Popper, we may have learned that theories are always matters of 'choice' and 'convention' that require scrupulous testing in the face of a potential entrenchment. But that was to presume that we have more legislative power than post-Kuhnians are willing to grant. Indeed, it would seem that our subjectivity has been put into receivership as we are reduced to grateful legatees and faithful inscription devices – a rather literal interpretation of 'reception theory'.

The complementary acritical position that passes for criticism is the sheer recognition of relatively independent alternative traditions, or simply 'relativism'. To be sure, such recognition is 'critical' in a rather weak and specific sense – namely, of those who claim that all traditions are always already pursuing the same ultimate ends. Geertz is a master of relativism in this sense. Nevertheless, it studiously avoids making normative claims about the relations in which the traditions stand to each other. In practice, a default libertarianism seems to operate, whereby each tradition is presumed entitled to pursue its own trajectory as long as it does not interfere with the trajectories of other traditions. While this 'separate but equal' doctrine may make for a tolerant cultural policy, tolerance is mainly a virtue for those who care not or dare not confront their differences. Critics are confrontational because they have a stake in what the criticized stands for. The rise of the critic as a formal social role in the eighteenth century corresponds to the emergence of aesthetics as the normative science of perception, whose principles both the producers and consumers of art works claimed to uphold. In short, the critic and the criticized aspire to the same ideals but disagree over their adequate realization. In this respect, true critics are better seen as disinherited members of a common tradition than representatives of 'subaltern' traditions. Theirs is a 'Tory history', the mirror image of the Whig history that postmodern post-critics have gladly relinquished (Fuller 2003: chap. 9).

When the critic's understanding diverges from the dominant understanding of her time, she must construct an alternative counter-history, which typically involves the redistribution of praise, blame and significance across a wide range of agents, acts and events. These counter-histories, often called 'revisionist', require considerable skill at juggling counterfactuals, especially ones relating to the sort of unactualized possibilities presupposed in the assignment of negative responsibility. The results are bound to be controversial in two senses. A good counter-history like Howard Zinn's *A People's History of the United States* (1980) challenges both received normative judgements about the past (and hence the legitimation they can offer the present) and received standards of evidence and inference, especially in terms of what may be inferred from the absence of evidence, either because it was never recorded or it has been subsequently suppressed.

Significantly, Zinn (1980) is not about intellectuals but entire subcultures of American life that have been written out of the official histories. The absence of counter-historiography is much more pronounced in intellectual history than in social, economic and political history. In the latter, there are established traditions of counterfactual reasoning, often drawing on quantitative arguments and even computer simulations. As we have seen, much has been made of the difficulties in tracking the causal trajectory of ideas, given their elusive ontological status. This fact would seem to foil methodologically rigorous assignments of responsibility, which typically depend on clear attributions of causation. Yet, such ontological elusiveness may also point to the ultimately self-serving character of intellectual life. Therefore, a symmetrical treatment of history's winners and losers is required – however politically controversial – lest those of us who fancy ourselves 'intellectuals' cause our readers to wonder, 'Who minds the minders?'

In summary, debates over the social role of the intellectual tend to erupt whenever intellectuals appear to have betrayed their calling. The sense of intellectual obligation that informs my critique was developed by considering the negative example set by Thomas Kuhn, whose disengagement from the political implications of his ideas is still sometimes mystified as indicative of how a 'pure inquirer' ought to act. Yet, even the very content of Kuhn's theory – his socially conformist and self-contained account of scientific practice – undermined the spirit of critical inquiry. This is not to deny that critique requires specific institutional settings that need to be carefully maintained. Indeed, the biggest problem with sustaining intellectual life comes not from political repression but the failure of intellectuals to connect with target audiences. In conclusion, I shall examine the methodology of intellectual critique (i.e. the critique of intellectuals) implied in the foregoing analysis, especially its relationship to postmodernism and relativism.

In promoting the intellectual's distinctive social role I have been often accused of 'postmodernism', a label that for me refers more to the brute conditions of contemporary knowledge than a normative badge worn with honour. Thus, I can accept the title of postmodernist only if it is taken to imply proceeding from an empirically realistic starting point (Fuller and Collier 2004: Introduction). Nevertheless, one agreeable aspect of postmodernism pertains to the ideal of 'equal time' for all positions, which now defines the epistemic horizon of the mass media. It concerns the negative implication that *any* position becomes politically dangerous, and hence deserving of intellectual critique, the more that power is concentrated in it. What makes positions problematic is not their guiding ideas per se but the amount of force at their disposal that both enhances their chances of success and shields them from any adverse consequences.

This, if you will, a 'postmodernist' sensibility underwrites my attraction to 'symmetrical' explanations of intellectual life, a principle associated with the relativism of the Strong Programme in the Sociology of Scientific Knowledge (Bloor 1976). The principle was introduced as an antidote to the tendency to assign privileged explanations to historical winners, as when the persistence of Newtonian mechanics is explained in terms of its 'truth' (at least for ordinary physical motion). The normative force of invoking symmetry is, so to speak, to balance the epistemic ledger, which I have called 'Zen historicism', whereby everyone's beliefs turn out to be true relative to their respective contexts (Fuller 2000b: 24–25). It follows that all intellectual conflict implies a failure of context specification, something that the conflict itself may resolve or, if not, remains as a task for future historians. I associate Zen historicism with the standpoint of the professional historian because even history's losers would prefer to have won than to have split the difference (in context) with the winners. Thus, the kind of 'neutrality' fostered by 'symmetry' in this sense shores up the historian's authority, arguably at the expense of the contesting historical agents. I reject this sense of symmetry as diametrically opposed to the attitude of the engaged intellectual.

This attitude is an important alternative to the widely held view that certain ideas – say, racism – should be banned from public intellectual life because *the very ideas* are thought to have politically negative consequences. Such an animistic view of ideas harks back to a pre-modern era to which we should never return. The best response to racism is the response to any other disagreeable idea – to argue against it on its own terms. Related to racism's periodic political triumphs has been the failure of *bien pensant* intellectuals to take its ideas sufficiently seriously to subject them to persistent public scrutiny, thereby resulting in a 'spiral of silence' (Noelle-Neumann 1982).

As for postmodernism's intellectual co-conspirator, relativism, I am prepared to accept its normative force once it is itself properly relativized, and hence symmetry once converted from a static to a dynamic principle. In other words, intellectual critique aims not simply to redress but also to reverse the balance of epistemic power. The anchor point for my position is the original source of relativism, the Athenian sophists, proto-intellectuals whose practices predate the ontology of ideas (Fuller 2005: chap. 1). The sophists claimed they could teach the art of public defence to enable wrong-footed clients to shift the burden of proof, or redistribute advantage, in an argument. This skill is captured by the slogan that Aristotle pejoratively attributed to Protagoras of 'making the weaker argument the stronger'. The sophist's typical client – someone accused of an error in judgement or action – is naturally forced into a reflexive position: if I am right, why am I positioned as wrong? The answer involves analysing access to the means of defence: behind the client's 'error' may be a lack of access to vindicating evidence, perhaps because the charge has been designed to preclude the consideration of such evidence. In that case, attention needs to be drawn to this feature of the context that positions the client as underdog. The sophists referred to it as *kairos*, or 'timing': he who frames the argument often wins it. As against this tendency, the sophists deployed what Plato subsequently demonised as 'rhetoric', the spirit of which survives in the dialectical tradition of philosophy, including Lukacsian 'oppositional consciousness' and Ricoeurian 'hermeneutics of suspicion' – all exemplary weapons in the modern intellectual's critical arsenal.

I hold that it is not possible to pass judgement on ideas – and to credit or blame the appropriate agents for them – without first grasping the social conditions under which those ideas are generated. Otherwise, it is not even clear what those ideas are. This point applies equally to those who privilege and discount the role of an author's intention in interpretation. Even Rorty's purely pragmatic criteria for judging ideas, according to which 'genius' is bestowed honorifically on, say, Heidegger for ideas of his we find useful, presupposes a comparative evaluation of candidates for satisfying a niche in our – or at least Rorty's – conceptual framework. I wish to make this assumption methodologically explicit: what is this niche? And what are the candidates, in relation to which Heidegger's ideas have been deemed superior? However these questions are answered, it is clear *pace* Rorty that they cannot be addressed *merely* by a close reading of one or more Heideggerian texts: his texts also need to be compared with those of other authors who are related by a common context of evaluation. To fail to make such a comparison is to succumb to that sociological superstition 'the weight of tradition'.

My approach to intellectual critique is certainly 'relativistic' in one sense. I do not assume a fact of the matter about which ideas are contained in which texts, and hence which texts are superior to which others. To claim that *The Structure of Scientific Revolutions* (Kuhn 1970) is the profoundest book about the nature of knowledge in the twentieth century is simply to say that the book surpasses it rivals according to criteria it helped to establish. Indeed, characteristic of a text deemed 'canonical' is that other texts are read in terms of it, which then serve to reinforce its canonical status through invidious comparison. Thus, even the best of Popper, Feyerabend, Lakatos or Toulmin is bound to look deficient if *Structure* sets the standard for scientific epistemology. However, if we apply other criteria, derived from other texts, then Kuhn appears in a different, probably diminished light. Indeed, this is not idle speculation, but the usual terms in which a text like *Structure* is at first evaluated. A similar fate befell Heidegger's *Being and Time*, originally read as a metaphysically bloated version of existentialism but nowadays honoured as having heralded the postmodern condition. As Kuhn himself would have it, a generational shift normally needs to occur before a recent text has a chance to set a new standard. This social fact about intellectual history reveals the arbitrariness of judgements of 'lasting significance', but equally it should embolden each generation of intellectuals to replace the current standards with ones suited to the future they would help bring about.

However, my methodology is decidedly *not* 'relativistic' in a different sense. I wish to revive the 'legislative' posture of the intellectual that Bauman (1987) has brought into disrepute. The crucial feature of this posture for intellectual critique is that the critic takes responsibility for constructing the standard according to which the intellectuals under scrutiny are held accountable. In other words, as the critic exposes others, she also exposes herself. This is the intellectual equivalent of the dialectic of policy-making and office-holding that is grounded in the electoral process of parliamentary politics, a great eighteenth-century innovation. This reflexive aspect of the Enlightenment fascination with legislatures is overlooked when we stereotype the period as fixated on benevolent despots, for whom 'legislative' simply means 'law-giving' without any concern for the relevant institutional checks and balances. From my standpoint, Bauman's alternative 'interpretive' stance looks like professionalized cowardice, since here the intellectual presents herself as marching to someone else's tune – namely, the authorities whose intertextual relations define the limits of our thought. To be sure, there is plenty of room for disagreement among the interpreters. But the source texts – be they Aristotelian, Biblical or Foucaultian – are, like Milton's Satan, only made stronger by the presence of discord.

'Cowardice' may seem like a strong word to use in this context. But here it is worth underscoring that the political responsibilities of intellectuals go beyond a generic category like 'citizenship'. Intellectuals have a special obligation to speak truth to power because of their social position. Karl Mannheim and Joseph Schumpeter, the one approvingly the other more cynically, pointed to the intellectual's relative detachment from the means of production. Whereas intellectuals may resemble other members of society in the sorts of ideas they have, intellectuals are distinguished by their protected status. Intellectuals are less likely to die, or even suffer, for their ideas than non-intellectuals. When intellectuals have fallen into dire straits, they have usually crossed the line into practical politics and came to be treated accordingly. More typical is that intellectuals are rewarded or otherwise encouraged to advance ideas that challenge conventional wisdom, whatever the outcome of these challenges. The intellectual's protected status may come from several sources. Some intellectuals are independently wealthy or the beneficiaries of patronage. Others like Sartre manage to communicate in ways that supply a market for anti-establishment thought. But the most common and least risky strategy has been the institution of academic tenure. As long as academics have not attempted to undermine the university's legitimacy, they have been allowed – indeed, professionally obliged – to advance the cause of Enlightenment.

Of course, the history of academic tenure has featured boundary disputes over when a reflexively generated critique of university culture shades into a more general condemnation of the state, the board of trustees or corporate sponsors that sustain the university's existence. Yet despite some notorious US cases in the early twentieth century and during the Cold War, what stands out is how *rarely* these boundaries have been tested. Instead of actively seeking new horizons for thought, perhaps by giving voice to silenced positions, academic intellectuals have generally settled for the safe havens of scholasticism and normal science. In this way, academics renege on their obligations as intellectuals just as wealthy capitalists fail the economy when they watch the interest on their bank accounts grow and refuse to expose their assets to the market by making risky investments. (George Soros, a former Popper student, is one capitalist who understands this ethic well.) The sense of 'humility' relevant to the intellectual is the willingness to expose one's knowledge claims to public scrutiny, which is an expression of *noblesse oblige* for a social position that is already marked as privileged. The more modest forms of humility urged by postmodernists like Donna Haraway (1997) strike me as either sociologically misinformed or morally evasive. On the one hand, contemporary culture is sufficiently democratized to make it unlikely that outspoken intellectuals will be taken *too* seriously, the traditional reason for a counsel of self-restraint. On the other hand, this perceived need for self-restraint may itself mask ordinary fears of ridicule and failure that intellectuals have a professional obligation to overcome.

This is a convenient point at which to consider the basis of the unabashedly moral judgements I make of particular intellectuals. Academics, no doubt reflecting on their own quiet lives, like to distinguish *advocacy* and *compliance* vis-à-vis a political regime. Given the ease with which intellectuals can be criticized for their political judgements, it is easy to imagine a 'judge not, lest ye be judged' attitude motivating their counsel of tolerance, whereby censure is reserved for the outright advocacy of a loathsome regime. It makes sense to extend such leniency toward people who could die or seriously suffer for expressing politically incorrect views. However, intellectuals have not generally been in this position. An intellectual has the talent and/or the status to convey disagreeable ideas in tolerable ways. Therefore, it is reasonable to treat advocacy and compliance as equally active responses that an intellectual can make to her social environment. Both are among the options available to the agent, in which she could have done otherwise; hence the significance I attach to the concept of negative responsibility: you are not an intellectual unless you have at your disposal a wide sphere of discretion over what you say (or do not say). To be sure, your life may be made easier by keeping silent about certain errors and injustices, and arguably were you *never* silent about these matters you might be committed to an asylum. Nevertheless, we should retain a clear distinction between *normatively desirable* and *statistically normal* behaviour among intellectuals. By analogy, even if most people cheat on their annual tax returns, it does not follow that the practice is desirable or that it should be excused when a person caught.

Of course, there is much room for an interesting disagreement about normatively desirable standards for intellectuals and the judgements made about particular intellectuals. Moreover, these disagreements will be forever fuelled by changes in our empirical understanding of how the past became the present, in terms of which each new generation tries to project a desirable future. But I would hate to see this line of inquiry closed down, or even attenuated, out of a fear of its reflexive implications. Admittedly, inquiries like the critique of intellectuals that are touched by the sociology of knowledge do have an unnerving tendency to leave the inquirer both wiser and dirtier. More serious and sullying questions can be asked of Heidegger than whether his philosophical insights and his Nazi sympathies flowed from the same sources: Sociologist Pierre Bourdieu (1991) along with Hugo Ott, Victor Farias and Richard Wolin – each part-philosopher, part-historian and part-journalist – have already revealed that common source. However, Heidegger's failure as an intellectual lay not in his Nazism but his cowardice.

In this respect, the moral judgements issued in the critique of intellectuals may diverge significantly from ordinary moral and political judgements. For example, Jean-Paul Sartre and Raymond Aron, though standing on opposite sides in the Cold War, probably deserve a comparable moral standing as intellectuals. In Fuller (2000b) I am much harsher towards the rather apolitical Thomas Kuhn than his Cold Warrior mentor James Bryant Conant. Whereas Conant openly defended a certain vision of democratic science ideologically suited to Cold War America, Kuhn refused to take a stand even after his work was embroiled in controversies around this issue. In Fuller (2003: 215), I observe that Kuhn's silence can be excused only if the USA of the Vietnam era was in a state of political repression.

Heidegger's Nazism is a moral problem for 'us' in that self-regarding sense of the word favoured by Richard Rorty, since 'we' want to both condemn Nazism as the twentieth century's biggest atrocity and acclaim Heidegger as the century's greatest philosopher. Rendering such a judgement coherent requires a strong dose of doublethink about how 'we' identify Heidegger's 'ideas'. But Heidegger's own moral problem was different: he openly supported the Nazis only as long as he thought they were listening to him. As soon as their paths diverged, he simply kept quiet, even when offered the opportunity to clarify his position after the war. As an intellectual, Heidegger was obliged either to restate or recant his former Nazism, but instead he dissembled.

However, Heidegger's moral failure as an intellectual also has reflexive implications for 'us'. To be sure, Heidegger's staunchest defenders appeal to his political naivete to explain his actions. But to take this explanation seriously is to question the secureness of Heidegger's grasp of the relationship between thought and being, a topic on which 'we' presume him to have said some significant things. In response, most philosophers are happy to adopt Rorty's convenient conclusion that all it shows is that intellectuals are human too. However, this charitable recognition of Heidegger's 'mortal coil' or 'crooked timbre' offers insufficient grounds to include him among the greatest philosophers. It provides at most a reason not to dismiss him out of hand. Truer to the critique of intellectuals is to conclude that Heidegger's legacy is a complete shambles that demands of 'us' the courage to consider whether it would be possible – and what it would be like – to have developed his allegedly deep insights without the Nazi animus. As I earlier observed, this is not a purely speculative question, as there are alternative historical exemplars in the form of Karl Jaspers, Jean-Paul Sartre and Paul Tillich, who were they to replace Heidegger would leave 'us' with a rather different sense of who 'we' are.

Pierre Bourdieu: The Academic Sociologist as Public Intellectual

Pierre Bourdieu (1930–2002) was the academic sociologist who, in recent times, had taken the role of public intellectual most seriously. Moreover, he gradually warmed to the role of 'universal intellectual' that has met with increasing disapproval by postmodernists, starting with Michel Foucault and exemplified in the attacks made in the media by Bourdieu's rival from the next generation, Bruno Latour. The full range of Bourdieu's interests reflected the main tendencies of the postwar period: the de-colonization of Algeria, the intensification of social distinctions in primary, secondary and tertiary education, the emergence of the artistic field as a mode of social reproduction and the mass media as the focus of public intellectual life, all reflecting the gradual eclipse of a distinctly French welfare state by a globalized neo-liberalism. A fair overall judgement is that Bourdieu was the French sociologist whose career trajectory and overall impact most resembled that of the field's academic founder, Emile Durkheim – a feat very unlikely to be matched soon in our increasingly decentred academic culture.

In his shrewd and semi-insider's guide to Bourdieu's corpus, Michael Grenfell observes that Bourdieu neither aspired to nor became a courtier to the leading edge of power, unlike, say, Anthony Giddens, who served as guru to Tony Blair's 'Third Way' (Grenfell 2004: 152–153). If nothing else, Bourdieu's attitude had consistently been one of *resistance*. A sympathetic leftist reading of Durkheim provides a precedent for this understanding of the sociologist's social role. Durkheim clearly saw himself as articulating an ideal of civic republicanism that France's Third Republic realized with variable success. From that standpoint, sociology proved its social value by reproducing knowledge of the ideal – especially in the next generation of teachers – and reminding society of the ideal when its practice falls short, as in the Dreyfus Affair, where Durkheim openly supported Émile Zola's famous accusation of a cover-up by the Foreign Office.

The assumption common to Durkheim and Bourdieu is that 'society' is more a normative than a descriptive term – specifically, a term for collective aspirations that deserve proper promotion but are sporadically or even routinely thwarted by actual social life. In this respect, Bourdieu's massive *La Misère du Monde* (1993) – translated into English as *The Weight of the World* (Bourdieu 1999) – was a worthy heir to Durkheim's more tightly focused *Suicide* (1897). On their face, the two works are quite different. Durkheim's is a *tour de force* in the interpretation of statistical data concerning the background of suicide victims, whereas Bourdieu's is an extended commentary on interviews with the working poor who are asked to reflect on their various failures. The diagnostic images that dominate the two works are also different: *Anomie* suggests the loss of definition that comes once the individual is released from family and religious bonds, while *Misère* reflects the individual's inability to resolve systemic contradictions that are due to a society that manufactures high expectations without providing the resources to realize them. Nevertheless, Durkheim and Bourdieu agreed that a strong welfare state was needed to redress the normative deficit of which the forms of social life they describe are symptomatic.

However, Bourdieu apparently did *not* see Durkheim as a fellow-traveller (Grenfell 2004: 15–16). Durkheim and Bourdieu worked at opposite ends of a century-long civic republican project. Durkheim spent his career trying to build a culture of hope that republicanism might constitute a definitive advance over the false nostalgia of the Bourbons and Bonapartists who led France to an ignominious defeat in the Franco-Prussian War. For the first time, so Durkheim thought, the postwar unification and secularization of the educational system would finally incorporate all French citizens into a common sense of 'solidarity', the word he used to convey the dual political-cum-scientific associations that Auguste Comte had bequeathed to the discipline he baptized as 'sociology'. However, this policy was expanded into the distinctive French colonial practice of 'assimilation', which aggressively encouraged the colonized peoples (especially in Africa) to adopt French culture.

It was during his stint in national service, when he was charged with documenting – including by photography – differences in Algerian tribal responses to assimilationism, that Bourdieu came to realize the political immaturity and hypocrisy that this Durkheim-inspired policy had bred. 'Informed' Algerians simply reproduced the ideological divisions they read about in French newspapers, regardless of their applicability to their own circumstances. Among other things, this led to an unhelpful amplification of the differences between secular and religious cultures – now transferred from a Christian to an Islamic setting. Even the intellectual inspirations for the Algerian resistance that emerged toward the end of Bourdieu's stint – Jean-Paul Sartre and Frantz Fanon – had to be anointed in Paris before they were taken seriously in Algiers. Such a mass production of false consciousness left an indelible mark on the young Bourdieu, who devoted much of his subsequent research to undoing the damage caused by the naïve imposition of a universalist secular educational policy, which often only succeeded in intensifying social maladjustment and personal self-loathing, albeit now in the name of republican 'solidarity'.

In this line of thought, including its negative historical appraisal of Durkheim, Bourdieu found a patron in the liberal polymath Raymond Aron. Like Bourdieu himself, Aron regarded sociology as the source of solutions to the problems posed by his original field of study, philosophy. Aron made Bourdieu his teaching assistant at the Sorbonne in 1960, upon the latter's return from national service, and supported his candidacy for the directorship of L'École des Hautes Études en Sciences Sociales, from which Bourdieu launched his successful bid (now with Michel Foucault's help) to the Chair in Sociology at the Collège de France in 1981. By Anglophone standards Aron clearly belonged to the centre-left of the political spectrum, but his supporters have tended to come from the centre-right, mainly due to his consistent scepticism about extreme leftist posturing – epitomized by his great rival Sartre – that succeeded only in justifying a hypocrisy and political instability that ultimately served no one's interests. This scepticism was inherited as a default sensibility by his protégé Bourdieu, who only gradually came to believe that, despite its imperfections, a strong welfare state remained the only vehicle for addressing social problems whose normalization has rendered them invisible, such as the reproduction of class differences through the education system. Much of Bourdieu's political activism in the last decade of his life can be understood as an attempt to mobilize various groups, especially fellow writers, to put pressure on states to defend the interests of society as a whole.

Those like myself who first learned about the history of sociology from Aron's masterful two volumes of Sorbonne lectures, *Main Currents in Sociological Thought* (1965), will recall that he traces a clear line of descent from the French Revolution of 1789 through Comte and Durkheim to totalising conceptions of society in the twentieth century that deny the reality of social conflict and hence the responsibility of actual humans for whichever way society goes. Though hard to appreciate at the time, Aron was at least as much an existentialist as Sartre – if not more so. After all, Sartre often wrote as if the capitalist oppressors sufficiently appreciated the 'logic of history' to know that their days were numbered. The presence of such 'dialectical reason' both explained their efforts at ideological subterfuge and inspired Communist efforts to promote the subjugated. In contrast, Aron imagined that people always acted in what they think at the time is in their best interests but, with the benefit of hindsight, may decide to change that course of action in the future. For Sartre in his more *Marxisant* moments, people simply decided on how later historians would judge their actions, since the course of history is itself objectively determined. As for Aron, people decided directly on their fate, largely because neither the forces that had previously thwarted them nor the forces that might now liberate them are as great as Sartre imagined. There is always everything to play for, even if the odds seem initially to be stacked against you. Bourdieu inherited this attitude from Aron, which allowed him to slide gracefully between a profoundly structuralist analysis of the social order and an increasingly voluntaristic vision of the scope for political action.

Aron, whose doctoral thesis was on the philosophy of history, believed that both Karl Marx (though not followers like Sartre) and Max Weber understood the dynamic character of history much better than Durkheim. The trace of this Aronian judgement began to surface in Bourdieu's thought in the 1980s, when he chaired a state commission for the reform of primary and secondary education. In this context, Bourdieu (unsuccessfully) called for the mass re-introduction of historical instruction, so that students might 'reappropriate the structures of their own thought' (Grenfell 2004: 75). Indeed, he viewed this proposal as an opportunity for teachers to stage a 'revolt from below' against the official guardians of epistemic power at the Sorbonne and Les Grandes Écoles. The guiding idea, which Aron had learned from Karl Mannheim's sociology of knowledge, was that most claims to social necessity – such as the class-based nature of society – were really mythified accounts of contingency (Fuller 1998). The advice might be epitomized as 'teach genealogy to immunise against teleology'. Here Bourdieu made a twofold advance on Mannheim and Aron:

1   He stressed the self-imposing character of class distinctions. Marxists believed that such distinctions were ultimately subjective reflections of different social relations to the mode of production that would disappear once those relations were somehow rendered more equal, or at least equitable. However, in shifting the economic focus of class identity from production to consumption, Bourdieu acknowledged that those supposedly oppressed by the class system are complicit in its reproduction by both a valorisation of the markers of class identity (the *raison d'être* of cultural studies) and, more importantly for Bourdieu, the 'misrecognition' that results from appearing as a 'fish out of water' when one tries to move between class identities. I shall say more about the latter below.

2   He identified education as the means by which class distinctions come to be systematically self-imposed. While children acquire their accents and mores from their families, it is the school system that provides them with a grid for locating themselves in relation to others, in terms of which everyone is a more-or-less failed version of the French *savant* whose ultimate realization is a perfect score in the national competitive examinations. Moreover, this sense of universal subsumption under an unrealizable ideal is enacted in the classroom as teachers routinely communicate with minimum redundancy, assuming that the students have understood everything they have been told previously. The students realize that the assumption is always false – but also always being made. They thus become fearful of being 'caught out' for falling much shorter of the ideal than they would like to appear. This leads students to adopt strategic modes of communication that reveal enough to seem clever but not so much as to seem ignorant. This attitude continues into adulthood, propelling the flow of 'symbolic capital' in society at large.

Broadly speaking, Bourdieu's account is Machiavellian, as the key to one's power appears to lie in the ability to persuade others not to test its limits – what in the more sanguine precincts of social theory is called 'trust'. However, Bourdieu significantly complicates the Machiavellian picture by observing that a measure of one's symbolic capital is the degree of tolerance accorded to one's performance for purposes of granting credit. Someone high in symbolic capital may receive credit for performances that would discredit someone low in symbolic capital. But conversely, the latter may fail to receive credit for performances that too obviously pursue the status held by the former. Bourdieu coined the terms 'hypocorrection' and 'hypercorrection' to capture these complementary phenomena, which are illustrated by, on the one hand, the conspicuous slovenliness of aristocrats and, on the other, the scrupulous (and parodied) attempts by lower class aspirants to emulate their 'betters' (Grenfell 2004: 29).

That underachievement might be rewarded and overachievement punished is indicative of the dynamic relationship between the two most famous terms in the Bourdieusan lexicon: *habitus* and *field*, roughly, one's ingrained personal resources and the market in which their social value is determined (Grenfell 2008: Part II). However, this relationship need not be as reactionary as the paradigm cases of hypo- and hypercorrection might suggest. In revolutionary times, such as the Impressionist movement of the 1860s and the student movement of the 1960s, a field's centre of gravity may have so shifted that *everyone*'s habitus is out of sorts, in which case other fields may serve, at least temporarily, to anchor estimations of social value. Thus, money may determine the value of art and power the value of knowledge.

Society, for Bourdieu, consists of a set of fields whose forces are normally aligned, such that one's habitus appears to instantiate social determinism, as one's class position is simply reproduced across fields. But ultimately fields do not exert the same amount of force over each other. This periodically provides opportunities for field realignments that are experienced as revolutions. Unfortunately Bourdieu confused matters by trying to make common cause with Thomas Kuhn's conception of 'scientific revolutions' (Grenfell 2004: 172). The problem is that scientific revolutions result from paradigm implosions, whereas fields are realigned by other fields. It is perhaps Durkheim's revenge that Bourdieu was spectacularly ineffectual in clarifying the big picture behind his sociological observations – especially his implicit 'social physics', which seems indebted to the intellectual godfather of the structuralist turn in the human sciences, Gaston Bachelard (Grenfell 2004: 99, cf. Fuller 2000b: chap. 7). This may explain why, despite his noisy productivity, Bourdieu's sociological legacy appears to be a mere cache of abstract concepts like habitus and field.

While much has been made of the self-imposed and even self-conscious character of habitus–field relations, less has been made of their ultimately *academic* source. Once elected to the Collège de France, and hence officially France's most important sociologist, Bourdieu rediscovered his existentialist roots by addressing his own complicity in the extra-mural reach of academic power. In the guise of 'reflexive sociology', Bourdieu attempted to assume Zola's mantle as the 'universal intellectual', partly to atone for academia's role in both administering and justifying the primary mode of domination and stratification in modern democracies, the school system. For Bourdieu, the choice was simple: you either try to repeat or correct the errors of the past – of course with the emphasis on 'try'.

Interesting cross-national differences emerge about the course of action taken by social scientists once they realize their own centrality to the reproduction of much of what they regard as oppressive. Take *Schooling in Capitalist America* (Bowles and Gintis 1976), a US work comparable to Bourdieu's critical sociology of education. However, after a brief flirtation with politics, the book's authors, two Harvard-trained professors at the University of Massachusetts' socialist Economics Department, joined the Santa Fe Institute, where they now construct computer simulations of alternative socio-economic worlds, having translated their original Marxist interest in life's 'material infrastructure' into a serious flirtation with sociobiology, evolutionary psychology and complexified versions of rational-choice theory.

For his part, Bourdieu never stopped promoting certain issues in the political field even after more practically minded fellow-travellers had moved elsewhere. For example, he consistently supported positive discrimination and compensation in educational policy, even though social discrimination tended to recur on new bases (Grenfell 2004: 91). While many self-avowed leftists came to be persuaded of the futility of any state-based quest for social justice, Bourdieu insisted that all this means is that the quest is without end, as the state takes an active role to ensure that the positively discriminated do not become the new elite by unintentionally marginalizing others. Of course, the politics of endless reformism is tricky, given that positive discrimination rarely translates across all fields spontaneously: for example, the state may enable more minorities to attend university without their tastes acquiring a status commensurate with their achievement.

At the same time, it is disappointing that Bourdieu never came around to appreciating the role played by Bernard-Henri Lévy, probably France's most photogenic intellectual who first made a splash as *l'enfant terrible* in the mid-1970s when he described socialism as 'barbarism with a human face' and then went on to document in gory detail the atrocities committed by allegedly liberating forces in Yugoslavia and Afghanistan (Grenfell 2004: 152). Here Bourdieu exhibited an unforgivable sense of academic snobbery. For him, Sartre and Lévy represented two opposing, but equally false, versions of the universal intellectual. Where Sartre had recourse to the party vanguard, Lévy resorted to the global media as their respective self-serving sources of 'universalization'. (It is thus easy to see why Foucault, given his own misgivings about universal intellectuals, would have supported Bourdieu's candidacy at the Collège de France.) However, given that he himself freely changed tack over his career, Bourdieu should have been more mindful of the Machiavellian maxim 'The end justifies the means'. Bourdieu denigrated Sartre's and Lévy's universalist aspirations as vanity projects, but this is just an uncharitable way of saying that they played to their strengths: they acted on their ideals where they thought it would have most effect.

Bourdieu, of course, did no less by founding a publishing house aimed at the popular market.

Nevertheless, a deeper but equally controversial point lies behind Bourdieu's opposition to the 'media effect' (Grenfell 2004: 24). He held the mass media responsible for destroying the intellectual power originally displayed by Zola in the Dreyfus Affair. Zola appeared to be speaking from a disinterested standpoint because he was neither a partisan nor an expert witness, but simply someone who read between the lines of the newspaper accounts and drew his own conclusions (Fuller 2005: 56). The 'universality' of his judgement rested on a claim to represent the articulate opinion of an informed member of the public – in a regime where public opinion officially mattered. According to Bourdieu, today's mass media have nullified Zola's role as they recognize only partisans and experts in trials that are often largely of their own creation. Bourdieu blamed the media for overstepping the line between informing and dictating the terms of public opinion. He never considered the less flattering alternative hypothesis that most academics and writers today are rhetorically inept, that is, unskilled in the art of proportioning means to ends when dealing with the public. But even if that hypothesis proves correct, Bourdieu nevertheless deserves credit for having organized an 'International Parliament of Writers' in 1993 to oppose the global forces of neo-liberalism (Grenfell 2004: 154). If nothing else, his heart was always in the right place – to quote the title of Germany's former Social Democratic Finance Minister Oskar Lafontaine's memoirs, 'It beats on the left' (Lafontaine 2000).

Finally, there is the status of the English-speaking world as the premier colonial battleground for French intellectual infighting at least since 1970 (Cusset 2008). In this all-important arena, Bourdieu's significance, if not undermined, has been systematically limited (e.g. Schinkel 2003). The battle over Bourdieu's Anglophone impact was engaged once he was elected to the Collège de France. Jon Elster's (1981) mixed review of *La Distinction* in the *London Review of Books* appeared three years before its English translation. Elster completed his PhD under Aron's supervision a decade after Bourdieu but was aligned with Bourdieu's rival, Raymond Boudon, who is known as France's leading rational-choice theorist, a perspective Elster subsequently imported into Marxism. Without denying Elster's insightful critical comparison of Bourdieu and Thorstein Veblen, he nevertheless managed to neutralize the negative import that Bourdieu had attached to the concepts of symbolic and cultural capital, which in turn helped paved the way for the acceptance of 'social capital' as a largely positive idea in the policy and academic circles of the neo-liberal 1980s and 1990s.

In recent years, the main source of hostility to Bourdieu has emanated from allies of his other great generational rival, the social movement theorist Alain Touraine. Touraine turns out to have been an early inspiration for Michel Callon's actor–network theory, the leading school of science and technology studies today (Barry and Slater 2002: 305). Both Boudon and Touraine may be seen as responding to the palpable failures of the welfare state in the late twentieth century. For Boudon the failure lay in a socialist ideology that was incapable of – and not necessary for – sustaining the successes achieved by modern liberal democracies. For Touraine, in contrast, the failure lay in the trust that had been placed in liberal-democratic procedures (i.e. voting), which the postmodern era had demonstrated to be an inappropriate vehicle for expressing genuine social interests. It is customary to stereotype the difference between Boudon and Touraine in terms of the individualism vs. communitarianism, but this would miss the point of their opposition to Bourdieu. Boudonian sociology calls for a very tight fit between the state and civil society, such that the state simply executes what society decides, whereas Tourainian sociology calls for a very loose fit between the two, whereby the state is merely one – and by no means the most powerful – agent amidst the self-organizing tendencies of civil society. Nevertheless, seen from Bourdieu's 'born again' civic republican standpoint, both positions short-change the state's capacity for good by redirecting statistically dominant social tendencies.

To conclude this career retrospective, let us contrast the spirit of Bourdieu's original field work in Algeria with that undertaken nearly twenty years later in the Ivory Coast by another then-fledgling ethnographer, Bruno Latour, actor–network theory's most celebrated practitioner. Both were concerned with the distinctly French problem of assimilation, indeed, specifically the impact of French managerial knowledge on native farming practices. It was here, for example, that Bourdieu first used the term *'déracinement'* to refer to the 'uprooting' of indigenous agricultural knowledge but later extended this to cover the full range of alienation caused by assimilationist policies (Grenfell 2004: 44).

However, Bourdieu's was a late colonial and Latour's a post-colonial Africa. Whereas Bourdieu wanted the Algerians to recover their autonomy from the French, Latour was more interested in enabling the Ivorians to incorporate French practices into their own, so as to facilitate trade relations. Latour found that French instructors were more likely to succeed at this goal if they worked with what the Ivorians already knew and did not try so hard to be 'French' in their top-down abstract presentation of economics and engineering (Latour and Woolgar 1986: 273–274). At the time, Latour's ethnography was seen as yet another blow against Eurocentrism in the tradition of Bourdieu's earlier efforts. Indeed, Latour's classic ethnography of the scientific habitat, *Laboratory Life* (Latour and Woolgar 1986), first published less than a decade after Latour's African fieldwork, bears the influence of Bourdieu's 'circulation of capitals' model of scientific credibility. However, under Callon's influence and once Bourdieu trounced Touraine at the Collège de France, Latour shifted to what his ethnography had really been all along, namely, a case study on how to open up markets by extending networks in a global neo-liberal order that is *both* post-colonial and post-French, thereby dissipating the conception of society Bourdieu had heroically striven to uphold.

4

The Improvisational Nature of Intellectual Life

Academics Caught Between Plagiarism and Bullshit

The canonical form of academic communication is the oral delivery of a written text. Powerpoint may be increasingly used but the general idea remains the same: academics think out loud by following a script. We take this sort of activity as indicative of deliberate thought, careful reasoning and, not least, respect for the audience. But perhaps all it shows is that academics literally do not know what they are talking about. We are the ugly autocuties. More to the point, it may prove that we are not very intelligent – or at least don't know how to recognize or value intelligence. Truly intelligent people know how to improvize well. Academics don't.

One would think that a life spent single-mindedly immersed in a subject matter would make academics at least as much adept as performers as professional actors who spend much less time ranging over many more roles – and possibly leaving a much more lasting impression. On the contrary, the one aspect of academic life in which such skills might be cultivated, classroom lecturing, tends to be treated with considerable suspicion, especially if it elicits a strong response, either positive or negative, from student audiences. Education may well play second fiddle to research in academia today. But even those who claim to defend education quite happily dump the lecture as a medium of instruction. I suppose they think that if the score is all that matters, then the difference between a virtuoso and a novice performer doesn't matter, as long as the right notes are struck most of the time.

Alas, improvisation is a skill that goes unrewarded, if not actively despised, in academia. When in doubt, we quickly reach for the 'bullshit detector' to belittle the improviser. Yet, too much of what passes for intellectual activity in our own quarters is little more than meeting well-defined expectations, if not sheer template-matching. We decry rote memorization merely because it is old-fashioned. But aren't today's cut-and-paste Powerpoint presentations even dumber? No wonder hope springs eternal for mechanical models of artificial intelligence!

Moreover, administrators are not to blame for this behaviour. If anything, they might be thanked for rewarding tendencies that academics already spontaneously display. But perhaps our gratitude is already expressed in the ease with which we adapt to each new academic audit regime. Maybe only then do we become good at improvisation. We hate when students ask what counts as a good answer, but only because they correctly realize that exam-taking is little more than literary marksmanship.

At a slightly more sophisticated level, shadows may be cast over an academic's entire body of work, especially within one's own discipline, by showing that she has failed to say or do particular things just right. To use the crypto-moral, pseudo-rigorous term that academics prefer on these occasions, such a colleague is 'unreliable'. But why should a failure to conform in detail be taken as indicative of anything deeper than minor errors? No known theory of rationality supports a harsher judgement. But then theories of rationality tend to value accuracy only insofar as it bears on something relevant, while academics value relevance insofar as it accurately hits their expertise.

There was a time – say, 500 or more years ago – when it made sense for academics to, quite literally, 'do things by the book'. Back then reading from a prepared text provided students with an opportunity to copy something required for their studies that they would otherwise not possess. But this was before the printing press, personal libraries, cheap paperbacks, let alone the worldwide web. Yet, those bygone days of primitive knowledge transmission persist not merely in our bad lecturing habits but in the very fact that we call it a 'lecture', which derives from the Latin for reading out loud.

Of course, there is nothing wrong with an academic using a pile of books as a prop, from which she pulls one out 'at random' to read a few sentences sonorously and then launches into a riff that is the intellectual equivalent of virtuoso jazz or the actor John Sessions at his best on the early 1990s British TV improvisational revue *Whose Line Is It Anyway?* The attractiveness of this practice, more so in Franco-German than English circles, rests on the idea that imitation may be the sincerest form of domination.

When old school humanists complain that today's students read more literary criticism than literature, they are not merely bemoaning the search for intellectual quick fixes. After all, much literary criticism is at least as difficult as the literature it claims to criticize. Rather, the humanists begrudge the talents of the academic improviser whose own performance can make the original text look much less interesting by comparison – should one then bother to read it. Indeed, the literary critic Harold Bloom made his career at Yale by using a little Freud to generalize this point into a strategy for achieving literary greatness. In *The Anxiety of Influence* (1973), Bloom argued that all poets live in the fear that their dead intellectual fathers – that is, the people whose work they have plagiarized – will be discovered. Great poets turn out to be the ones whose improvisational skills allow them to get away with murder.

In the case of academic culture, the recent metastasis of the plagiarism taboo into a full-blown moral panic over the security of intellectual property rights suggests that behind the disdain for improvisation may lurk an admission of intellectual weakness. After all, would the stealing of text and ideas appear so criminal if we took seriously that, regardless of its provenance, any product of the mind is open to multiple novel uses and that, in any case, there are always many more things to think and say? Here we catch sight of the sin that the improviser commits: she refuses to say exactly what she knows or know exactly what she says. On the one hand, she presents the established as if it were novel. That's plagiarism. On the other, she presents the novel as if it were established. That's bullshit. From this unholy alliance of plagiarism and bullshit, the improviser conspires to make a virtue out of unreliability.

A more relaxed view towards matters of reliability can often be found among those outside the academic's home discipline, a safe distance away from its guild pieties. To be sure, this can quite literally result in 'fabulous' judgements of the intellectual merit of people's work. A good case in point is Thomas Kuhn, the populariser of 'paradigm' and 'scientific revolution', who was the most influential theorist of science in the second half of the twentieth century. Kuhn is celebrated as a historian, philosopher, sociologist and even psychologist of science. However, as someone trained only in physics, he skated on thin ice in all these fields and, by practitioner standards, often fell through the cracks. Yet, he is hailed as a genius.

And Kuhn *would* have been a genius, if what he achieved was what he had set out to do. He would have been a great improviser who started from clear themes in various disciplines, taking them in novel directions that ignored or contradicted actual developments in those disciplines. Like the great actors and musicians given to improvisation, his genius would have then rested on having demonstrated enough technical mastery to allow his audience to ignore any remaining deficiency. Why? The freedom permitted by that deficiency resulted in something superior to what would have resulted from merely doing things right. But Kuhn proved to be more idiot than savant. He was completely flummoxed by his reception and refused to play along with it. Indeed, his subsequent work left the impression that his magnum opus, *The Structure of Scientific Revolutions* (1970), had been a fluke. The true improviser, if he admits to bluffing at all, would do so only at the end of his career.

In contrast, consider Kuhn's French contemporary, Louis Althusser, the most influential Western Marxist of the 1970s, who admitted in his memoirs that most of what he knew about Marx came from hearsay and his students' essays. To be sure, his star has fallen much more precipitously than Kuhn's. Even worse than an idiot is a savant who makes everyone else look like an idiot. But that trait alone need not be damning, if others eventually come along and play your role straight, with everything laid out in good academic order. Unfortunately, Althusser's improvisational skills were devoted to intellectually engaging defences of Marxism's most totalitarian tendencies. Had the Communists won the Cold War, he might still be considered a genius.

Lest I unduly discourage would-be academic improvisers, let me turn now to the grandmaster of the species, someone whose exquisite sense of world-historic timing allowed him to stay one step ahead of his doubters, while remaining one step behind his vindicators. I refer to that icon of the Scientific Revolution, Galileo Galilei, who was full of what the Italian Renaissance called *sprezzatura*, a broad term for the improviser's art that runs the gamut from 'making it up on the spot' to 'thinking for oneself'. The data of Galileo's famed experiments were massaged, when not outright manufactured. He claimed great powers for a telescope whose images were blurry and whose optics he could not explain. On top of all that, Galileo did not merely propose an alternative view of the cosmos. Unlike his timid precursor Copernicus, he explicitly said that his view should replace the Church's. No doubt, had the next two generations of scientists not been inspired to make good on Galileo's improvisations, his reputation would now be languishing either in Purgatory, alongside Kuhn's, or in Hell, alongside Althusser's.

The stories of Kuhn, Althusser and Galileo – and their varying fates – highlight improvisation's unique brand of intelligence. Its genius can be maintained only by sustained engagement with the audience, since it is quite literally an art that is made up as one goes along. Often that interaction consists in reassuring the audience that each strange turn is indeed for the better, as the suspension of disbelief is rewarded by a pleasant surprise that causes one to reassess all that had previously transpired. In that respect, as we saw with Galileo, the improviser is always playing for more time.

So what would an improvisation-friendly academia look like? Certainly standards of public performance would shift. We would become more tolerant of people who speak crudely without notes, if they can improve as they take questions from the audience. But we would equally become less tolerant of people who refuse to take questions simply because they stray from their carefully prepared presentation. Instead of 'sloppy/rigorous', we would apply the binary 'expansive/limited' to describe the respective intellects of these people.

This shift in standards may have some interesting knock-on effects. Academics might question the 'value added' of inviting a speaker who does little more than rehearse well-publicized writings. They might become more assertive in propozing to speakers topics outside their intellectual comfort zones, perhaps even as a condition of their invitation. Overall these developments might convert the lecture from the usual re-hydration of freeze-dried thought into an occasion for full-blooded inquiry.

My first taste of academic improvisation came in maths class in a Jesuit high school. Students were invited to complete a geometric proof. Even if the first student got it right, the teacher would continue to ask, 'Does anyone think otherwise?' Without fail, many of us would propose all sorts of ingenious – usually wrong – alternatives. The teacher would wait for us to run dry and then break the bad news. But he would go on to show that most, if not all, of those alternatives had a sound basis that worked in other contexts. None of us knew what to expect of each other in such classroom encounters, yet they almost always worked. After all, the cause of inquiry is better served by being interestingly wrong than being reliably right.

Bullshit: A Disease Whose Cure Is Always Worse

Harry Frankfurt's (2005) *On Bullshit* is the latest contribution to a long, distinguished, yet deeply problematic line of Western thought that has attempted to redeem the idea of intellectual integrity from the cynic's suspicion that it is nothing but high-minded, self-serving prejudice. I say 'problematic' because while Plato's unflattering portrayal of poets and sophists arguably marked the opening salvo in the philosophical war against bullshit, Plato availed himself of bullshit in promoting the 'myth of the metals' as a principle of social stratification in his *Republic*. This doublethink has not been lost on the neo-conservative followers of the great twentieth-century Platonist Leo Strauss.

To their credit, some of history's great bullshit detectors – though not Frankfurt nor his role model Ludwig Wittgenstein – have pled guilty as charged without hesitation. Friedrich Nietzsche and his great American admirer the journalist H.L. Mencken, who coined the euphemism 'bunk', come to mind. It helped that they were also cynics. They never held back from passing a moral judgement on those they debunked. Moreover, both even tried to explain the adaptive advantage of specific forms of bullshit: bullshitters may be craven but they are not stupid. Jews, Christians and Muslims – or, more precisely, their clerics – may lack any definitive proof of a transcendent deity, but the sheer possibility of its existence does wonders to focus the mind and discipline the body in often politically effective ways.

Nietzsche's and Mencken's multifarious pronouncements invited others to judge them: does either the mentally unstable Nietzsche or the hard-drinking Mencken inspire confidence in our ability to live in a bullshit-free world? More generally, does the dogged pursuit of bullshit refine or coarsen one's sense of humanity or, for that matter, raise or lower one's likelihood of recognizing the truth if confronted with it? For everyone who saw Nietzsche and Mencken as exposing false prophets, there were others who viewed them as the ultimate Doubting Thomases. If bullshit is too easily found, and found to run too deep, the bullshit detector's own judgement is reasonably called into question. Henrik Ibsen's classic dramas *The Wild Duck* and *Hedda Gabler* explored this prospect in terms of the need for a 'life lie'. For their part, both Nietzsche and Mencken have been dubbed 'nihilists' by their detractors, who reverse the harsh light of truth to reveal the bullshit detector as a self-appointed absolutist who happens to take an unhealthy interest in people whose minds he is incapable of either respecting or changing. Scratch a nihilist, and you get a dogmatist in exile.

The bullshit detector aims to convert an epistemic attitude into a moral virtue: reality can be known only by the right sort of person. This idea, while meeting with widespread approval by philosophers strongly tied to the classical tradition of Plato and Aristotle, is not lacking in dissenters. The line of dissent is best seen in the history of 'rhetoric', a word Plato coined to demonize Socrates' dialectical opponents, the sophists. The sophists were prepared to teach anyone the art of winning arguments, provided you could pay the going rate. As a series of sophistic interlocutors tried to make clear to Socrates, possession of the skills required to secure the belief of your audience is the only knowledge you really need to have. Socrates famously attacked this claim on several fronts, which the subsequent history of philosophy has often conflated. In particular, Socrates' doubts about the reliability of the sophists' techniques have been run together with a more fundamental criticism: even granting the sophists their skills, they are based on a knowledge of human gullibility, not of reality itself.

Bullshit is sophistry under this charitable reading, which acknowledges that the truth may not be strong enough by itself to counteract an artfully presented claim that is not so much outright false as, in the British idiom, 'economical with the truth'. In stressing the difference between bullshit and lies, Frankfurt clearly has this conception in mind, though he does sophistry a disservice by casting the bullshitter's attitude toward the truth as 'indifference'. On the contrary, the accomplished bullshitter must be a keen student of what people tend to regard as true, if only to cater to those tendencies so as to serve her own ends. What likely offends Frankfurt and other philosophers here is the idea that the truth is just one more tool to be manipulated for personal advantage. Conceptual frameworks are simply entertained and then discarded as their utility passes. The nature of the offence, I suspect, is the divine eye-view implicated in such an attitude – the very idea that one could treat in a detached fashion the terms in which people normally negotiate their relationship to reality. A bullshitter revealed becomes a god unmade.

The theological overtones are deliberate. In the hierarchy of Christian sins, bullshit's closest kin is *hypocrisy*, the official target of Nietzsche's and Mencken's ire. However, as Max Weber famously observed with regard to the rise of capitalism, Christians were not uniform in their condemnation of hypocrisy. Some treated it more as an unfortunate by-product in the efficient pursuit of ends. Benjamin Franklin's *Autobiography* developed this position with striking explicitness. Indeed, Franklin modelled his understanding of 'economical with the truth' on the economy one might exercise in the use of any valuable resource. A lesson he claimed to have learned in life was that one's truthfulness should always be proportional to the demands of the speech situation. It is always possible to say either too much or too little, speaking truthfully in each case, yet ending up appearing as either incompetent or dishonest. Such verbal misfirings benefit no one, though it may have served to represent some abstract sense of 'truth'. (For an updated defence of Franklin's position, epitomized as 'the civilizing force of hypocrisy', see Elster 1998.)

Franklin's advice is often read as a counsel of cynicism, but it marked a crucial transition in the conception of the human mind from a passive receptacle to a creative agency. Like many other US founding fathers,

Franklin's Christianity veered toward Unitarianism, according to which the person of Jesus signifies that the human and the divine intellects differ in degree not kind. Just as the biblical God communicated with humans on a 'need-to-know' basis without total revelation, in part to stimulate our own God-like powers as free agents, so too should be the ethic that governs secular human communication. The result is that we elicit from each other our own creative potential. The success of this injunction can be measured by advertising's colonization of corporate budgets in modern times: what sells is ultimately not intrinsic to the product but one's idea of the product, which advertising invites the consumer to form for herself.

Whatever one makes of Franklin's theology, it is clear that bullshitters *qua* hypocrites are rough cognitive equals of liars and truth-tellers, not people who lack a specific competence that, were they to possess it, would inhibit their propensity to bullshit. I stress this point because bullshit detectors gain considerable rhetorical mileage by blurring the epistemic and ethical dimensions of the phenomenon they wish to root out. Often this involves postulating a psychologically elusive state of *integrity*. To be sure, in these democratic times, bullshit detectors are rarely so overt as to declare that bullshitters lack 'good character', which might suggest something objectionable, let alone unprovable, about the bullshitters' upbringing or even genetic makeup. Nevertheless, the emerging literature in 'virtue epistemology' courts just such uninhibited judgements (Zagzebski and Fairweather 2001).

But the same impression can be conjured by other means. For example, ten years ago, Alan Sokal notoriously argued that French literary philosophers and their American admirers would not have so easily inferred postmodern conclusions from cutting-edge mathematical physics had they been scientifically literate: if you knew more, or were better trained, you would behave better (Sokal and Bricmont 1998). But notice what 'behave better' means: it is not that the Francophile philosophers should have derived *anti*-postmodern conclusions from cutting-edge science; rather, according to Sokal, they should have refrained from drawing any conclusions whatsoever, since the science does not speak directly to the wider cultural issues that interest the Francophile philosophers. (Of course, this position is harder to maintain with a straight face when such great scientists as Bohr and Heisenberg seem to have crossed the line themselves.)

Thus, while it is convenient to focus on the lightly veiled incompetence of bullshitters, bullshit detectors are ultimately disturbed by what they take to be the lack of self-discipline revealed by the bullshitter's verbal camouflage. When venturing into terrain yet to be colonized by a recognized expertise, where 'true' and 'false' are not clearly signposted, bullshitters assert authoritatively rather than remain silent. What accounts for this difference in attitude? A distinction borrowed from Kant and conventionally used to understand the history of early modern philosophy comes to mind: bullshitters and bullshit detectors examine the same uncertain knowledge situation from, respectively, a *rationalist* and an *empiricist* perspective. Bullshitters see the resolution of uncertainty in terms of selecting one from a number of already imaginable alternatives, whereas bullshit detectors seek some externally caused experience – a.k.a. evidence – to determine where lies the truth. I shall argue that the scientific method is largely a 'dialectical synthesis' of these two attitudes, by which I mean that each cancels out the excesses of the other to produce a more powerful form of knowledge than either could provide alone.

Bullshit detectors take comfort in the fact that the time required to master a body of knowledge virtually guarantees the initiate's loyalty to its corresponding practices and central dogmas. Moreover, the overarching discipline may have been crafted over the years to render as difficult as possible the contrary 'truth' a bullshitter might wish to advance. In Thomas Kuhn's hands, this tendency was enshrined as 'normal science'. According to Kuhn, a radical alternative to the scientific orthodoxy must await the self-destruction of the dominant paradigm, which may take a very long time, as ill-defined conceptual objections (a.k.a. bullshit) struggle against the paradigm's made-to-order empirical successes. Equally, the self-transformation from potential critic to compliant subject is a matter of reducing what social psychologists call 'cognitive dissonance': how could all that scientific training effort have been in vain, especially once it has resulted in a secure social identity and (perhaps less secure) means of employment? The mathematician Blaise Pascal's famous wager is a very general version of this line of thought: we should bet our lives on God's existence by adopting a Christian lifestyle that would then make us receptive to any signs of divine presence, should they ever appear. As in science, so too in religion: discovery favours the prepared mind.

But what if it were made easier to assert and challenge knowledge claims without having to undergo the personal transformation required of, say, doctoral training? In the absence of such institutionalized immunity to bullshit, the result would be a sophist's paradise. Truth would be decided on the day by whoever happens to have the stronger argument or survives some mutually agreed test. Never mind prior track records or prima facie plausibility: show me here and now. The scientific method was developed largely in this frame of mind, one deeply distrustful of all forms of authority, be it based on a canonical text or some canonical representation of collective experience. This distrust fed on the frequently observed failure of authoritative statements to accord with what one's spontaneously thinks, feels or experiences.

The signature moment in the Western tradition for this sentiment, which made the hearer's conscience – and not the speaker's sincerity – the final court of appeal, was the guilt that Martin Luther continued to feel even after having been exonerated of sin in the Catholic sacrament of Penance. This provoked a more wide-ranging questioning of Catholicism's royal road of ritual to divine salvation. The result was Protestantism's greater tolerance for bullshit, with the understanding that everyone skates on thin ice in this life. The phrase 'playing it by ear' captures well the inevitably improvisational character of attending to conscience as a guide to truth. In the end, there is only one bullshit detector: God. Accept no substitutes.

The bullshit detector believes not only that there is a truth but also that her own access to it is sufficiently reliable and general to serve as a standard by which others may be held accountable. Protestants appeared prepared to accept the former but not the latter condition, which is why dissenters were encouraged – or perhaps ostracized – to establish their own ministries. The sophists appeared to deny the former and possibly the latter condition as well. Both Protestants and sophists are prime candidates for the spread of bullshit because they concede that we may normally address reality in terms it does not recognize – or at least do not require it to yield straight 'yes-or-no', 'true-or-false' answers. In that case, we must make up the difference between the obliqueness of our inquiries and the obtuseness of reality's responses. That 'difference' is fairly seen as bullshit. When crystallized as a philosophy of mind or philosophy of language, this attitude is known as *antirealism*. Its opposite number, the background philosophy of bullshit detectors, is *realism*.

The difference in the spirit of the two philosophies is captured as follows: do you believe that everything you say and hear is bullshit unless you have some way of showing whether it is true or false; or rather, that everything said and heard is simply true or false, unless it is revealed to be bullshit? The former is the *antirealist*, the latter the *realist* response. Seen in those terms, we might say that the antirealist regards reality as inherently risky and always under construction (*Caveat credor:* 'Let the believer beware!') whereas the realist treats reality as, on the whole, stable and orderly – except for the reprobates who try to circumvent the system by producing bullshit. In this respect, *On Bullshit* may be usefully read as an *ad hominem* attack on antirealists. Frankfurt himself makes passing reference to this interpretation near the end of the essay (Frankfurt 2005: 64–65). Yet, he appears happy to promote the vulgar image of antirealism as intellectually, and perhaps morally, slipshod, instead of treating it as the philosophically honorable position that it is.

A case in point is Frankfurt's presentation of Wittgenstein as one of history's great bullshit detectors (Frankfurt 2005: 24–34). He offers a telling anecdote in which the Viennese philosopher objects to Fania Pascal's self-description as having been 'sick as a dog'. Wittgenstein reportedly told Pascal that she misused language by capitalizing on the hearer's easy conflation of a literal falsehood with a genuine condition, which is made possible by the hearer's default anthropocentric bias. Wittgenstein's objection boils down to claiming that, outside clearly marked poetic contexts, our intellectual end never suffices alone to justify our linguistic means. Frankfurt treats this point as a timeless truth about how language structures reality. Yet, it would be quite easy, especially recalling that this 'truth' was uttered seventy years ago, to conclude that Wittgenstein's irritation betrays a spectacular lack of imagination in the guise of scrupulousness.

Wittgenstein's harsh judgement presupposes that humans lack any real access to canine psychology, which renders any appeal to dogs purely fanciful. For him, this lack of access is an established fact inscribed in a literal use of language, not an open question answers to which a figurative use of language might offer clues for further investigation. Nevertheless, scientists informed by the Neo-Darwinian synthesis – which was being forged just at the time of Wittgenstein's pronouncement – have quite arguably narrowed the gap between the mental lives of humans and animals in research associated with 'evolutionary psychology'. As this research makes more headway, what Wittgenstein confidently declared to be bullshit in his day may tomorrow appear as having been a prescient truth. But anyone holding such a fluid view of verifiability would derive scant comfort from either Wittgenstein or Frankfurt, who act as if English linguistic intuitions, circa 1935, should count indefinitely as demonstrable truths.

Some philosophers given to bullshit detection are so used to treating any Wittgensteinian utterance as a profundity that it never occurs to them that Wittgenstein may have been himself a grandmaster of bullshit. The great bullshit detectors whom I originally invoked, Nietzsche and Mencken, made themselves vulnerable to critics by speaking from their own self-authorizing standpoint, which supposedly afforded a clear vista for distinguishing bullshit from its opposite. Wittgenstein adopts the classic bullshitter's technique of *ventriloquism*, speaking through the authority of someone or something else in order to be spared the full brunt of criticism.

I use 'adopts' advisedly, since the deliberateness of Wittgenstein's rhetoric remains unclear. What was he trying to do: to speak modestly without ever having quite controlled his spontaneously haughty manner, or to exercise his self-regarding superiority as gently as possible so as not to frighten the benighted? Either way, Wittgenstein became – for a certain kind of philosopher – the standard-bearer of linguistic rectitude, where 'language' is treated as a proxy for reality itself. Of course, to the bullshitter, this description also fits someone whose strong personality cowed the impressionable into distrusting their own thought processes. As with most successful bullshit, the trick is revealed only after it has had the desired effect and the frame of reference has changed. Thus, Wittgenstein's precious concern about Pascal's account of her state of health should strike, at least some readers today, as akin to a priest's fretting over a parishioner's confession of impure thoughts. In each case, the latter is struck by something that lies outside the box in which the former continues to think.

If Wittgenstein was a bullshitter, how did he manage to take in professed enemies of bullshit like Frankfurt? One clue is that most bullshit is forward-looking, and Wittgenstein's wasn't. The bullshitter normally refers to things whose prima facie plausibility immunizes the hearer against checking their actual validity. The implication is that the proof is simply 'out there' waiting be found. But is there really such proof? Here the bullshitter is in a race against time. A sufficient delay in checking sources has salvaged the competence and even promoted the prescience of many bullshitters. Such was the spirit of Paul Feyerabend's (1975) notorious account of Galileo's 'discoveries', which concluded that his Papal Inquisitors were originally justified in their scepticism, even though Galileo's followers subsequently redeemed his epistemic promissory notes.

In contrast, Wittgenstein's unique brand of bullshit was backward-looking, always reminding hearers and readers of something they should already know but had perhaps temporarily forgotten. Since Wittgenstein usually confronted his interlocutors with mundane examples, it was relatively easy to convey this impression. The trick lay in immediately shifting the context from the case at hand to what Oxford philosophers in the 1950s called a 'paradigm case' that was presented as a self-evident standard of usage against which to judge the case at hand. That Wittgenstein, a non-native speaker of English, impressed one or two generations of Britain's philosophical elite with just this mode of argumentation remains the envy of the aspiring bullshitter. Ernest Gellner (1959), another émigré from the old Austro-Hungarian Empire, ended up ostracized from the British philosophical establishment for offering a cutting diagnosis of this phenomenon as it was unfolding. He suggested that Wittgenstein's success testified to his ability to feed off British class anxiety, which was most clearly marked in language use. An academically sublimated form of such language-driven class anxiety remains in the discipline of sociolinguistics (Bernstein 1971–77).

Yet, after nearly a half-century, Gellner's diagnosis is resisted, despite the palpable weakening of Wittgenstein's posthumous grip on the philosophical imagination. One reason is that so many living philosophers still ride on Wittgenstein's authority – if not his mannerisms – that to declare him a bullshitter would amount to career suicide. But a second reason is also operative, one that functions as an insurance policy against future debunkers. Wittgenstein is often portrayed, by himself and others, as mentally unbalanced. You might think that this would render his philosophical deliverances unreliable. On the contrary, Wittgenstein's erratic disposition is offered as evidence for his spontaneously guileless nature – quite unlike the controlled and calculated character of bullshitters. Bullshit fails to stick to Wittgenstein because he is regarded as an *idiot savant*. In contrast, bullshit detectors direct their fire at those capable of making a strategic distinction in their own minds between the current state of evidence and the state of belief in which they would like to leave their interlocutors. We have seen this mentality before. It is best called by its classical name: 'hypocrisy', a word that derives from the masks actors wore in Greek dramas.

The bullshitter is the consummate hypocrite. This sounds damning if you imagine that on the masked side of the hypocrite's mental divide is a clear sense of where the weight of evidence lies. But if you imagine instead that behind the hypocrite's mask lurks a deep uncertainty about the truth, then the outward image is a defiant, though possibly doomed, gesture to inject some order into an otherwise chaotic world. At this point, some readers might query the wisdom of portraying bullshitters as heroic Existentialists, bluffing their way out of the abyss. After all, on most matters, don't we usually have a reasonably clear sense of which way the evidence points? If so, the only relevant decision is whether to admit, deny, or spin what one believes. However, as might be expected, the bullshitter's take on evidence is not so straightforward. It is influenced by the sophistic principle that to control the moment of decision is to control its outcome. The first line of sophistry, then, is to call the question when the balance of arguments is to one's advantage. But provided there is sufficient time, resources and wit, the truth of *any* proposition can be demonstrated – or so the sophists presumed. The problem is that we are rarely afforded these luxuries, and so there is a strong temptation simply to declare for what strikes us now as most evident.

Bullshitters stress the impressionistic character of this decision, since contrary to promiscuous appeals to 'reliability' in both philosophical and public discourse, we are usually in no position to assess the actual track records of those who would lay claim to our beliefs. We might be able to access a partial record or, more likely, recall our personal experience, as coloured by the vagaries of memory. Perhaps this is why epistemologists have increasingly leaned on the quasi-moral concept of 'trust', and affiliated theological notions of 'witness' and 'testimony', to make up the difference between our genuine strength of feeling towards a proposition and the actual paucity of our evidence in its favour (e.g. Kusch and Lipton 2002). Under the benign interpretation of the Scottish cleric Thomas Reid, the spark of the divine in the human (a.k.a. common sense) ensures that, in the main, humans are reliable sources of information. But under the malign reading of those touched by the more heretical Kierkegaard, the prevalence of such concepts simply betrays our cowardice, as we delegate to others the responsibility for beliefs we should take personally, admitting error when shown wrong but otherwise accepting modest credit for having expressed them. Among those touched by Kierkegaard in this way was the young Karl Popper, whom consequently I have dubbed a 'scientific existentialist' (Hacohen 2000: 83–84; Fuller 2003: 100–110). In any case, by papering over the gap between evidence and belief, reliability would appear to be a bullshit concept – a problem, of course, only for those like Frankfurt keen on eliminating bullshit.

It is possible to detect the bullshit in the bullshit detectors by setting up an analogy between the *epistemic economy of evidence* and the *moral economy of sensation*. Evidence for what is true and false is typically described in the same terms of 'compelling experience' as sensations of pleasure and pain. But why should we be so easily moved by evidence in spheres of knowing, when most philosophers would not have us automatically succumb to sensation in spheres of acting? For example, Utilitarianism, the modern ethical theory most closely tied to a moral economy of sensations, explains welfare in terms of the deferment of immediate gratification in favour of a more substantial good projected in the long term. Thus, the redistribution of income afforded by taxation insures against our tendency to discount the value of our future selves or, for that matter, future generations.

Similarly, the bullshitter's imperviousness to the current weighting of the evidence may be understood as an attempt to forgo the opportunity costs associated with discounting what might turn out to be, in the fullness of time, a more promising line of inquiry. Analogous to taxation here would be an 'affirmative action' strategy that would handicap better evidenced positions so as to give weaker ones a chance to develop. In terms of the inter-temporal comparison of the evidence base for knowledge claims in the known present and the imagined future, one would therefore sacrifice a short-term adherence to 'only the truth' in favour of a long-term commitment to 'the whole truth'. (For a discussion of this as a trade-off between 'correspondence' and 'coherence' theories of truth, see Fuller 2005: 51–60.) As Franklin might put it, the virtue exemplified in both the moral and the epistemic economies is *prudence*: the one saves for the future, whereas the other plays for time.

The Scientific Method as a Search for the (Piled) Higher (and Deeper) Bullshit

The natural conclusion to draw from these considerations so far is that bullshit abounds, not least among those keen on detecting and removing it. But must this be such a bad thing? The success of Francis Bacon's invention of the scientific method suggests that it might not be so bad, as long as everyone admits upfront they are producing bullshit, and decisions about what is and is not bullshit are left to a third party. Bacon wrote as the top lawyer to England's King James I in the early seventeenth century, a period we now describe as having been in great scientific and religious ferment, though the difference between these two sources of unrest was not so clear at the time. Bacon realized as much. Radical religious thinkers often proposed and occasionally proved knowledge claims of general scientific merit. Yet, they typically insisted that only those sharing their religious commitments were fit to test and appreciate the validity of those claims. Bacon saw that the public interest was best served by devising a way to test the validity of knowledge claims without having to accept whatever controversial metaphysical assumptions might have motivated the claimants. This procedure – the scientific method – was modelled on a trial, indeed, of the sort conducted in the inquisitorial legal systems of Continental Europe, which Bacon admired (Franklin 2001: 217–218).

What distinguishes the inquisitorial from the accusatorial system traditionally favoured in England is that the judge, as opposed to the plaintiff, frames the terms of the trial. This typically means that before a verdict is reached, the judge will have conducted his own investigation of, say, what counts as normal conduct in the relevant sphere of life, in order to determine whether the defendant is being held to an unreasonably high standard – or, equally, a reasonable standard that few people actually meet. Thus, it is not sufficient for the plaintiff to prove her case on its merits. In addition, it must be clear that the defendant is not being unfairly singled out for something that, for better or worse, is routinely tolerated. After all, the defendant may be guilty as charged but others are potentially guilty of much worse, in which case the judge must consider how – and whether – justice is served by making an example out of the defendant.

A notorious recent example of how a shift from an accusatorial to an inquisitorial perspective can significantly affect the disposition of a case is that of the political scientist Bjørn Lomborg, whose international best seller *The Sceptical Environmentalist* (Lomborg 2001) was brought before the Danish Research Council's Committee on Scientific Dishonesty by an entrepreneur in alternative energy sources who held that Lomborg had systematically distorted research findings in ways that undermined his business. Lomborg's basic message was that the future of the global environment is not nearly as desperate as most ecologists make it out to be. The plaintiff received major foreign support from, among others, *Scientific American* magazine and E.O. Wilson, founder of sociobiology and latter-day champion of biodiversity.

Lomborg was initially found guilty, but the verdict was overturned on appeal – indeed, the very purpose of the Committee on Scientific Dishonesty was called into question – because it appeared that Lomborg was unfairly targeted, given that in the field of environmental studies, the politicization of research is the norm not the exception. Lomborg was guilty of little more than having extrapolated from the relevant statistical data a much more optimistic ecological forecast than usual. But all such extrapolations are ultimately speculative and motivated to raise consciousness among research funders, policy makers and the general public. In other words, no special legal action is necessary because these matters are already fairly aired and debated, leaving audiences to draw their own conclusions (Fuller 2007b: 159–170).

The history of the Lomborg case beautifully illustrates how a legal proceeding can foster both the manufacture and removal of bullshit. The plaintiff held the defendant uniquely responsible for an event backed by the testimony of impressive experts, while the defendant professed his own purity of motive and questioned the politics of his accusers. Bullshit abounds here on both sides. In his inquisitorial role, the judge (in this case, a panel) was expected to devise a test that would conclusively decide between the two parties by virtue of incorporating their shared assumptions and eliminating the ones they contested. Transferred to the scientific realm, this is what Bacon called a 'crucial experiment'. The great virtue of the crucial experiment, as extolled by the various intellectual movements that have travelled under the banner of 'positivism', is that it forces a clear distinction to be drawn between theory and method: a scientific society may be divided by theories but it is united in method. But there is also a political point about *free expression* close to the heart of democracy, what Karl Popper called the 'open society': everyone can bullshit to their heart's content, as long as there is an agreement on how to clean up after it.

I stress 'free expression' because, as Franklin would have been the first to observe, the relevant freedom includes the freedom to say what one believes needs to be said, even if one does not quite believe it oneself. Some signature moments of public intellectual life have been defined in these terms. For example, when Emile Zola publicly accused the French War Office of framing Captain Dreyfus (*J'Accuse!*), he had no more evidence than the court that had convicted Dreyfus of treason. He simply read between the lines and took a chance that there was more than met the eye. Zola turned out to be right, but it was only after the confession of the perpetrators that he discovered why. However, his pre-emptive declaration served to stimulate others to re-open the case, resulting in evidence that corroborated Zola's claims, while all the while he was exiled in London. Zola's fate was not so different from Galileo's, whose house arrest after the Inquisition prompted natural philosophers across Europe to take up his hypotheses, which were finally vindicated in Newton's *Principia Mathematica*.

However, Bacon's vision has been realized only imperfectly. In particular, his idea that theory and method should always be distinguished in each case has metamorphosed into the idea they should be distinguished in the same way in all cases. Thus, in the positivist imagination, the inquiring judge whose discretion determines how the distinction is anchored in each case came to be replaced by a mechanical procedure that could be applied to all cases. To a large extent, this transition is traceable to the political failure of Bacon's project (Lynch 2001). After all, Bacon envisaged a royally sanctioned science court, whereas the best a weakened English monarchy could manage after the Civil War was to charter a self-policing private body, the Royal Society of London, whose loyalty to the Crown was demonstrated by its appeal to 'method' to exclude potentially controversial matters from the outset.

One feature of the original Baconian model that remains today has often proved a thorn in the side of the legal system: a liberal policy toward the admission of expert witness testimony, much of which would be discounted as hearsay, if it came from the mouth of an ordinary witness (Golan 2004). This pro-bullshit policy, derided by some as producing 'junk science', is in principle desirable, if only because even orthodox claims to reliable knowledge can rarely, if ever, be evidenced first hand. Such a policy positions the judge as an inquisitor empowered to set up an independent standard by which to detect bullshit in the case at hand. However, if the judge sees herself as no more than a referee between two adversaries, the typical position in Anglo-Saxon law, then the balance of arguments as defined in the terms raised by the plaintiff is likely to prevail. Of course, this does not mean that the plaintiff automatically wins her case, but if she happens to represent the dominant viewpoint on the contested issue, that certainly increases her chances. Thus, Bacon's intention may be undermined in practice.

In conclusion, consider a case in point: the string of US court cases concerning the disposition of evolution and creation – and, more recently, intelligent design – in the high-school curriculum. A landmark ruling occurred in 1982, *McLean v. Arkansas*, in which the presiding judge appealed to a philosophical definition of science, as provided by Michael Ruse, to justify the exclusion of creationism from the science curriculum. This was the first time a judge did not simply defer to the weight of scientific experts but, realizing that the nature of science itself was at issue in the case, tried to arrive at a standard that was genuinely neutral to the contesting parties. What matters here is neither that the judge appealed to an oversimplified definition of science, nor that his reasoning reinforced the general pattern of court rulings against creationism. Rather, it is that he turned to a standard that even the creationists had to agree was reasonable. The judge managed to cut through the bullshit on both sides.

Unfortunately, the judicial precedent set in *McLean* has not stuck. In *Kitzmiller v. Dover Area School District* (2005), the judge's ruling was based largely on a philosophically customized definition of science supplied by the plaintiffs with the blessing of the US National Academy of Sciences. The definition was 'customized' in that the operative doctrine, 'methodological naturalism', while lacking a clear meaning within philosophy, was crafted specifically to exclude intelligent design theory and other forms of scientific creationism (Fuller 2007c: chap. 4).

Philosophers have questioned both why an adherence to scientific methodology requires naturalism and why an adherence to naturalism must remain merely methodological. These two points are made, respectively, in Schick (2000) and Pigliucci (2003). 'Naturalism' is normally regarded as a metaphysical doctrine, a species of monism opposed to supernaturalism. The doctrine has been historically hostile to monotheistic world-views for their postulation of a transcendent deity, resulting in an unforgivable dualism. This point joins, say, Spinoza and Dewey in common cause as naturalists, regardless of their many other differences. However, the prefix 'methodological' is meant to soften the blow by suggesting that only the conduct of science – not all aspects of human existence – presupposes naturalism. But this too is false, as any honest appraisal of the metaphysical realist (a.k.a. supernaturalist) strand in the history of science makes clear.

It is no coincidence that now basic concepts in scientific research like gravity and genes presupposing a depth to reality beneath surface appearances were proposed by theorists with strong theological commitments – Newton and Mendel, respectively (Fuller 2008). In fact, the closest semantic cousin of 'methodological naturalism' in mainstream philosophical usage – *normative naturalism* – implies that a truly naturalistic approach to science would take seriously science's historic track record in discovering entities and processes that challenge previously taken-for-granted modes of understanding empirical reality, which in turn makes it difficult to issue any generalizations about 'The Scientific Method' beyond a few weak inductive principles (Laudan 1987). While it is to be expected – and even encouraged – that adversaries make arguments that put their case in the best possible light, justice is served by acknowledging the bullshit on *both* sides and cutting through it in an equitable fashion. This aspect of the Baconian legacy, where science and law meet, is all too rarely realized in cases where the truth is deemed to rest with the side whose bullshit is piled higher and deeper.

Conclusion: How to Improvize on the World-historic Stage

The phrase 'MO' (short for *modus operandi*), so well popularized in television legal dramas, deserves greater currency in intellectual life. It suggests that understanding an agent's style of operation offers insight into her motive, if not identity. What, then, is the MO of a truth-seeker? For example, is it to believe what highly reliable and esteemed people believe about some matter? In that case, my beliefs should shift as the experts' do. Or, is it to appear respectful to all views, especially those at the extremes of credibility, i.e. those whose minority or majority status is clearly flagged? In that case, I should treat my conformity to expert belief as a private matter (which will be vindicated in the aggregate anyway) and allow others their differing beliefs as long as they are not foisted upon everyone else.

I find neither option satisfying because there is no reason to think that the truth has anything to do with what I believe. This doesn't mean I stop believing what I do or, as a sceptic or Buddhist might, stop holding beliefs altogether. And it certainly doesn't mean that the truth is ultimately beyond my comprehension. Rather, I take seriously the idea that holding beliefs, understood as informed mental dispositions, is only one among several ways at our disposal to access, however fallibly, the truth. Another, occasionally more effective, way is to defend a position one does *not* believe. Needless to say, you will find it hard to accept my argument, if you regard a Romantic virtue like *sincerity* as part of the MO of a truth-seeker.

But why does the idea of an insincere truth-seeker seem so intuitively implausible? Two reasons stand out.

The first source of implausibility is our default epistemic egoism: we presume that we would not have survived long enough to address this very question, were not most of our beliefs true. On such a view, most of the falsehoods we utter are lies, that is, statements that contradict our beliefs. In that case, insincerity works at best as a brief ironic interlude against an otherwise epistemically reliable backdrop of sincere belief. While such a position undoubtedly flatters us, it also renders mysterious the idea that truth is something that must always be strived for, not least because it so easily eludes our grasp. Epistemic egoism is much too complacent to sustain the idea that truth is something 'sought' rather than simply 'revealed'.

The second reason we intuitively recoil from the idea of insincere truth-seeking is that we routinely conflate the verbal assertions entailed by our beliefs and statements we are willing to defend publicly. This conflation is achieved via an omnibus category of 'intellectual responsibility' that compels us to say what we believe and believe what we say. But for purposes of truth-seeking, what really matters is that we are willing to defend, ideally justify, whatever we say – regardless of whether we believe it. A deep but unappreciated point about the history of epistemology is that the inventor of the scientific method, Francis Bacon, was a lawyer by training who regarded experimentation as an inquisition conducted on nature: one's mettle – human or otherwise – is proven exclusively by the integrity of one's responses to the inquisitor's probes.

I draw a strong distinction between what I believe and what I believe needs to be said. The distinction presupposes that knowledge is a collective enterprise, all of whose members potentially benefit from any one of them managing to achieve, or at least approximate, the truth. However, it does not follow that the best way to do this is by trying to establish the truth for oneself as a fixed belief and then making it plain for all to hear or see, so that it might spread like a virus, or 'meme', as Richard Dawkins might say. In the case of deep or complex matters, it might take too long to form a belief that one is willing to promote as true. But potentially more worrisome is that one might form beliefs too quickly and stick to them too tenaciously, which might attract followers but for the wrong reasons – namely, a desire to conform to a position whose apparent strength is also likely to attract others: a.k.a the herd mentality.

So, how best to contribute to the knowledge enterprise? My answer is that you should say what needs to be said in a situation where you are well positioned to say it. If knowledge is indeed a collective enterprise of indefinite longevity, then each of us plays an extended walk-on role. The hard part is figuring out the plot of this soap opera. Intellectual history is certainly written this way. Characters make a difference to what Richard Rorty (1979) popularized as 'the conversation of mankind' by responding in interesting and pertinent ways to other characters. But how do you know they have done so? Turn the page – or tune in next week! Is it important whether, say, Kant believed his transcendental arguments as much as Hume believed his sceptical ones? Of course not. For all we know, Kant and Hume were lying or bluffing. But, epistemologically speaking, all that matters is that they prompted others to respond in ways that we take to have moved us all closer to the truth. That's what makes them, quite literally, great philosophical *actors*.

So, then, how do I determine what to say? Here is a handy step-by-step procedure:

1 What has been already said – especially said well and recently? Whatever you do, don't say those things.
2 What could you say of significance that has not been said?
3 Of those things, which ones could you get away with saying?
4 Of those things, which ones are you willing to develop further in the face of various forms of resistance?
5 Of those things, which ones come with a pretext likely to promote maximum exposure, participation and impact?
6 That's what you say – and Godspeed!

If you are scandalized by this MO, then you may secretly harbour a religious need for a mental transparency that would render your words a window to your soul. Transparency of this sort has always dampened free critical inquiry. Publicity of thought is fine: back up what you say with something we can see. But to ask, however innocently, 'Do you really believe what you're saying?' is to restrict the terms of discourse by forcing an immediate resolution of all the ambiguities, qualifications and reservations that might otherwise play themselves out in a more liberal context of inquiry.

It is easy to forget nowadays that the original eighteenth-century Enlightenment was not a time when people measured their words according to their beliefs. On the contrary, it was a golden age of irony, role-playing and, indeed, considerable scepticism – most famously Hume's – about the very existence of a soul that might deliver a coherent statement of belief. What made the Enlightenment so controversial in its day was not so very different from what makes postmodernism so controversial today: both suspend the belief in established epistemic authority without necessarily endorsing an alternative. The difference is that nowadays the Vatican has been replaced by the Royal Society, and the critical function of something called 'Reason' by something else called 'Deconstruction'.

The most influential school of the philosophy of science in the twentieth century, logical positivism, also insisted on this strong distinction between transparency of mind and publicity of thought. For the positivists, only the latter mattered to the conduct of science. This led them to focus, perhaps to exaggeration, on the role of testing theories against the evidence, ideally in the form of experimental hypotheses. Whatever their shortcomings, the positivists were clear that proposing a scientific theory was *not* like taking a loyalty oath or professing a religious commitment. A young fellow-traveller of the positivists, Karl Popper, turned this point into a general philosophy of the 'open society', on the basis of which he criticized the likes of Michael Polanyi and Thomas Kuhn for treating science as a kind of faith-based community.

These abstract points of social epistemology acquire concrete purchase in the US Supreme Court ruling *Edwards v. Aguillard* (1987), which set the precedent for the *Kitzmiller* ruling against intelligent design (ID) theory raised in the previous section. In *Edwards*, the justices decided that the mere presence of a religious motivation is sufficient to disqualify a theory from science instruction in state-supported schools. To philosophical eyes, this looks like a blatant commission of the genetic fallacy, especially given how much of today's science was the product of religiously inspired inquirers. However, the justices specifically set their sights on Christian fundamentalists who reject Darwin's theory of evolution simply because it contradicts the Genesis account of divine creation. But in that case, why not simply ban the teaching of false science rather than worry about the perpetrators' motives?

As it turns out, over the years Creationists have come to take seriously Francis Bacon's original idea that the scientific method is content-neutral. In other words, once a theory, whatever its religious or ideological origins, has passed certain publicly observable trials, it becomes scientifically respectable – no matter how much that upsets the established scientific community. Creationists are helped by the fact that today's secular school systems presume the validity of Darwin's theory. Positioned as underdogs, they are now defending the right for their alternative theory to be taught alongside *not* instead of Darwin's. This in turn has spawned a 'teach the controversy' approach to biology instruction, epitomized in a new textbook promoted by Seattle's Discovery Institute, *Explore Evolution* (Meyer et al. 2007). Even Creationism's strongest opponents admit that its arguments are getting harder to defeat as Creationists play more by the rules of science. However, because the US Constitution mandates a separation of church and state, these efforts at scientific gamesmanship can be short-circuited by simply citing the ultimately religious motivation for 'Creation science'.

In this context, the version of Creationism known as intelligent design theory has made life especially difficult for the US legal system because it casts all of its arguments in scientific terms, often capitalizing on biological phenomena that Darwinists admit they find difficult to explain. Moreover, the specific focus on design tapped into historically deep regulative ideals of science, notably what Leibniz and Kant called 'the intelligibility of nature' – that is, the idea that nature is constructed so that we may understand it. The most obvious source of this assumption is that humans have been created in the image of the divine creator: we can make systematic sense of reality because our own minds are micro-versions of the creator's. To be sure, an assumption is hardly a proof. Nevertheless, in a time when films like *The Matrix* and philosophers like David Chalmers have popularized the idea that reality may be the output of a complex cosmic computer, and indeed that simulation is increasingly replacing the laboratory and the field at the site of original scientific research, ID's version of the 'God Hypothesis' is not without a certain intuitive plausibility.

Here my own MO as a truth-seeker comes into play. I agreed to serve as an expert 'rebuttal' witness in the first US trial to test ID as fit for public science instruction, *Kitzmiller*. In other words, my testimony addressed the arguments of those who thought ID had no place in science classes. As a tenured professor steeped in the history, philosophy and sociology of science, I was well prepared for the task and relatively immune to whatever adverse consequences might follow, which even now has never gone beyond personal abuse. Given the suspicions of ID as 'warmed over' Creationism, I had no illusions that this was anything other than a thankless task. At the same time, I held no strong personal views about whether life was 'intelligently designed' (in some sense) or, as Darwinists maintain, the product of 'chance-based processes' (in some sense). If anything I was slightly biased to the latter. So I was genuinely curious what the Darwinian response to a robust defence of ID's inclusion in the curriculum would look like.

As it turns out, and somewhat to my surprise, the arguments invoked to oppose ID were remarkably weak – at least from a philosophical standpoint. Of course, the religious motivation of ID supporters was easy to spot, and that settled the matter for a judge who simply upheld the *Edwards* judgment that religiosity is tantamount to original sin in the pursuit of science.

What made the anti-ID arguments so philosophically weak were their repeated reliance on a winner-take-all approach to the history of science. Thus, Darwinism, by virtue of its current dominance in biology, is presumed to be exclusively entitled to interpret all research in the discipline to its advantage, even though much of it had been done, and might now be used, by those opposed to Darwinism. Moreover, without this exclusive epistemic licence, Darwinism is open to familiar questions from the philosophy of science about how evidence from heterogeneous sources can be integrated in support of highly general claims. In particular, how are results produced under the artificial conditions of today's labs or computers supposed to 'confirm' events and processes that took place in the mists of time, especially when the closest we have to direct evidence of the evolutionary past – the fossil record – requires the interpretation of radiometric data that are themselves contestable?

To be sure, lower-level disputes of interpretation regularly occur in each of the natural sciences relevant to the case for evolution. However, it seems that Darwinists, now aided and abetted by the US legal system, wish to prevent these pressure points in the theory from possibly coming together to inspire an alternative to the Darwinian orthodoxy. Indeed, the US National Academy of Sciences would make allegiance to the metaphysical position underlying evolution – naturalism – a condition for any scientifically sanctioned dissent. Thus, an exceptionally disagreeable feature of the current controversy is the tendency for evolutionists to call the more scientifically literate ID theorists 'liars', which pre-empts the need to answer ID's substantive charges by presuming that not even its own supporters believe them – that is, they 'know better'. But when did science enter the confession box, such that I don't need to take your arguments seriously unless they are served up with the right sincerely held beliefs?

One of the few historical generalizations on which philosophers of science agree is what Hilary Putnam (1978) originally dubbed the 'pessimistic meta-induction': all theories of wide explanatory scope in science are eventually shown to be empirically false, usually because they overreach their grasp. From that standpoint, Darwinists appear to be postponing the inevitable. Of course, that doesn't make ID true, but ID may be well positioned to point out the deep systemic flaws in Darwinism that Darwinists themselves have no incentive to recognize, let alone explore. If that's true, then insofar as truth-seeking is a collective enterprise at least partly detachable from the scientific fashions of the day, then someone who considers themselves part of that enterprise should do what needs to be done to ensure that Darwinism is dialectically foiled. And that may be a role that has my name written on it, and ID may be my prop.

Summary of the Argument

The Sociology of Intellectual Life is organized around the three central concepts that underwrite the Humboldtian ideal of the modern university. These concern the nature of the institution itself (Chapter 1), its ideological justification (Chapter 2) and the sort of person it tries to produce (Chapter 3). Chapter 4 defends a crucial but widely despised feature of intellectual life – its improvisational nature.

In Chapter 1, the university is introduced as an institutional solution to the modern problem of knowledge in society – namely, how knowledge can have a universal purchase on reality (as 'science') and yet be universally accessible (as 'democracy'). For Plato, this was not a problem because for him science was by nature undemocratic, i.e. an elite possession that entitled one to power over others. In contrast, Humboldt reinvented the university as a sociological correlate to Kant's philosophical vision of the Enlightenment, whereby access to universal knowledge is necessary for each individual to complete his or her personal development. However, over the last hundred years, the Humboldtian project has been undermined by the alienation of knowledge from the person – first by disciplinary specialization and then by the instrumentalization of knowledge according to various market-driven demands. In many respects, universities have been complicit in these developments, as their own secular power has increased by becoming clearinghouses for the dispensing of credentials and other forms of epistemic authorisation. Moreover, the most popular academic ideology of the past quarter century – postmodernism – is itself an anti-university movement that has provided a protective colouration for the reorientation of the institution towards the marketplace. My own defence of the Humboldtian university turns on seeing the institution as manufacturing knowledge as a public good through the 'creative destruction of social capital'. In other words, academia's teaching imperative democratizes its complementary research imperative by redistributing the advantage that new knowledge initially accrues to its producers. This supports the university's more general historic role as an agency of 'affirmative action' in society at large. But this vision can be realized only against the backdrop of a robust sense of 'academic freedom' that enables both academics and students to inquire freely in each other's company.

Chapter 2 focusses mainly on the sociological fate of philosophy in the Anglophone world in the twentieth century. However, this topic is embedded in a larger discussion of the social conditions of knowledge production, or 'social epistemology'. The idea of philosophy as the foundational academic discipline out of which the special sciences emerge is an ideological invention associated with the Humboldtian university that was first championed by the German idealist successors of Kant. (Theology had previously performed that role.) This often overlooked fact comes through clearly in Randall Collins's magisterial *The Sociology of Philosophies* (1998), whose strengths and weaknesses are surveyed with an eye to mounting an alternative sociology of philosophy that counters the canonical histories by stressing the discipline's value-driven, or 'axiological', animus, which would allow for a broader range of social influences on philosophy. This corrective helps to provide a critical perspective on the global ascendancy of Anglophone over Germanophone tendencies in the discipline over the past century. In a nutshell, German themes were typically translated into English terms, sometimes – courtesy of two world wars – by the original principals themselves, with attendant claims for the superiority of English 'clarity' as a philosophical language that bear ironic comparison with earlier German claims for the 'depth' of its language. Sociologically speaking, this shift reflects philosophy's decline from a discipline that 'grounds' what can and perhaps must be done to one that merely 'clarifies' what has been already or is likely to be done. After all, the stylistic obscurity associated with claims to 'depth' makes sense if one imagines that inquiry is still in its relatively early stages. From the Humboldtian standpoint, the Anglophone stress on clarity as philosophy's premier virtue implies that the discipline has ceded its prerogative to the special sciences. Indeed, a 'Retro-Humboldtian' like Heidegger would say that the turn to clarity is a sure sign of philosophy's death wish. Nevertheless, a relatively wealthy US academic environment makes it easy to overlook all this, especially once philosophy's diminished socio-epistemic status is repackaged as yet another exotic technical interest.

Chapter 3 considers the role of the intellectual as someone who is clearly of academic descent but not necessarily of academic destiny. At the outset, I identify the intellectual with the Shakespearean fool who can speak truth to power because he performs entirely at the behest of the sovereign without any power of his own. More modern ways of bringing about a similar state-of-affairs include lifelong academic tenure as well as the sort of marketplace success enjoyed by a popular but respected author like Emile Zola, for whom the word 'intellectual' was virtually invented. In other words, a socio-economic precondition for robust intellectual life is the ability to exercise 'the right to be wrong'. Zola is such an exemplary intellectual because, from a strictly legal standpoint, his notorious *J'Accuse!* charge against the French Foreign Office during the Dreyfus Affair was unfounded yet his underlying suspicions were later proven correct. However, it is unlikely that the case would have been reopened, had someone in Zola's privileged position not stepped in to sow the requisite seeds of doubt. Zola's practice as an intellectual can be seen as a microcosm of what universities try to do for society as a whole – namely, to redistribute authority and ultimately power in a more equitable direction. However, academics routinely undermine this role at the meta-level by treating the possession of an idea as a matter of reception (e.g. the product of a social contagion) rather than creation (e.g. the result of an active weighing up of evidence). Although the Humboldtian ideal of *Lehrfreiheit* ('freedom to teach') was meant to highlight the judgemental character of lecturing, in practice it has licenced a relatively passive reproduction of established beliefs. This overall lack of intellectual risk-taking among academics can be explained in one of two ways: either they are scared by the possible consequences of their public utterances or, more simply, they are attracted to the insular affairs of their disciplines. In times of plenty, the two motives may be difficult to distinguish, but against both I put forward the ethic of 'negative responsibility' – that you can be reasonably blamed for your inaction, if had you acted you would have substantially benefited others without having harmed yourself. Adherence to this ethic provides the true normative measure of the intellectual. Pierre Bourdieu counts as an academic sociologist who increasingly came to see his own rights and duties in exactly these terms.

Chapter 4 extols and elaborates the centrality of improvisation in intellectual life. If the life of the mind is meant to inform social action, on the basis of which institutions are made and remade, then the practice of educated thinking in public – including what is often derided as bullshit – needs to be encouraged and emulated, along with appropriate responses to the perceived errors and exaggerations inevitably generated by such practice. In this respect, the publication and reception of academic knowledge could learn much from the heterogeneous standards employed by the mass media. But in any case, intellectual life as a whole suffers as long as the entry costs for either proposing or criticizing knowledge claims remain too restricted. As a result, it becomes too easy both to defer to the orthodoxy and to discount its dissenters. The chapter and book close by proposing that the cause of truth is best promoted in the long term by saying not what one believes but what one is well positioned to say and defend. This counter-intuitive maxim epitomizes the improvisational nature of intellectual life, while driving home the deep epistemic point that things are rarely as they seem.

References

Aron, R. (1957). The Opium of the Intellectuals. Garden City, NY: Doubleday.

Austin, J.L. (1961). *Philosophical Papers*. Oxford: Oxford University Press.

Barry, A. and D. Slater (2002). 'Technology, Politics and the Market: an Interview with Michel Callon', *Economy and Society*, 31(2): 285–306.

Bauman, Z. (1987). *Legislators and Interpreters*. Cambridge: Polity.

Beck, U., A. Giddens and S. Lash (1994). *Reflexive Modernization: Politics, Tradition and Aesthetics in the Modern Social Order*. Palo Alto, CA: Stanford University Press.

Bell, D. (1966). *The Reform of General Education*. New York: Doubleday.

Bell, D. (1973). *The Coming of Post-Industrial Society*. New York: Basic Books.

Berkson, W. and J. Wettersten (1984). *Learning from Error: Karl Popper's Psychology of Learning*. La Salle, IL: Open Court.

Bernard, J. and T. Kuhn (1969–70). Correspondence. 29 November to 10 February. *Thomas Kuhn Papers*, MC 240, Box 4, Folder 7, MIT Archives and Special Collections.

Bernstein, B. (1971–77). *Class, Codes, and Control: Theoretical Studies towards a Sociology of Language*, 3 vols. London: Routledge & Kegan Paul.

Bloom, H. (1973). *The Anxiety of Influence*. Oxford: Oxford University Press.

Bloor, D. (1976). *Knowledge and Social Imagery*. London: Routledge.

Bourdieu, P. (1991). *The Political Ontology of Martin Heidegger*. Cambridge: Polity.

Bourdieu, P. (1999 [1993]). *The Weight of the World*. Oxford: Polity Press.

Bowles, S. and H. Gintis (1976). *Schooling in Capitalist America*. New York: Basic Books.

Boyd, R. and P. Richerson (1985). *Culture and the Evolutionary Process*. Chicago: University of Chicago Press.

Braunstein, P. and M.W. Doyle (eds) (2001). *Imagine Nation: The American Counter-Culture of the 1960s and 1970s*. London: Routledge.

Bruner, J. (1983). *In Search of Mind: Essays in Autobiography*. New York: Harper & Row.

Bruner, J., J. Goodnow and G. Austin (1956). *A Study of Thinking*. New York: John & Wiley & Sons.

Bühler, K. (1930 [1919]). *The Mental Development of the Child*. New York: Harcourt, Brace & Company.

Cahn, S. (ed.) (1995). *The Affirmative Action Debate*. London: Routledge.

Callebaut, W. (ed.) (1993). *Taking the Naturalistic Turn*. Chicago: University of Chicago Press.

Cassirer, E. (1950). *The Problem of Knowledge: Philosophy, Science, and History Since Hegel*. New Haven, CT: Yale University Press.

Cavell, S. (1992). *The Senses of Walden*. Chicago: University of Chicago Press.

Chisholm, R. and W. Sellars (1957). 'Intentionality and the Mental: Chisholm-Sellars Correspondence on Intentionality', in H. Feigl and W. Sellars (eds), *Minnesota Studies in the Philosophy of Science*, vol. II. Minneapolis: University of Minnesota Press, pp. 521–539.

Chomsky, N., I. Katznelson, R. Lewontin, D. Montgomery, L. Nader, R. Ohmann, R. Siever, I. Wallerstein and H. Zinn (1997). *The Cold War and the University.* New York: New Press.

Cohen, I.B. (1985). *Revolutions in Science.* Cambridge, MA: Harvard University Press.

Cohen, L.J. (1986). *The Dialogue of Reason.* Oxford: Clarendon Press.

Cohen, M. and E. Nagel (1934). *An Introduction to Logic and the Scientific Method.* New York: Routledge & Kegan Paul.

Colllini, S. (1979). *Liberalism and Sociology.* Cambridge: Cambridge University Press.

Collins, R. (1979). *The Credential Society.* New York: Academic Press.

Collins, R. (1998). *The Sociology of Philosophies: A Global Theory of Intellectual Change.* Cambridge, MA: Harvard University Press.

Collins, R. (2000). 'Reflexivity and Embeddedness in the History of Ethical Philosophies', in Kusch (2000), pp. 155–178.

Collins, R. (2004). *Interaction Ritual Chains.* Princeton: Princeton University Press.

Conant, J.B. (1970). *My Several Lives: Memoirs of a Social Inventor.* New York: Harper & Row.

Cooper, D.E. (1996a). *World Philosophies: An Historical Introduction.* Oxford: Blackwell.

Cooper, D.E. (1996b). 'Verstehen, Holism and Fascism', in A. O'Hear (ed.), *Verstehen and Humane Understanding* (pp. 95–108). Cambridge: Cambridge University Press.

Cusset, F. (2008). *French Theory: How Foucault, Derrida, Deleuze & Co. Transformed the Intellectual life of the United States.* Minneapolis: University of Minnesota Press.

Dahrendorf, R. (1970). 'The Intellectual and Society: The Social Function of the Fool in the 20th century', in P. Rieff (ed.), *On Intellectuals* (pp. 53–56). Garden City, NY: Doubleday.

Dahrendorf, R. (1995). *LSE.* Oxford: Oxford University Press.

Dawkins, R. (1976). *The Selfish Gene.* Oxford: Oxford University Press.

Dawkins, R. (1983). *The Extended Phenotype.* Oxford: Oxford University Press.

Delaney, C. (ed.) (1977). *The Synoptic Vision: Essays in the Philosophy of Wilfrid Sellars.* South Bend, IN: Notre Dame University Press.

Dennett, D. (1995). *Darwin's Dangerous Idea.* New York: Simon and Schuster.

Descombes, V. (1980). *Modern French Philosophy.* Cambridge: Cambridge University Press.

Diggins, J.P. (1994). *The Promise of Pragmatism.* Chicago: University of Chicago Press.

Drahos, P. (1995). 'Information Feudalism in the Information Society', *The Information Society*, 11: 209–222.

Dummett, M. (1993). *The Origins of Analytic Philosophy.* London: Duckworth.

Edwards, P. (1996). *The Closed World: Computers and the Politics of Discourse in Cold War America* Cambridge, MA: MIT Press.

Eisenstein, E. (1979). *The Printing Press as an Agent of Change.* Cambridge: Cambridge University Press.

Elster, J. (1981). 'Snobs', *London Review of Books*, 3(20): 10–12.

Elster, J. (1983). *Sour Grapes: Studies in the Subversion of Rationality*. Cambridge: Cambridge University Press.

Elster, J. (1998). 'Deliberation and Constitution Making', in J. Elster (ed.), *Deliberative Democracy* (pp. 97–102). Cambridge: Cambridge University Press.

Feyerabend, P. (1970). 'Consolations for the Specialist', in I. Lakatos and A. Musgrave (eds), *Criticism and the Growth of Knowledge* (pp. 197–229). Cambridge: Cambridge University Press.

Feyerabend, P. (1975). *Against Method*. London: Verso.

Feyerabend, P. (1979). *Science in a Free Society*. London: Verso.

Frank, A.G. (1997). *Re-Orient*. Berkeley: University of California Press.

Frankfurt, H. (2005). *On Bullshit*. Princeton: Princeton University Press.

Franklin, J. (2001). *The Science of Conjecture: Evidence and Probability before Pascal*. Baltimore: Johns Hopkins University Press.

Frisby, D. (1983). *The Alienated Mind: The Sociology of Knowledge in Germany, 1918–1933* London: Routledge.

Fukuyama, F. (1992). *The End of History and the Last Man*. New York: Free Press.

Fuller, S. (1985). 'Bounded Rationality in Law and Science', PhD in History and Philosophy of Science: University of Pittsburgh.

Fuller, S. (1988). *Social Epistemology*. Bloomington: Indiana University Press.

Fuller, S. (1993 [1989]). *Philosophy of Science and Its Discontents*, 2nd edn. New York: Guilford Press.

Fuller, S. (1995). 'Is there Life for Sociological Theory after the Sociology of Scientific Knowledge?' *Sociology*, 29: 159–166.

Fuller, S. (1996). 'Recent Work in Social Epistemology', *American Philosophical Quarterly*, 33: 149–166.

Fuller, S. (1997). *Science*. Milton Keynes: Open University Press.

Fuller, S. (1998). 'Divining the Future of Social Theory: From Theology to Rhetoric via Social Epistemology', *European Journal of Social Theory*, 1: 107–126.

Fuller, S. (2000a). *The Governance of Science: Ideology and the Future of the Open Society*. Milton Keynes: Open University Press.

Fuller, S. (2000b). *Thomas Kuhn: A Philosophical History for Our Times*. Chicago: University of Chicago Press.

Fuller, S. (2001). 'Looking for Sociology after 11 September', *Sociological Research On-Line*, 6(3): http://www.socresonline.org.uk/6/3/fuller.html

Fuller, S. (2002a). *Knowledge Management Foundations*. Woburn, MA: Butterworth-Heinemann.

Fuller, S. (2002b). 'Making Up the Past: A Response to Sharrock and Leudar', *History of the Human Sciences*, 15(4): 115–123.

Fuller, S. (2003). *Kuhn vs Popper: The Struggle for the Soul of Science*. Cambridge: Icon Books.

Fuller, S. (2005). *The Intellectual*. Cambridge: Icon Books.

Fuller, S. (2006a). *The New Sociological Imagination*. London: Sage.

Fuller, S. (2006b). *The Philosophy of Science and Technology Studies*. New York: Routledge.

Fuller, S. (2007a). *The Knowledge Book: Key Concepts in Philosophy, Science and Culture*. Stocksfield: Acumen.

Fuller, S. (2007b). *New Frontiers in Science and Technology Studies*. Cambridge: Polity Press.

Fuller, S. (2007c). *Science vs Religion? Intelligent Design and the Problem of Evolution*. Cambridge: Polity Press.

Fuller, S. (2008). *Dissent over Descent: Intelligent Design's Challenge to Darwinism*. Cambridge: Icon Books.

Fuller, S. and J. Collier (2004 [1993]). *Philosophy, Rhetoric and the End of Knowledge*, 2nd edn. (Orig. 1993, by Fuller). Hillsdale, NJ: Lawrence Erlbaum Associates.

Galison, P. and D. Stump (eds) (1996). *The Disunity of Science*. Palo Alto, CA: Stanford University Press.

Gane, M. (1988). *On Durkheim's Rules of the Sociological Method*. London: Routledge.

Geertz, C. (1973). *The Interpretation of Cultures*. New York: Basic Books.

Geertz, C. (1995). *After the Fact: Two Countries, Four Decades, One Anthropologist*. Cambridge, MA: Harvard University Press.

Gellner, E. (1959). *Words and Things: A Critical Account of Linguistic Philosophy and a Study in Ideology*. London: Victor Gollancz.

Gellner, E. (1992). *Reason and Culture: The Historic Role of Rationality and Rationalism*. Oxford: Blackwell.

Gibbons, M. Limoges, C., Nowothy, H., Schwartzman, S., Scott, P., Trow, M. (1994). *The New Production of Knowledge*. London: Sage.

Giddens, A. (1976). *New Rules of the Sociological Method*. London. Hutchinson.

Giere, R. (1996). 'From *Wissensschaftliche Philosophie* to Philosophy of Science', in R. Giere and A. Richardson (eds), *Origins of Logical Empiricism* (pp. 335–354). Minneapolis: University of Minnesota Press.

Gigerenzer, G. (1999). *Simple Heuristics that Make Us Smart*. Oxford: Oxford University Press.

Gladwell, M. (2000). *The Tipping Point*. New York: Little and Brown.

Glaser, B. and A. Strauss (1967). *The Discovery of Grounded Theory*. Chicago: Aldine.

Glover, J. (1984). *What Kind of People Should There Be?* Harmondsworth: Penguin.

Golan, T. (2004). *Laws of Men and Laws of Nature: The History of Scientific Expert Testimony in England and America*. Cambridge, MA: Harvard University Press.

Goldgar, A. (1995). *Impolite Learning: Conduct and Community in the Republic of Letters, 1680–1750*. New Haven, CT: Yale University Press.

Goldman, A.I. (1986). *Epistemology and Cognition*. Cambridge, MA: Harvard University Press.

Goldman, A.I. (1992). *Liaisons: Philosophy Meets the Cognitive and Social Sciences*. Cambridge, MA: MIT Press.

Goldman, A.I. (1999). *Knowledge in a Social World*. Oxford: Oxford University Press.

Goodson, I. (1999). 'The educational researcher as a public intellectual', *British Educational Research Journal*, 25: 277–297.

Gould, S.J. (1981). *The Mismeasure of Man*. New York: Norton.

Gouldner, A. (1970). *The Coming Crisis in Western Sociology*. New York: Basic Books.

Gouldner, A. (1979). *The Future of the Intellectuals and the Rise of the New Class*. London: Macmillan.

Grenfell, M. (2004). *Pierre Bourdieu: Agent Provocateur*. London: Continuum.

Grenfell, M., (ed.) (2008). *Pierre Bourdieu: Key Concepts*. Stocksfield: Acumen.

Grundmann, R. and N. Stehr (2001). 'Why is Werner Sombart not part of the core of classical sociology?' *Journal of Classical Sociology*, 1: 257–287.

Habermas, J. (1971 [1968]). *Knowledge and Human Interests*. Boston, MA: Beacon.

Hacking, I. (1975). *Why Does Language Matter to Philosophy?* Cambridge: Cambridge University Press.

Hacking, I. (2002). *Historical Ontology*. Princeton: Princeton University Press.

Hacohen, M. (2000). *Karl Popper: The Formative Years, 1902–1945* Cambridge: Cambridge University Press.

Haraway, D. (1990). *Simians, Cyborgs and Women*. London: Free Association Books.

Haraway, D. (1997). *Modest Witness@Second Millenium*. London: Routledge.

Hawking, S. (1988). *A Brief History of Time*. New York: Bantam.

Heidelberger, M. (2004). *Nature from Within*. Pittsburgh: University of Pittsburgh Press.

Herf, J. (1984). *Reactionary Modernism*. Cambridge: Cambridge University Press.

Hinde, J. (1999). 'Patents provide universities with slender returns', *Times Higher Education* Supplement, 5 February, p. 4.

Hirsch, F. (1977). *Social Limits to Growth*. London: Routledge & Kegan Paul.

Hirst, P. (1975) *Durkheim, Bernard and Epistemology*. London: Routledge.

Horowitz, D. (2006). *The Professors*. Washington, DC: Henry Regnery.

Horowitz, D. (2007). *Indoctrination U.: The Left's War against Academic Freedom*. New York: Encounter Books.

Husserl, E. (1954 [1937]). *The Crisis of the European Sciences and Transcendental Phenomenology*. Evanston, IL: Northwestern University Press.

Hylton, P. (1990). *Russell, Idealism, and the Emergence of Analytic Philosophy*. Oxford: Clarendon Press.

Jacob, M. and T. Hellstrom (eds) (2000). *The Future of Knowledge Production in the Academy*. Milton Keynes: Open University Press.

Johnson, D. (2005). 'British Intellectual Life Today', *The New Criterion*, 24: 9, September.

Jones, R.A. (1994). 'The Positive Science of Ethics in France: German Influences on *De La Division Du Travail*', *Sociological Forum*, 9: 37–57.

Judt, T. (1994). *Past Imperfect: French Intellectuals 1944–1956*. Berkeley: University of California Press.

Kimball, R. (1990). *Tenured Radicals*. New York: HarperCollins.

Kitch, E. (1980). 'The law and the economics of rights in valuable information', *The Journal of Legal Studies*, 9: 683–723.

Klemperer, V. (2000). *The Language of the Third Reich*. London: Athlone.

Kolakowski, L. (1972). *Positivist Philosophy: From Hume to the Vienna Circle*. Harmondsworth: Penguin.

Krause, E. (1996). *The Death of the Guilds: Professions, States, and the Advance of Capitalism*. New Haven: Yale University Press.

Kuhn, T.S. (1970 [1962]). *The Structure of Scientific Revolutions*, 2nd edn. Chicago: University of Chicago Press.

Kuhn, T.S. (1977a). *The Essential Tension*. Chicago: University of Chicago Press.

Kuhn, T.S. (1977b). Letter to Arnold Thackray, 7 April, in *Thomas Kuhn Papers*, MC 240, Box 12, Folder 1. MIT Archives and Special Collections.

Kuklick, B. (1984). 'Seven Thinkers and How They Grew', in R. Rorty, J.B. Schneewind and Q. Skinner (eds), *Philosophy in History* (pp. 125–140). Cambridge: Cambridge University Press.

Kuklick, B. (2001). *A History of Philosophy in America*. Oxford: Oxford University Press.

Kusch, M. (1995). *Psychologism*. London: Routledge.

Kusch, M. (1999). *Psychological Knowledge: A Social History of Philosophy*. London: Routledge.

Kusch, M. (ed.) (2000). *The Sociology of Philosophical Knowledge*. Dordrecht: Kluwer.

Kusch, M. and P. Lipton (eds) (2002) Special Issue on Testimony, *Studies in History and Philosophy of Science*, Part A. 33(2): 209–423.

Lafontaine, O. (2000). *The Heart Beats on the Left*. Cambridge: Polity.

Latour, B. (1987). *Science in Action*. Milton Keynes: Open University Press.

Latour, B. (1997). 'A Few Steps toward an Anthropology of the Iconoclastic Gesture', *Science in Context*, 10: 63–83.

Latour, B. (2002). 'Gabriel Tarde and the End of the Social', in P. Joyce (ed.), *The Social in Question*. London: Routledge.

Latour, B. and S. Woolgar (1986 [1979]). *Laboratory Life*, 2nd edn. Princeton: Princeton University Press.

Laudan, L. (1987). 'Progress or Rationality? The Prospects for Normative Naturalism', *American Philosophical Quarterly*, 24: 19–33.

Lave, J. and E. Wenger (1991). *Situated Learning*. Cambridge: Cambridge University Press.

Lehman, D. (1991). *Signs of the Times: Deconstruction and the Fall of Paul De Man*. London: Andre Deutsch.

Lessig, L. (2001). *The Future of Ideas: The Fate of the Commons in a Connected World*. New York: Random House.

Lilla, M. (2001). *The Reckless Mind: Intellectuals in Politics*. New York: New York Review Press.

Locke, J. (1959 [1690]). 'Epistle to the Reader', *An Essay Concerning Human Understanding*, vol. 1. New York: Dover.

Lomborg, B. (2001). *The Sceptical Environmentalist*. Cambridge: Cambridge University Press.

Lutz, M. (1999). *Economics for the Common Good*. London: Routledge.

Lynch, W. (2001). *Solomon's Child: Baconian Method in the Early Royal Society of London*. Palo Alto, CA: Stanford University Press.

Lyotard, J.-F. (1983 [1979]). *The Postmodern Condition*. Minneapolis: University of Minnesota Press.

MacIntyre, A. (1984 [1891]). *After Virtue*, 2nd edn. South Bend, IN: Notre Dame University Press.

Mannheim, K. (1936 [1929]). *Ideology and Utopia*. New York: Harcourt Brace & World.

Marcus, G. and Fischer, M. (1986). *Anthropology as Cultural Critique*. Chicago: University of Chicago Press.

McCumber, J. (2001). *Time in the Ditch: American Philosophy in the McCarthy Era*. Evanston, IL: Northwestern University Press.

McGuire, W. and D. Papageorgis (1961). 'The Relative Efficacy of Various Prior Belief-Defense in Producing Immunity against Persuasion', *Journal of Abnormal and Social Psychology*, 62: 327–337.

Menand, L. (2001). *The Metaphysical Club*. New York: Farrar, Straus and Giroux.

Merz, J.T. (1965 [1896–1914]). *A History of European Thought in the 19th Century*, 4 vols. New York: Dover.

Metzger, W. (1955). *Academic Freedom in the Age of the University*. New York: Random House.

Meyer, S. Minnich, S., Moneymaker, J., Nelson, P., Seelke, R. (2007). *Explore Evolution: The Arguments for and against Neo-Darwinism*. Melbourne, Australia: Hill House.

Mirowski, P. (2001). *Machine Dreams: Economics Becomes a Cyborg Science*. Cambridge: Cambridge University Press.

Murray, M. (1973). 'Heidegger and Ryle: Two Versions of Phenomenology', *Review of Metaphysics*, 27: 88–111.

Nader, L. (1997). 'The Phantom Factor: Impact of the Cold War on Anthropology', in Chomsky et al. (1997), pp. 106–146.

Noelle-Neumann, E. (1982). *The Spiral of Silence*. Chicago: University of Chicago Press.

Notturno, M. (2000). *Science and the Open Society: In Defense of Reason and Freedom of Thought*. Budapest: Central European University Press.

O'Connor, J.R. (1973). *The Fiscal Crisis of the State*. New York: St Martins Press.

Passmore, J. (1966). *A Hundred Years of Philosophy*, 2nd edn. Harmondsworth: Penguin.

Pigliucci, M. (2003) 'Methodological vs. Philosophical Naturalism', *Free Inquiry*, 23: 53–55.

Pinker, S. (2002). *The Blank Slate: The Modern Denial of Human Nature*. New York: Vintage.

Polanyi, M. (1957). *Personal Knowledge*. Chicago: University of Chicago Press.

Popper, K. (1945). *The Open Society and Its Enemies*. London: Routledge & Kegan Paul.

Popper, K. (1972). *Objective Knowledge*. Oxford: Oxford University Press.

Price, C. (1993). *Time, Discounting and Value* Oxford: Blackwell.

Price, D. de S. (1978). 'Toward a Model for Science Indicators', in Y. Elkana et al. (eds), *Toward a Metric of Science* (pp. 69–96). New York: Wiley-Interscience.

Proctor, R. (1991). *Value-Free Science? Purity and Power in Modern Knowledge*. Cambridge, MA: Harvard University Press.

Putnam, H. (1978). *Meaning and the Moral Sciences*. London: Routledge & Kegan Paul.

Quinton, A. (1999). 'My Son the Philosopher', *The New York Review of Books*, 8 April. Vol. 46: 6.

Ravetz, J. (1971). *Scientific Knowledge and Its Social Problems*. Oxford: Oxford University Press.

Rawls, J. (1971). *A Theory of Justice*. Cambridge, MA: Harvard University Press.

Reichenbach, H. (1938). *Experience and Prediction*. Chicago: University of Chicago Press.

Ricoeur, P. (1970). *Freud and Philosophy*. New Haven, CT: Yale University Press.

Ringer, F. (1969). *The Decline of the German Mandarins*. Cambridge, MA.: Harvard University Press.

Ringer, F. (1979). *Education and Society in Modern Europe*. Bloomington, IN: Indiana University Press.

Rorty, R. (1979). *Philosophy and the Mirror of Nature*. Princeton: Princeton University Press.

Rorty, R. (1982). *The Consequences of Pragmatism*. Minneapolis: University of Minnesota Press.

Rorty, R. (1988). 'Taking Philosophy Seriously', *The New Republic*, 11 April: 31–34.

Ross, D. (1991). *The Origins of American Social Science*. Cambridge: Cambridge University Press.

Ryle, G. (1949). *The Concept of Mind*. Oxford: Oxford University Press.

Samuelson, P. (1969). 'Pure Theory of Public Expenditures and Taxation', in J. Margolis and H. Guitton (eds), *Public Economics* (pp. 98–123). London: Macmillan.

Saracci, R. (2001). 'Introducing the History of Epidemiology', in J. Orsen et al. (eds), *Teaching Epidemiology*. Oxford: Oxford University Press.

Schick, T. (2000). 'Methodological Naturalism vs. Methodological Realism', *Philo*, 3(2): 30–37.

Schinkel, W. (2003). 'Pierre Bourdieu's Political Turn?' *Theory, Culture and Society*, 20(6): 69–93.

Schnädelbach, H. (1984). *Philosophy in Germany, 1831–1933*. Cambridge: Cambridge University Press.

Schreiterer, U. (2008). 'Trust Matters: Democratic Impingements in the City of Knowledge', in N. Stehr (ed.), *Knowledge and Democracy* (pp. 67–86). New Brunswick, NJ: Transaction.

Schumpeter, J. (1950 [1942]). *Capitalism, Socialism and Democracy*, 2nd edn. Harper & Row: New York.

Shils, E. (ed.) (1974) *Max Weber on Universities: The Power of the State and the Dignity of the Academic Calling in Imperial Germany*. Chicago, IL: University of Chicago Press.

Sidgwick, H. (1966 [1874]). *The Methods of Ethics*. New York: Dover.

Smart, J.J.C. and Williams, B. (1973). *Utilitarianism: For and Against*. Cambridge: Cambridge University Press.

Smith, B. (1994). *Austrian Philosophy: The Legacy of Franz Brentano*. La Salle, IL: Open Court Press.

Söderqvist, T. (ed.) (1997). *The Historiography of Contemporary Science and Technology*. Amsterdam: Harwood Academic Publishers.

Sokal, A. and J. Bricmont (1998). *Fashionable Nonsense: Postmodern Philosophers' Abuse of Science*. London: Profile Books.

Sperber, D. (1996). *Explaining Culture: A Naturalistic Approach*. Oxford: Blackwell.

Stehr, N. (1994). *Knowledge Societies*. London: Sage.

Stewart, T. (1997). *Intellectual Capital*. London: Nicholas Brealy.

Swanson, D. (1986). 'Undiscovered Public Knowledge', *Library Quarterly*, 56(2): 103–118.

Thayer, H.S. (1968). *Meaning and Action: A Critical History of Pragmatism*. Indianapolis: Bobbs-Merrill.

Toews, J. (1985). *Hegelianism*. Cambridge: Cambridge University Press.

Toulmin, S. (2001). *The Return to Reason*. Cambridge, MA: Harvard University Press.

Tversky, A. and D. Kahneman (1974). 'Judgment under Uncertainty: Heuristics and Biases'. *Science*, 185: 1124–1131.

Urry, J. (2000). *Sociology Beyond Societies*. London: Routledge.

Valsiner, J. and R. van der Veer. (2000). *The Social Mind: Construction of the Idea*. Cambridge: Cambridge University Press.

Weber, M. (1958 [1918]). 'Science as a Vocation', in H. Gerth and C.W. Mills (eds), *From Max Weber* (pp. 129–158). Oxford: Oxford University Press.

Werskey, G. (1988 [1978]). *The Visible College: Scientists and Socialists in the 1930s*, 2nd edn. London: Free Association Books.

White, M. (1957). *Social Thought in America: The Revolt against Formalism*. Boston, MA: Beacon Press.

Wilson, E.O. (1998). *Consilience: The Unity of Knowledge*. New York: Knopf.

Wolin, R. (1990). *The Politics of Being*. New York: Columbia University Press.

Wolin, R. (2000). 'Untruth and Method', *The New Republic*, 15 May: 36–45.

Wolin, R. (2001). *Heidegger's Children*. Princeton: Princeton University Press.

Wuthnow, R. (1989). *Communities of Discourse*. Cambridge, MA: Harvard University Press.

Zagzebski, L. and A. Fairweather (eds) (2001). *Virtue Epistemology: Essays on Epistemic Virtue and Responsibility*. Oxford: Oxford University Press.

Zinn, H. (1980). *A People's History of the United States*. New York: Harper & Row.

Index

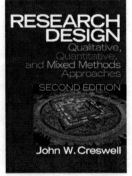

The Qualitative Research Kit

Edited by Uwe Flick

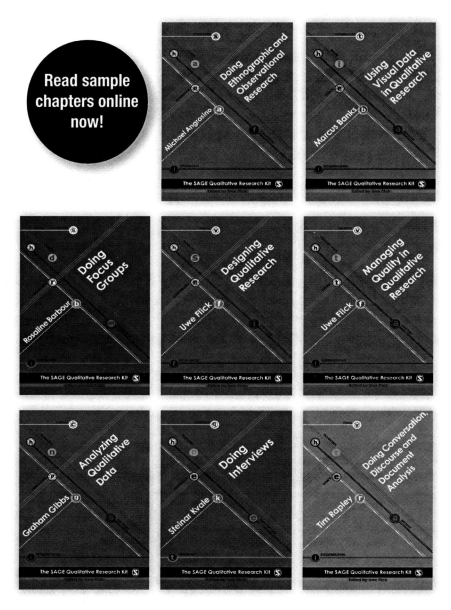

Read sample chapters online now!

Doing Ethnographic and Observational Research — Michael Angrosino — The SAGE Qualitative Research Kit

Using Visual Data in Qualitative Research — Marcus Banks — The SAGE Qualitative Research Kit

Doing Focus Groups — Rosaline Barbour — The SAGE Qualitative Research Kit

Designing Qualitative Research — Uwe Flick — The SAGE Qualitative Research Kit

Managing Quality in Qualitative Research — Uwe Flick — The SAGE Qualitative Research Kit

Analyzing Qualitative Data — Graham Gibbs — The SAGE Qualitative Research Kit

Doing Interviews — Steinar Kvale — The SAGE Qualitative Research Kit

Doing Conversation, Discourse and Document Analysis — Tim Rapley — The SAGE Qualitative Research Kit

www.sagepub.co.uk

Supporting researchers for more than forty years

Research methods have always been at the core of SAGE's publishing. Sara Miller McCune founded SAGE in 1965 and soon after, she published SAGE's first methods book, Public Policy Evaluation. A few years later, she launched the Quantitative Applications in the Social Sciences series – affectionately known as the "little green books".

Always at the forefront of developing and supporting new approaches in methods, SAGE published early groundbreaking texts and journals in the fields of qualitative methods and evaluation.

Today, more than forty years and two million little green books later, SAGE continues to push the boundaries with a growing list of more than 1,200 research methods books, journals, and reference works across the social, behavioral, and health sciences.

From qualitative, quantitative, mixed methods to evaluation, SAGE is the essential resource for academics and practitioners looking for the latest methods by leading scholars.

www.sagepublications.com